JIM BROWN

JIM BROWN

The Fierce Life of an American Hero

MIKE FREEMAN

WM
WILLIAM MORROW
An Imprint of HarperCollins*Publishers*

HarperCollins books may be purchased for educational, business, or sales promotional use. For information please write: Special Markets Department, HarperCollins Publishers, 10 East 53rd Street, New York, NY 10022.

FIRST EDITION

Designed by Laura Kaeppel

Library of Congress Cataloging-in-Publication Data

Freeman, Michael, 1966–
    Jim Brown: the fierce life of an American hero/Mike Freeman.
      p. cm.
    ISBN-13: 978-0-06-077682-4
    ISBN-10: 0-06-077682-X
    1. Brown, Jim, 1936–   2. Football players—United States—Biography.   I. Title.

GV939.B75F74 2006
796.332092—dc22
[B]   2006049515

06 07 08 09 10 WBC/RRD 10 9 8 7 6 5 4 3 2 1

To Kelly,

the greatest woman in the world,

who stands by me through thick and thin

Once, after a blast of six or seven yards, Brown was the first to regain his feet. When he got back to the huddle he was blowing hard—but the inert figures of three Giants marked the trail where he had passed, like the breadcrumbs on the forest path of Hansel and Gretel. For mercurial speed, airy nimbleness, and explosive violence in one package of undistilled evil, there is no other like Mr. Brown.

—**Red Smith,**
Pulitzer Prize–winning writer

CONTENTS

JIM BROWN

PROLOGUE

FOR MUCH OF HIS EXISTENCE, Jim Brown walked the planet with supreme arrogance. Each step was more confident and profound than the last. He did not believe in weakness or insecurity. He did not believe in hugging his own children. Only a soft man, he often thought when he was a player in the National Football League, ever cried in public. Brown was blessed with brains and biceps, and used both in equal proportions, on and off the various playing fields he dominated, physically intimidating both men and women. There have been few athletes smarter or more defiant or more controversial. Just as he left the crumbs of opponents scattered behind him on his blazing sprints on the football field, Jim Brown also cast aside the shells of stereotypes wherever he passed. First, he redefined the running game. Then, in quick succession, he redefined what it meant to be a movie star, a lover, a civil rights leader, an activist. He helped to redefine what it meant to live as a black man in America, from the 1950s until today.

Jim Brown is consumed with being special. Afraid of being remembered as mundane, Brown has had one concern for much of his life: to be the baddest, the smartest, the most lasting man ever.

A SCENE FROM the life of Brown. It was October 13, 1963. As he had done so many times before, in so many different ways, Brown was demonstrating that he was a physical being who had mastered a brutal sport.

Cleveland was in Yankee Stadium playing the New York Giants. Tickets to the game were tough to get because the Browns had won their first four games, and because Jim Brown was going to be on the field.

The old NFL was a different entity than the polished, image-conscious sport it has become. Then, the rules were few and the tactics cheap. Football was full of dirty players and optically challenged game officials. Punching, kicking, head slapping, biting—it all happened with disturbing regularity.

Brown experienced it all. As the most dangerous weapon on the Browns team, he drew the attention and the cheap shots from the most vicious enforcers. The Giants were no different. In the moments following Brown's first carry, one of the Giants defenders stuck several of his fingers inside Brown's woefully inadequate face protection. It was the NFL's long-retired two-bar face mask; the bars were several inches apart and rested just beneath his nose, offering the Giants more than enough room to attack his face.

The Giants players mostly went after Brown as he was going down to the ground. When Brown was underneath the massive piles, his arms pinned, practically defenseless, fingers jabbed and gouged and probed under Brown's face mask. As the game continued, it became clear that Brown's eyes—the sharp brown ones that allowed him to view the field with digital clarity—were under a planned, organized assault.

Over the course of the first half alone, Brown's eyes would be poked or hit a half dozen times, at least, by several Giants players, often in the large pileups. In a particularly vicious moment, one of the Giants players shoved his elbow inside the mask and jammed it into Brown's left eye. When Brown arose his vision was severely blurred, as if he were trying to see through a thin, closed curtain.

At halftime, Brown plodded over to a corner of the locker room and sat alone, gathering his thoughts. Brown had scored a 1-yard touchdown in the first half and Cleveland trailed only 17–14, but something was wrong with Brown. He was questioning himself. He was experiencing fear.

Everything changed in the second half. Brown's fear was gone, replaced by icy anger. He took a screen pass from quarterback Frank Ryan, ran over two Giants players, and burst for a 72-yard touchdown. All of those hands and fingers and elbows that had searched for his eyes were now grasping for air. On Cleveland's next possession, there was another Brown score. The Cleveland linemen, using an option blocking system, in which Brown picked his running lanes, freed Brown for a 32-yard touchdown. By now, the Giants had ceased their cheap shots. They were too stunned and broken by Brown to do anything except relent. Cleveland was victorious by 11 points.

Forty-eight hours after the game, Brown's vision was still blurry. Both of the fullback's eyes were swollen and aching. He had told no one in the media what was wrong except a reporter for *Sport* magazine. "It was my most satisfying game under the circumstances," Brown told the media. He declined to state just what those circumstances were.

Brown had asked one of the assistant coaches about going to a doctor but was told to wait until after practice. If his teammates became aware he was hurt, it could demoralize them. So Brown told only a few close friends on the team and one sports reporter, and swore them to secrecy.

His eyes throbbing through drill after drill, Brown waited until practice concluded, then quietly went to see a physician later that night.

A SCENE FROM the life of a sexual creature happily trapped in the middle of a revolution.

It was the 1960s. Everyone screwed everyone, or at least it seemed that way. In Cleveland, the players had a house called the Headquarters. They brought girlfriends on one night, their wives the next, one group unaware of the other. They had parties called the Night of a Thousand Fingers. Hands and feet and torsos cavorted across the several different rooms.

Brown would never smoke cigarettes, because of his health. He did not like to consume large quantities of alcohol, because he disliked being out of control, even if sometimes he did get that way. Yet at times, sex ruled him, overriding the controlling tendencies that worked so well in other aspects of his life. He purchased cocaine for women to arouse them but was repulsed by the idea of using the drug.

He liked his women young—ripe and firm, as he describes them. He had girlfriends who were nineteen when he was in his thirties. The women also knew this: Jim Brown was no one-woman man. His strong sexuality was a lure and a curse, leading to ruined relationships and at least one paternity suit. Yet for the next phase of his life, the one in which he became one of the most important leading men in the history of filmmaking, that sexuality was a tremendous asset.

Before Brown, a black man was not allowed to be sexual on the big screen. In 1960s America, it was not fear of a black planet. It was, as a film historian said in Spike Lee's movie about Brown's life, fear of a black penis.

Sidney Poitier was the reigning black movie star of the time. He was a splendid actor—warm, compassionate, and skilled. He was also safe for white audiences, who felt comfortable with Poitier because he was an emasculated black man, not a virile one. To the newly enlightened white moviegoer, it was okay for Sidney to come to dinner. Not Brown. When he made the daring move from football star to movie action hero, he broke onto the screen with his shirt off and his sexuality intact. He provoked gunfights, battled in brawls, and bedded Raquel Welch.

Poitier broke many barriers and walked through Hollywood's front door; Brown kicked in that door by being the uncompromising, forward-thinking man that he was, as a football star and a civil rights leader.

Brown wanted to be everything Poitier was not. Most of all, Brown wanted his characters to be sexual. Brown and Welch starred in the 1969 movie *100 Rifles*. Welch was the white woman every white man wanted to touch. The interracial love scenes between Welch and Brown remain one of the more significant turning points in cinematic history because a black man was having sex with America's white carnal queen. Welch, with her full breasts and flowing hair, and Brown, muscled and manly, did the voracious sex scene, complete with Brown sticking his tongue in Welch's ear, on the first day of shooting the film.

Brown's acting career would include a number of films. Often stone-faced and stiff in movies, he will not go down as the greatest thespian of all time, but he could be remembered as one of the most significant. He was a revolutionary presence, particularly to black film audiences, who for the first time saw someone on the screen who seemed more like them.

• • •

A SCENE FROM a justifiably paranoid life.

It was April 1970, and Brown sat stiffly in his chair, untrusting and unyielding, as an interviewer from the *New York Sunday News* lobbed questions at Brown about topics ranging from his prosperous film career to the possibility of a race war. Just as he never shied away from physical confrontations on the field, Brown never shrank in the face of tough questions. His opinions were always stout and forceful; his glares were menacing, his patience was short, when faced with a query he disliked; now was no different.

"The FBI, CIA, and the local police forces seem to be in cahoots," Brown was saying. "Anyone that speaks too loud is going to be tied down in a court case—or shot—or something. Because of this, I think people who would normally think of being actively involved in a race war or black uprising will have second thoughts about it. But they will think about how they can protect themselves against certain kinds of oppression. And they will utilize brainpower and resources to do that. Doing things in an intelligent way is a much greater threat than operating out of total emotionalism on the streets. This country has never seen intelligent black people committed to using the last resort, which you might refer to as violence or warfare. But if these people feel threatened by violence, they can only think of retaliation in the same form."

Brown was then asked about his being arrested several times and if he was being targeted unfairly by the police. "I'm singled out like any other black or white cat in America that speaks out too much," Brown responded. Then, thinking of a famous black boxer vilified in the 1910s for beating white opponents, Brown added: "Jack Johnson had to leave the country. He was forced out. Paul Robeson was forced out; Stokely [Carmichael] is gone; Cleaver's gone; [Ali] will probably have to leave. You can go right on down the line. The thing about me is that my philosophy can't really be attacked. They can't fight the philosophy, but they can cut off areas where funds must be obtained to develop black people economically. They don't want my independence to be used as an example for others to follow."

"You keep referring to they," the reporter asked. "Who are they?"

"Why, the Man, of course," Brown responded. "The Man. You see, I can't be controlled and I have an opinion. It's difficult to get me involved in things like riots or inciting riots because I'm not in those areas. I don't even talk about them. My activities can't be attacked, but with my private life it is different. They can take an incident and blow it up. I'm always attacked. They get you in any area they can. Now you know there isn't a man in this country who hasn't a private life that they could pin some headline on if they wanted to."

"So you're convinced that there's a concerted effort to make you look immoral and criminal?"

"Well, judge for yourself," Brown said. "Did you ever see any other movie star on the front page, shackled because of a car accident where no one was hurt and where no one was touched? A lot of papers carried the photo of me in handcuffs and chains. This was supposed to kill me. It was supposed to take my black manhood and put it on the ground. But when the jury heard the case, they took less than a half hour to find me not guilty. So I know they are singling me out. But it won't work, because my head won't drop down to my chest. You're going to say that I sound bitter. But I don't sound bitter, man, I'm just real."

You aren't paranoid if they really are out to get you, right?

And Brown had no idea just how correct he was. The FBI was watching.

A SCENE FROM a life spied upon.

They thought he was a threat, this powerful Negro, this

popular Negro. So they watched and monitored and probed. Where he went, they went. This continued for years, by one FBI agent's estimate. While they spied, he never knew.

They thought he was a threat, so they looked to smear him, if necessary, and to ruin him, if possible, and that's how the United States government's stalking of Brown began. Files were accumulated. Reports were written.

"The FBI thought strong African American sports heroes like Jim Brown were a threat," states a former FBI agent, who says he is familiar with the agency's spying on Brown and other prominent black athletes of the 1960s.

The agent maintains that FBI officials attempted to injure Brown's business ventures at that time by spreading disinformation with local and national business leaders, first claiming that Brown was secretly a member of the American Communist Party, and later that he was a radical Muslim. Much the way the FBI, spearheaded by its obsessive director J. Edgar Hoover, smeared and threatened Martin Luther King Jr., other black leaders were also thwarted. Brown was still able to secure limited loans and money for his programs, including the Negro Industrial Economic Union, later renamed the Black Economic Union, which was formed to help blacks become competitive in the business world.

"It was deplorable," says the former agent, who agreed to an interview only on the condition that his identity not be revealed. "The more vocal and powerful Brown got, the more he was watched. They made up crap. They looked for dirt to hurt him with when the time came."

The file the FBI accumulated on one chapter of Brown's Black Economic Union is eye-opening. (The file was declassified by the FBI in November of 2003 and transferred to the National Archives not long after that.) It shows that the FBI, the Secret Service, and various local police departments all worked together to spy on Brown's organization and on one chapter in particular.

The first indication that the FBI's motives in attempting to damage Brown were at least partially racially generated is that the files contain a UPI photograph of a bare-chested Brown standing provocatively over an almost-nude Raquel Welch. The picture was taken as part of the media publicity for the Brown and Welch movie *100 Rifles*. The idea of Brown filming love scenes with a white woman was, according to the former FBI source, "infuriating to members of the bureau."

The FBI engaged in a sly but effective plot to frame Brown's Black Economic Union as a group of radical extremists. The group, however, was anything but. It was the first organization started by a professional athlete solely dedicated to improving the economic fortunes of a group of people, in this case, black people.

One FBI field agent wrote in a report dated June 26, 1968, that in one meeting attended by BEU members, an FBI spy indicated "that the meeting lasted approximately five or six hours and should be more properly described as a ritual or a ceremony, rather than a meeting. The source said the ceremony consisted of chanting the word 'Black' or 'Blackness' and the leader . . . asking questions such as, 'Who buys most of the Cadillacs and who buys the $60.00 shoes.' In each instance the group chanted a reply, 'The Negro.'

"Source stated that some type of book by Che, whose last name is Guevarra [*sic*], Castro leader who was killed in Bolivia, was laying [*sic*] on the table," says the report. "This source stated that the whole atmosphere of the ritual was one of brotherhood on the part of the Negro opposition to the 'White Hunkie.'"

Of course the field agent meant the racially derogatory term "honky."

What was collected on Brown and his group remains sensitive

to this day. One document in the file, five pages long, is marked "ACCESS RESTRICTED."

"In review of this file this item was removed because access to it is restricted," the notice states.

The date of this document was August 19, 1968. Almost forty years after the document's production, the government is still concealing it.

What caused the FBI to consider a football player to be such a formidable threat to national security?

"The FBI did not see him as just an athlete," the agent says. "The FBI believed that one day he was going to become a significant political force. I know this sounds silly now, but back then, they saw his strength and push for African Americans to fight for themselves and their independence as a major threat. There was no way they were going to let some football nigger get power. That's what one other agent once told me. They were going to hurt him as much as possible."

A FINAL SCENE from the life.

Brown was speaking from the Ventura County Jail in California, and the irony did not escape him. Normally when the Hall of Fame running back stepped into a prison, he was counseling inmates, preparing them for the day when their sentence would end and they would have the chance to become functioning members of society. Now, Brown was not an adviser who would stay for a short time, then depart. He was locked up in a cell the size of a walk-in closet. His uniform was a flimsy light blue jumpsuit over a white T-shirt. He wore a thick ID tag on his right arm. The teacher, it seemed, had become the prisoner.

Brown's violent temper had led to his being locked in that

hell—there is no other word for jail. On the football field, Brown's disposition was always cool and calm. Off of it, he was fiery, his anger sometimes erupting. Brown has been accused at least five times of using physical violence, sometimes against girlfriends and wives. As one of Brown's friends stated: "Sometimes, when it comes to women, Jim can be one crazy motherfucker."

Art Modell, the former owner of the Cleveland Browns, the team where Brown established himself as the best football player of all time, remembers instances when Brown "got into trouble because of, shall we say, a rough social encounter with a gal, or two, or three."

When Brown spoke to the author from prison, he sounded worn, perhaps from the effects of what he called a fourteen-day spiritual cleansing. Others believe Brown, always defiant, always stubborn, was undergoing a hunger strike to protest what he believed was an unfair prison sentence: the six-month jail term he received after refusing to undergo court-ordered counseling and community service resulting from a conviction for vandalizing the car of his then twenty-five-year-old wife, Monique, in 1999. During his two-week cleansing, or strike, Brown consumed only water. The prison nurses pleaded with Brown to eat. He refused. They told him he risked serious health problems if he did not. Again, he declined.

Under California law, a prisoner has the right to decline both food and medical attention. At one point, some seventeen days into Brown's hunger strike, or cleansing, the state considered acquiring a court order that would force Brown to eat. But soon after, Brown relented and began consuming food again.

The entire episode was typical Brown. Even then, at sixty-six years old, he still possessed the qualities, in abundance, that made him one of the most important athletes of the last century. Brown's hardened will was the catalyst that molded him into such a superb football player, and provided him with the confidence to become an unflinching, uncompromising symbol of black pride and self-reliance.

In this situation Brown's stubbornness, however noble he may have felt, landed him in jail. On January 5, 2000, Brown was ordered to prison for misdemeanor vandalism after smashing the windows of Monique's Jaguar with a shovel. Judge Dale S. Fischer, who called Brown's actions the worst case of vandalism she had ever seen, sentenced Brown to a year of domestic-violence counseling. Brown was also instructed to spend forty days on a work crew cleaning up city streets around Los Angeles, put in four hundred hours of community service, pay $1,800 in fines, and serve three years' probation. Brown refused to go to counseling, saying he did not need it, and the notion of a proud Brown picking up garbage along a highway, well, that was never going to happen.

"They offered me three deals," Brown said, "and I refused."

Brown's athletic career helped him become a new kind of American hero, a new kind of black hero. But even a superhero of vast character and strength has his flaws.

INTRODUCTION

AS THE *SPORTING NEWS* once wrote, Brown came, he saw, he conquered. And then, shockingly, he left the game as quickly as he had risen to dominance, disappearing from professional football with every rushing record tucked neatly under his beefy arms. Brown's legend remains as sturdy as the body-scattering runs that lifted him to prominence as the Cleveland Browns' most significant offensive weapon from the years 1957 through 1965. There is no doubt about it: he was the greatest pure football player the sport has ever known.

"One of the true measures of a great player is what other great players who played against you say," said Dallas Cowboys Hall of Famer Randy White. "I never played against Jim, but I talk to people who did all the time, and they say he was the toughest son of a gun they ever saw. I think Jim Brown could have dominated in any era, any year, anywhere."

Brown was blessed with an eighteen-inch neck, broad, imposing shoulders, and a chest that was measured at forty-five inches. His large thighs carried him around the field with the grace and power of a sprinter or champion skier. Dr. W. Montague Cobb, a former Howard University anatomist, said in the 1960s, "Jim Brown's bone structure must resemble forged vanadium steel—the hinging of ankles, knees, elbows; the 'crawl' of muscles, the dynamism of effort easily tapped are all in immediate evidence." Brown ran with head held high, legs pumping and broad arms swiping away tacklers. He ran over linemen and defensive backs alike. Often, quite simply, opponents were afraid to tackle him.

Brown was an athletic gem who played multiple sports at Syracuse University, including lacrosse, which he loved; but football was his passion. He plowed through the NFL as a rookie in 1957, rushing for 942 yards, earning the first of eight rushing titles over a remarkable but brief nine-year career. He never missed a full game—or practice—despite severe injuries, painful lacerations and muscle aches that sideline many athletes today. He played hard because it was Brown's nature, but also because Brown knew if he ever missed a contest, Cleveland would have little chance of winning.

His top seven yearly rushing totals would become the standard for all the greats that would follow: 1,863, 1,544, 1,527, 1,446, 1,408, 1,329, and 1,257 yards. What made Brown's accomplishments so stunning was that teams knew he was getting the ball, and defenders were programmed to stop him, and mostly only him; still, he galloped across the field, usually unchallenged, often untouched.

He once told Baltimore Colts tight end John Mackey: "Make sure when anyone tackles you, he remembers how much it hurts." No one who tried to tackle Brown ever forgot the encounter.

Brown was equally intimidating off the field. There were times when you would need to subpoena his smile; his glares and scowls were often nuclear in intensity. When he spoke out about race, whites thought he was bitter and resentful, while blacks felt he was honest and true. Neither group was aware of just how threatening Brown seemed to the government. Today, all these decades later, many members of both races feel the same primordial and often different stirrings when Brown's name is mentioned.

In 1966 Brown casually delivered the stunning news of his retirement from football while on the movie set of *The Dirty Dozen*. He was just thirty: unlike many of today's athletes, who often hang on far too long, Brown knew when to exit.

"It was the right time to retire," he told the media then. "You should go out on top."

And he was at the pinnacle, the owner of a championship ring and twenty NFL records. Brown is the only player to be inducted into the pro football, college football, and lacrosse Halls of Fame. Recently, Syracuse University announced two Jim Brown scholarships.

Brown's life has resembled a tough, sprawling drama, and includes the seeds of activism that shaped him. In Cleveland in the 1960s, Brown helped found the Negro Industrial and Economic Union (later renamed the Black Economic Union) to assist black-owned businesses. "When you came to the Cleveland Browns, if you were black, you had to come a certain way," he has said. "That meant being responsible off the field and being serious about playing on the field. We had to be about something."

In a 1968 interview with *Ebony* magazine, Brown explained in no uncertain terms why he began the Black Economic Union. "Dealing with the white man economically is one of the things we're teaching brothers through the [BEU]. See, we believe that the closest you can get to independence in a capitalist country is financial independence. See, we've got to find a way to stop begging, just like we've got to stop wasting all our energy and money marching and picketing and doing things like camping-in down in Washington on a Poor People's Campaign. They didn't accomplish a single thing down there. They got a little attention and lots of condescending pats on the back from white liberals who wanted them to keep as quiet as possible and hurry up and get out of town. That's all. . . . We've got to get off the emotional stuff and do something that will bring about real change. We've got to have industries and commercial enterprises and build our own sustaining economic base. Then we can face white folks man-to-man and we can deal."

Players today, Brown says, are dramatically different from the players of his generation, as modern athletes are too blinded by lucrative contracts to care about what's going on in their own communities. "The money is so big," he says. "Most of these individuals have no concept of history, of who opened the door for them." This has long been a Brown theme, one of many that makes him such an interesting character to study.

Brown's list of charitable actions is as long as the list of his rushing records, or of the contradictions in his life. He embraces society's lowest citizens, encouraging gang members and prisoners to transform their lives, to reclaim their humanity. But Brown's many sons and daughters have spoken of their father's distant nature and of the years they were not a true part of his life.

When I spoke to him in prison, he was charming and brilliant, yet to some Americans he has always seemed threatening. His recurring displays of anger added to that reputation. Brown was fined $500 and briefly jailed for beating up a male golf partner in 1978, and he has faced assault charges against several women over the last four decades; in most cases the charges were either dropped or he was acquitted after his female accusers decided not to testify against him.

Brown's coaches and teammates from the lacrosse, football, and basketball teams at Manhasset, Long Island, High School and Syracuse vividly recall Brown's extraordinary athletic feats. He starred in four sports while with the Orangemen, scoring 43 points once in a football game and leading the country in goal scoring in lacrosse. He was exciting on the field and glamorous off of it. Stars like Raquel Welch spoke of his enticing appeal, which enabled Brown to crush previously taboo sexual images of black men in Hollywood. It was Brown who became the first black action star, with leading roles in *The Dirty Dozen, Ice Station Zebra,* and many other films. As film historian Donald Bogle has pointed out, where Poitier was polished and nonsexual, Brown was pure testosterone, a strong, confident black man creating tough, sexy characters audiences hadn't seen before—unintentionally helping give rise to the blaxploitation movement of the early 1970s (in which he also participated, in films such as *Slaughter, Black Gunn,* and *Three the Hard Way*). In many respects, today's black cinema actors owe a portion of their stardom and fortunes to Brown.

Brown's life wasn't always so sexy. He was born on February 17, 1936, on St. Simons Island off the southern coast of Georgia. He was abandoned by his father about two weeks after his birth, and his mother left when he was two years old to take a job as a housekeeper on Long Island. Brown's great-grandmother raised him, and they shared a house with his grandmother, who was an alcoholic. When he was four, he attended school, segregated from the white kids he played with, in a two-room shack. When Brown turned eight, his mother came back for him; it was the first time they had seen each other in six years.

Ed Walsh, the Manhasset athletic director and a man Brown has looked up to as much as anyone in his life, said that when Brown was a teenager, he would walk the streets all night rather than come home to his mother and her dates. Some coaches on the football staff at Syracuse didn't want to allow Brown on the team unless Walsh got him to adhere to ten rules, the first one being that Brown could not date white girls. "Not unless you have [the same rules] for every guy on the team," was Walsh's reply. Brown attended

Syracuse anyway, not on a scholarship, but on money raised by Ken Molloy, a Long Island man who would become another of Brown's friends and champions. Another white man, Roy Simmons, was also a champion of Brown's.

Despite so many historic and interesting aspects of his life, aspects that make for fascinating analysis, no independent biography of Brown had been written as of late 2006, and the last book about the star player was a children's book done in 1996. The reason? I believe it is Brown's stoic stubbornness. Brown wants no stinkin' writer chronicling his life unless he says so (he believes many writers are parasites living off the exploits of others). Besides, Brown believes he could write the story himself, and word in the publishing industry is that he was attempting to do just that. He's already penned two autobiographies, using other writers to help him. In Brown's mind, there is nothing he cannot do. Remarkably, many times, over the course of a remarkable life, that belief has proven true.

THERE IS JUST one great dilemma and challenge in writing this book: How do you call a man a hero when he has been accused of serious incidents of domestic violence? How do you label him a leader, a brilliant mind, after he allegedly tossed a much smaller and weaker human being off a condo balcony?

"With me Jim was always gentle, kind, and sweet," said Stella Stevens, who shot a love scene with Brown in *Slaughter.*

"He was great to me despite his reputation for being big, bad, and mean," she said.

"Besides being one of the greatest athletes of the twentieth century," said Roy Simmons Jr., a standout Syracuse lacrosse star who played with Brown and whose father coached Brown in the same sport, "he was one of the most inspirational people I have ever met."

"The Jim Brown I know is a wonderful human being," says close friend and former Cleveland Browns teammate John Wooten, who, like dozens of people who have known Brown for decades, remains extremely loyal to him. "He is generous and always thinks of other people before himself. He helped black businesses, black athletes, and black people in general. When others ignore what is happening to poor people and others, Jim spends his life helping them. He is one of the most impressive people I have ever met."

Others disagree. Katherine Redmond, head of the National Co-alition Against Violent Athletes, believes it is not possible to call Brown a hero, because of the allegations of violence against women. "Here is a man who represents African-Americans and has fought for their rights. And yet, he maintains an arrogance, as well as an antiquated view of women as property," she wrote in an e-mail. "The irony is that while America, at the time of Jim Brown's hype, had been embroiled in a painful, violent struggle for freedom and prosperity for all, regardless of race, Jim Brown was an active pro-ponent and symbol of the oppression he confronted and conquered—but towards women. And eventually, himself.

"Jim Brown's life, in effect, has been little more than a complex paradox of values," Redmond continued. "Much like some of his successors and colleagues, the fame, glory and power that come from being a sports idol often enable a lifestyle based on entitle-ment, and when it comes to relationships, a need to conquer. It is arguable that Brown sees women as adversaries and property. How he views them, and treats them, is no different than the treatment he so condemned of his enslaved ancestors. Slaves were property. Their very lives existed at the whim of their master. Intimidation kept them in line and the threat of violence loomed over their heads. So, too, were the experiences of the women in Brown's life. What readers of this book must understand, is the same NFL that condoned Brown's idea that women were enemies who needed to be conquered, is still instilling that belief in today's players. Brown is a product of his environment, much like today's athletes. The flagrant lack of accountability coupled with a significant amount of power comes at a price that their victims must pay."

"All heroes seem to have tragic flaws; some are obvious and others are yet to be exposed," said David Belkin, a nationally known sports psychologist who has worked with hundreds of high school, college, and professional athletes. "This is because, at first, we only get to know the most salient feature of their persona. The talented and free-spirited rock star that lives life in the moment is a hero to those who feel constricted in their lives. That moment-to-moment pleasure-seeking that we find so compelling is also what allows him to get hooked on dope, have children out of wedlock, and ultimately ruin his life. We only discover this as we delve deeper into his human side. A hero is a hero because he represents an ideal, the best of something in humankind. He can be at best only a representation of the idea, never the real thing. The hero often falls short in other areas, because he is tragically human.

"Those same traits that make us heroic in one arena are often character flaws in another," Belkin continued. "Jim Brown's dogged determination, the force of his will, his unwillingness to accept any outcome other than the one he wanted, served to make him a hero on the field and in the fight for causes that he believed in. At the same time, this character trait may have tarnished his personal relationships, where considering the feelings of others and sometimes submitting to the will of another may be necessary or desirable. Maybe the appropriate adjective to describe Jim Brown's life is exceptional, but certainly not heroic."

That is the way many may feel about Brown—they see it as impossible to describe someone with Brown's history of domestic violence as a hero. I disagree with Belkin and Redmond, two highly reputable and knowledgeable people. It is possible for Brown or any other person to be both heroic and flawed; Brown's alleged acts of domestic abuse, or simply violence against others, indeed scar him, but they do not define him.

Perhaps he is more the Shakespearean kind of hero, a tragic hero, whose larger-than-life power makes him utterly compelling, yet certainly troubling. Think of Macbeth, thirsty for power; Hamlet, pure in vengeance; Othello, perhaps, awe-inspiring both in his military valor and in his jealous rage.

BROWN FACED A battery of racial double standards during his playing and acting careers, which created an understandably high level of resentment and distrust of many whites, even as white football fans adored him. Like many blacks who have experienced severe racism in their lives, Brown was caught between two extreme and conflicting emotions. For every white person who was decent and honest, he encountered many other whites who were racist and cruel. In the 1950s and 1960s, Brown struggled with these polar opposites. His moods alternated between appreciating the white men like Ed Walsh who helped him overcome race-related obstacles, and despising those who targeted him solely because of the color of his skin, such as college lacrosse opponents who called him a "nigger" and other racial slurs dozens, maybe hundreds, of times. At one point, frustrated by these experiences, he raised a wall of aloofness that only a few close friends ever scaled.

When the subject of race and truth arose during a 1966 interview, Brown told the white reporter: "I speak the truth. If you deny me, you're my enemy. Maybe [the truth] is what Cassius Clay says when he calls all white men the devil. That could be the truth. I can't buy it." That answer is typical Brown: he floats back and forth across the color line.

Then, in the next breath, we see another part of Brown. He used a common Vietnam-era phrase to demonstrate the side of him that distrusted whites. Leaning forward, he pointed a finger in the interviewer's face and declared: "Listen, you're Charlie, baby. I'm fighting you."

No athlete—not Jackie Robinson, not Jack Johnson, not Joe Louis, and not even Muhammad Ali—has addressed the issue of racism and society's historical mistreatment of blacks and the poor as boldly and consistently as Brown has for decades.

His on-field heroics; his groundbreaking movie roles; his social activism; and perhaps just as important, his willingness to talk publicly about race, both in 1950s America and now, all these decades later, make Brown the most significant black athlete—and maybe the most significant athlete, period—in the history of American sports. Jackie Robinson's contribution was vital and historic, as were Muhammad Ali's and Jack Johnson's. Johnson was the boxer once described by the *Chicago Tribune* as "the black peril." The level of ugliness he faced was unjust. Johnson's feats were accomplished at a time when race relations in America were at their lowest since slavery. Johnson might be the sole athlete in the history of this country who faced being murdered on a daily basis because of the color of his skin.

Babe Didrikson Zaharias dared to play golf on the men's tour in the 1930s. The *New York World–Telegram*'s Joe Williams wrote about her: "It would be better if she and her ilk stayed at home, got themselves prettied up and waited for the phone to ring." Jimmy Winkfield was the first black jockey to win the Kentucky Derby, and racism forced him to flee America for Russia and eventually Paris. Baseball great Hank Aaron faced numerous death threats as he approached Babe Ruth's home run record. Each time Joe Louis fought, it was like a national holiday for blacks, as millions sat around their radios and cheered on their hero. Louis fought bravely while facing great racism as well. One of the many ugly names he was called was the "Tan

Tarzan." Ring announcers would glibly state, before announcing his impressive credentials, "Although colored . . ."

What makes Brown's accomplishments more impressive than others' is that Brown's activism has been the most lasting. For five decades he has used the platform of his various careers and businesses, as well as his eloquence, to further his causes and beliefs. No athlete has done all of these things as well or as long as Brown. Not even Ali.

Most would point to Ali's lasting greatness as proven by his being awarded the Presidential Medal of Freedom by President Bush in 2006. He was also recognized by the World Economic Forum in Switzerland, which promotes dialogue and understanding between the Muslim and Western worlds. Yet Ali has become more popular than Brown because the less the historic boxing champion has been able to speak because of his tragic Parkinson's disease, the more America has warmed up to him.

Brown will never be as liked as Ali because of Brown's violent past and because of his continued outspokenness. But that outspokenness puts today's athletes to shame. Brown does not dodge racial booby traps and double standards. He confronts them forcefully and unblinkingly. The modern athlete is fat from corporate dollars and is unaware of, or indifferent to, the sacrifices made by athletes like Brown. Tiger Woods, Michael Jordan, LeBron James, and many others have the financial and social clout to jump-start a much-needed racial conversation, but none has done so. The only high-profile athlete who has touched the issue is Barry Bonds, and his words are often dismissed as simple belligerence (as the words of Brown once were by some whites).

ESPN.com writer Scoop Jackson wrote of this phenomenon:

We live in the era of the soundless athlete. An era in which the highest-profile figures in sports not only say nothing about the condition of the sociopolitical landscape their fan base resides in, but worse—they have *nothing* to say. They'll speak of love and hate in Nike commercials, they'll save women falling from buildings in Adidas spots. They'll dunk cantaloupes in carts in grocery store aisles, they'll chase Afro'd dolls through parties trying to get a Sprite. They'll put tats on their bodies proclaiming love for loved ones and those they've lost; they'll go on "Oprah" or "Jay Leno" and shed tears about their past and how they were lost; they'll do one-on-ones with chosen sportscasters to promote their CDs; they'll form opinions about dress codes. Saying nothing. And, bottom line? Ain't none of them wrong. That's what they are supposed to do. Their silence has emancipated them. Taken them places past their American dreams. Made them our heroes. Some our leaders. To them we look for answers; answers we find in their silence. We applaud their performances, make sure our kids always choose them on "NBA Ballers"; Live '06 them, Xbox them, DS them, PSP them. All the while accepting their silence. Because their silence has gone past golden. It's now platinum.

Brown has been extremely angry at the reluctance of black athletes to invest money in the dilapidated neighborhoods from which they came. He told the *Syracuse Herald-Journal* in 1993 that modern black athletes are "the most embarrassing collection of individuals I have ever known."

While many high-profile athletes see no evil, Brown works tirelessly attempting to end the annihilation of the black lower class (and to some degree the lower class in general), entering the cracks and crevices of society, the prisons and slums; in other words, places where even a Tiger dare not tread. Brown is not the only athlete or ex-athlete to do this; in one of the toughest neighborhoods in Jacksonville, Florida, a place called Durkeeville, former Wimbledon finalist MaliVai Washington has quietly established one of the most successful after-school programs for disadvantaged kids in the nation. There are other athletes who donate their time and money, but far too few, and none have done what Brown has done for as long as he has done it.

The biggest missing ingredient in today's America, Brown believes, is the black father. To many prisoners and poor people he has touched, poor black people, Brown is that father.

You cannot discuss the life of Brown—any scene, any touchdown, any movie role—without that discussion involving the context of race. Thus, race (and to some degree sex) is a central subtext of this book.

What is clear is that after dozens of interviews, the careful review of FBI files, and the reading of approximately a thousand newspaper and magazine articles about Brown, there is no single category into which Brown neatly fits. He is the kind of man who is both clearly identifiable and difficult to describe. He is the football star who was cheered by hundreds of thousands of Cleveland fans but was not allowed to eat in the same restaurants with them. He was a movie star but a loner. He loved women yet was accused of physically abusing some of them. He was confident and powerful, yet sometimes insecure. He is dedicated to helping the downtrodden, the poor, the imprisoned, giving perfect strangers a helping hand, yet at times Brown has been strangely distant from his own flesh and blood.

Still, above all, Jim Brown has been a pure individual, one who has lived a fierce life.

1950

EVOLUTION

His physique resembled that of a Greek god
with dark skin.

—John Burger,
who played lacrosse with Brown
at Syracuse University

P aul Brown stood on a choppy practice field, hands on his hips, his eyes fixed on a player several feet away. The man many people called Jimmy Brown was stretching on the scruffy green canvas. Paul watched, showing a brief smile, his full cheeks fattening as Jim had moved from stretching to jumping jacks and then graduated to running sprints at half speed. His quickness, despite running at a lower gear, was more than evident. Paul was still stunned, even after months of watching Brown: how could a man his size be so fleet of foot?

Paul had an unremarkable face with thinning hair and a long chin. His personality was just as nondescript. He was an unemotional man, often distant from his players, and not prone to intense emotional outbursts or grandiose statements.

So the beginning of practice on August 1, 1958, was unusual because of something Paul said to a small group of reporters. "There," Paul declared, slightly nodding in the direction of the galloping Jim, "is the best draft choice we ever made. Can you think of a better football player we've drafted?"

Jim was within earshot and could not help but smile awkwardly. His relationship with Paul had started warmly but quickly cooled. Paul would later come to believe that Jim caused the team to divide along racial lines, and Jim felt strongly that Paul had little if any emotional connection with the players who shed blood for him, particularly the black players. Jim appreciated Paul's strong will. A football team needs a leader. Yet Paul was sometimes too unyielding and uncompromising. "If I ever coach one day," Jim told teammates, "I would do it 180 degrees differently than Paul."

That summer's day marked just the beginning of Jim's second year in the NFL, but he already possessed the confidence—actually, the cockiness—of a player far more experienced. Then again, there were few players who were like him, and Jim knew it. He believed strongly in his physicality, and not just his taut muscles. To Jim, the brain was a weapon, and he decided quickly that being poised but quiet was better for a football player than acting gregarious and chatty. There were often several days a week in which Jim spoke to few of his teammates, even the ones who would become close friends. He would stand alone in practice, several feet to the side of the nearest man, or sit alone on a bench or at his locker. Brown had loner elements to his personality, but some of what he did was also contrived. He wanted people, even some of his own teammates, to believe he was unbalanced, ready to pop off at any moment. Many teammates gave Brown a wide berth and then spread the word to friends on other teams around the league about Brown's seemingly unbalanced mind-set. This reputation, Brown knew, would work to his advantage in games if opponents thought he was a little anomalous, in addition to being a brutish, skilled athlete.

Brown had learned early in his life that stoicism could convey messages of intimidation as well as calm. "What's with Jim today?"

was a question often asked by Brown's Cleveland teammates, until they realized nothing was wrong with him. Moodiness was as much a part of Brown's pathology as were his power and speed.

Brown's face itself gave mixed messages. He possessed a caramel-colored, soft complexion with light brown eyes and very occasionally a smile that resembled a confident smirk. Jim kept his hair military short and trimmed on the sides in his early days in Cleveland, like the good ROTC driller he had been at Syracuse. His mouth and lips were full, and his face was usually stubble-free. He looked like a cross between a movie heartthrob and a young, sterling army officer, simultaneously inviting and standoffish.

Considering the conservative decade, the 1950s, in which his rise to prominence and stardom began, women, black and white, flocked to Brown with shocking forwardness. It was only a few years before the freedom of the 1960s, but the straitlaced 1950s were not easily relinquishing their hold. Conservative dress and attitude were still the order of the day in the Midwest. Still, each Brown appearance in public was met with aggressive flirtations and correspondence shoved into his hands or pockets from women seeking a physical relationship with the football star.

When he reported to training camp in 1958, Jim was a powerful 220 pounds, slightly more muscled up than in his rookie season; ten days into camp, he had added an additional 8 pounds. When the Browns used a hand timer to check his speed in the 40-yard dash on one of the first days of practice, he ran it in a blistering 4.5 seconds while wearing his entire uniform, including shoulder pads and helmet, and entering the sprint from a three-point stance. Before Jim, the fastest player on the Browns was running back Ray Renfro, who ran his heat in 4.7 seconds. Renfro was approximately 40 pounds lighter than Jim.

In a second race against other running backs, Renfro won with a time of 4.6, still slower than Jim's. After hearing that Renfro had won his heat, Jim went to Paul and pleaded with the coach: Let me race Renfro. Brown was the fastest man on the squad, but he was irritated because someone else came close to his speed.

"No," Paul told Jim, "you two would bust a leg trying to beat each other."

In actuality Paul did not want Renfro's ego to be mangled, because Jim would have embarrassed Renfro in front of the entire team by beating him. Later, when Big Ten hurdles champion Bobby Mitchell joined the team, Paul had the two men race on the first day of training camp. Brown may have outweighed Mitchell by forty pounds, just as he did Renfro, but he would beat Mitchell. They would race several times, with Brown and Mitchell beating each other equally, and each race drawing a crowd of excited Browns players to view perhaps the two fastest men in football.

When Paul made the uncharacteristically public (and, for him, passionate) pronouncement that Brown was the best draft pick in franchise history, it was an interesting statement at the time. Paul's intimation was clear. He was not simply saying that Brown was the best draftee; he was hinting that, already in his young career, Brown might be the best Browns player ever. Now, with decades of hindsight, such words do not seem like hype. Paul was always careful to choose his public utterances carefully. He often refused to compare Jim to another great Cleveland fullback, Marion Motley, one of the most outstanding runners the Browns had ever seen. There were other great Browns: Edgar Jones, Lou Rymkus, Mac Speedie, Dante Lavelli, and, of course, quarterback Otto Graham. Yet, Jim's talent had so mesmerized Paul that the coach was already putting Jim ahead of some of them.

Paul and his staff had studied Jim incessantly, which is what Paul did with every draft pick. When the Browns first entered the National Football League, the year was 1950, and teams gathered for the draft inside a cramped ballroom in a Philadelphia hotel.

Preparation was prehistoric, and so was the planning for it. There were teams that actually made their selections for the draft by paging through a football magazine that listed the players and briefly described their skills.

When the Cleveland staff entered that ballroom they initially drew snickers; later they won praise. They were carrying stacks of notebooks that contained the name of each potential draftee, his school, his position, his strengths, and a ranking of where the team thought he might be drafted. After that draft, teams mimicked what Paul had started.

Despite the team's extensive draft preparation, Jim actually tumbled into Cleveland's lap following two lucky and completely coincidental occurrences. The Los Angeles Rams had the first opportunity to draft Brown, but in one of those curious blips of sports history, Sid Gillman, the innovative offensive mind who envisioned Brown as a mallet that would compliment his team's wispy passing game, was stabbed in the gut by his owners, who did not want Brown, and forced Gillman to take a popular, hometown Southern Cal player.

Cleveland had finished tied with Pittsburgh the season before, and a coin toss determined which of the two teams would pick first. The Steelers won the toss and grabbed Len Dawson from Purdue. Paul wanted a quarterback as well, but Dawson was the last highly rated thrower on the Browns' board—running back Paul Hornung had already been selected by Green Bay, and quarterback John Brodie was also gone—so Paul Brown decided to take the best available player. That meant Jim.

Paul could actually have had his great quarterback as well. Two years earlier, in 1955, the Browns' coach was sitting in his office when a player named John Unitas phoned him. Unitas had just been cut by the Pittsburgh Steelers and was calling teams to see if they were interested. "Can you get me in for a tryout?" Unitas asked.

Paul was polite but firm. "We have Otto," Paul said, "but you can come back next year." Paul liked Unitas, but his loyalty to Graham was unswerving, as was Unitas's eventual path to the Hall of Fame.

In his rookie season Jim demonstrated power, speed, and the ability to play through pain and injuries at levels that shocked even the coaching staff that had studied him so extensively. One of Cleveland's staff members, Dick Gallagher, detail-oriented and thorough, had seen four of Brown's games at Syracuse. Gallagher's reports to Paul dripped with anecdotes and details of Jim's exploits. "He is the best player in the country, by far," Gallagher informed Paul. When Paul began his own intense film examinations of Brown, he saw the speed and balance, noticing how defenders trying to tackle him seemed as if they were teetering on a balance beam.

Paul saw something else on film that few others studying Jim bothered to notice. Everyone who saw Jim play knew he was a powerful, fast athlete who was slippery once he broke into the open field. But Jim also had great courage. The majority of his runs at Syracuse were between the tackles, meaning he was always attacking the strength of a defense, and every time he did so, the defense bulged, cringing outward, with Jim acting as a pummeling force against a much weaker and thin obstacle.

It was Jim's lateral movement that distinguished him from any previous football player. In practices and games, he would approach the line of scrimmage, and if the running lanes were crammed with bodies, Jim would simply bounce rapidly from side to side until there was a small crack, and then use his sprinter speed to burst through. When defenders reached to grab him, he would break any arm tackle, and if they snagged a leg, he would allow that leg to become temporarily lifeless, and the tackler would simply slip off. He was both oily and powerful.

Jim had a genetic advantage that harmonized with his stubborn courage and high tolerance for pain. The Browns, rather awkwardly, had closely examined Jim's massive thighs, measuring and poking the thick, tightly coiled muscles as if they contained the answer to some great mystery. His thighs were Jim's secret weapon, generating his power. Jim did not believe in extensive stretching, and indeed as the press later began to learn of the rift between Jim and Paul, they pointed to Jim's disdain for the leg-stretching exercises mandated by Paul during practice as one of the original sources of friction. The stretches were an intense form of calisthenics. Before practice, the Browns would line up in long rows, wearing their mostly white practice uniforms, and do leg extensions, which were the centerpiece of an advanced conditioning program. They looked a little like the Rockettes, kicking one leg as high as possible in the air, then turn, take two steps, and flip the other leg into the air, repeating this dozens of times. Because Jim's thighs were so taut, and because he was often so sore and battered, he could sometimes lift his legs no more than eighteen inches off the ground during the leg drills. This ignited the belief that Brown was a lackadaisical and sloppy practice player, though that was hardly the case.

Leg stretching aside, the Browns had indeed lucked into Jim. Paul knew this. He was fond of reminding people around the Cleveland organization: "Sometimes you get kicked upstairs." He meant that the luck of many NFL teams when it came to the draft was dismal, and errors led to staffs getting canned.

Paul had more grandiose thoughts about Jim but kept those close. Paul knew that Brown was not just a good running back but something far different. In 1957, his rookie season, Jim led the NFL in rushing with 942 yards, doing so on athletic ability alone. One game that year typified his season. In Cleveland on November 24, before 65,407 people on a blustery thirty-five-degree day, Browns quarterback Tommy O'Connell was badly injured early in the first quarter against the Los Angeles Rams. Jim had already scored one touchdown early in the game, and after O'Connell was blasted, Paul turned over the game to Jim, something that would become a recurring theme throughout Jim's career. Starting on their own 31-yard line, Paul called a draw play for Jim, and just as he took the football from new quarterback Milt Plum, he was hit from opposite sides by two blitzing Rams linebackers, Larry Morris and Dick Daugherty. Daugherty hit Jim so hard that Daugherty's helmet popped off. Brown stumbled for one quick moment, then broke loose of both linebackers' grips and ran 69 yards for a touchdown. After fumbling the football in the third quarter, Jim redeemed himself by scoring two more touchdowns and setting up two others as well as one field goal. He finished the game with four touchdowns and an NFL record 237 yards.

Knowing that his physical prowess would take him only so far, Jim used the weapon in his vast arsenal that served him best: his brain. Practically by himself, with little coaching, Jim began to study his own running style, and noticed that as he approached the holes in the line, he danced around for one or two seconds, looking for an opening. This inevitably led to Brown's beating one tackler, but the hesitation allowed the remainder of the defense to catch Brown from behind, thus negating his speed advantage.

Brown changed all of that just one season later. By 1958, beginning in training-camp practices in Hiram, Ohio, Jim had organized a drill: he recruited Browns defenders to jam the running lanes, and he would practice aggressively charging the hole, whether it was plugged by a body or not. If a man was there, Brown would simply run him over or break the tackle, then use moves and speed in the open field. In a run against the New York Giants in the first game of the season, Brown used this technique to burst for a 58-yard run after breaking three tackles near the line of scrimmage. His new running style would not change for the remainder of his career.

That season Brown rushed for a record 1,527 yards, beating the former record held by Steve VanBuren by almost 400 yards. The

Associated Press named Brown the player of the year. He beat out Baltimore's Unitas. When Jim played Unitas in Baltimore on November 1, 1959, Jim scored five touchdowns on the day to four for Unitas. Many of the 57,557 Colts fans gave Jim a standing ovation.

In the mid-1950s players like Alan Ameche or Rick Casares were considered dominant runners. Then came Jim and the evolution. Paul saw before anyone—except maybe Jim himself—that Jim was taking the sport of football to a different plane by bringing skills to the running-back position that had not been seen before. Before him, running backs were smallish and slow, and their main purpose was to move piles and pick up three or four yards. Brown took the position and turned it on its head. He proved that a running back could be a threat on any down, in any situation, on any part of the field. Paul sent Jim on deep pass routes, and he would blow by defensive backs, who were usually neither fast nor agile.

Paul Brown's rules and coldhearted nature inspired respect, resentment, and fear. Behind his back players referred to him as "that bastard," and if they were really angry with him he became "that bald-headed bastard." Nowhere was the relationship between Browns coach and player rawer than between Paul and Jim. The Browns coach and his game-changing runner were two intensely strong-willed men who would experience numerous disagreements and personal clashes that resulted in a thorny, dysfunctional relationship. Their only piece of connective tissue was the firm belief that Jim was going to be one of the league's true stars and that the team, the entire franchise, was going to hitch a ride on those dangerous, broad shoulders all the way to a championship.

HE WAS A man impossible to tackle in an era when players were allowed to use every dirty method and nasty tactic possible to chop a runner down.

He took punches to the ribs and kidneys, often in full view of game officials. Kicks were delivered with cold fury to his groin; his fingers were purposely bent backward. Over his career, newspaper reports described Brown as being light-headed or dizzy. It is likely that he suffered many concussions, leading to moments when he saw nothing as he walked, almost like a zombie, slowly back to the huddle, readying his mind for the next play.

"I have never seen an athlete be as physically abused and still play at such a high level, as Jim Brown," remembered former owner Art Modell. "Things were done to Jim that today would lead to players getting arrested."

There were no warm and comfortable domes in which to play and practice in the winter. Day after day, practice after practice, game after game, in the chilling cold and wind of Cleveland's ugly winters, Brown played on. There was a fractured wrist so painful and limp that teammates had to help him tie his shoes. There was an entire season played with a broken toe. Brown did not tell the coaching staff about the injury until the season had concluded, because he knew that the coaches would have told him to get on the field anyway. So why bother with the lip service?

The injuries and physical abuse only stiffened Brown's resolve. But his dedication despite the devastating pain went beyond what was almost a genetic toughness. Brown was not just a powerful athlete, he was also an intellect. He knew that as the sole focus of Cleveland's run-oriented offense, he desperately needed to engineer tactics that helped him cope with the sustained violence.

Brown's cool exterior on the field was a part of a learned and calculated response to the hits his body absorbed and the verbal abuse his ears tolerated. "You ain't shit, motherfucker" was something Brown heard on more than a few occasions early in a game. No matter how much his elbow ached or his knees creaked or his heart told him to respond to a tackler who stated he was overrated,

Brown normally refused to show outward emotion. He did not want the defense to sense he was hurt or angry. In football, especially during that era, any sign of weakness only intensified the attack.

He was always the same, no matter how jarring the hit. After a play, whether it was a galloping run or a stuff for a loss, Brown rose from the ground slowly, deliberately. He called it "getting up with leisure." A defense would watch Brown closely, looking for a limp or a whimper, and the only thing they would see was Brown plodding back to the huddle, hiding behind his linemen so no one could witness just how much he hurt.

Brown violated his rule of self-control on just two known occasions. In 1965, near the end of his career, a young and darting running back named Gale Sayers was drafted in the first round by the Chicago Bears, out of Kansas. Brown and Sayers had actually met. Sayers heard Brown speak at a Rotary Club in Omaha, Nebraska. The two men talked afterward and initiated a friendship that has lasted until now.

The NFL was almost as startled by the abilities of Sayers as it had been when Brown arrived. Brown and Sayers were in an intense battle for the league lead in touchdowns. The Browns were playing in St. Louis in the team's last regular-season game. Cleveland was headed to the playoffs while St. Louis was not.

Late in the game, after a short run, Brown slowly lifted his body from the ground. Just after turning his back to the defense to prepare for his slow walk back to the huddle, an elbow smashed into the back of his head, causing searing pain. The elbow belonged to defensive lineman Alvis Joe Robb, a bruiser from Lufkin, Texas, who played for TCU in the 1959 Cotton Bowl against Air Force, an infamous game that ended in a 0–0 tie. Robb would end up as a decent but unremarkable player whose biggest claim to fame might be angering Brown.

Brown was ailing from the hit, but, as he wrote in his second autobiography, *Out of Bounds*, the pain did not dampen his rage. None of Brown's Cleveland teammates remember him ever being in an excitable state on the field. The angrier he got, the quieter and calmer he became. This was a portion of the Brown mystique that was part nature and part nurture. But it often confused teammate and opponent alike. Men in that time expressed their anger with curses and fisticuffs, not introspection.

After Robb's dirty hit, Brown did what he always did. He walked back to the huddle without saying a word and readied for the next play. A short time later a pass play was called. As the Cleveland players started to approach the line of scrimmage, Brown grabbed one of his tackles by the shoulder pad. He covertly pointed in Robb's direction and instructed the big man, softly and politely, to let Robb into the backfield.

As Robb came bursting through, Brown crouched down, just inches away from the turf, coiling his powerful torso into a tight bundle, before exploding upward, his forearm acting like the leading edge of an airplane wing, cutting through the air, and landing on Robb's jaw. As Robb stood there momentarily stunned, Brown then kicked him in the stomach. Robb was taken to the ground, Brown was tossed out of the contest by game officials, and Sayers won the touchdown race.

Brown's only other true moment of on-field fury came against New York. After the Giants had poked and battered his eyes in 1963, Brown swore to himself he would never take such abuse again. When Cleveland next met the Giants, one of New York's linebackers, Tom Scott, a two-time Pro Bowler, squeezed his chunky forearm inside Brown's helmet and began hitting Brown in the face. Brown used his own forearm to hit Scott on the side of his face, bloodying Scott's mouth. Brown was ejected.

"I think Brown handed out as much physical pain to our

players," the late Hall of Fame Giants owner Wellington Mara told the author years before his death, "as they did to him."

As much physical abuse as Brown endured, no one was a bigger self-bully. His retaliations against Robb and Scott notwithstanding, Brown believed in purging emotions on the field, and most of the time he stuck to this rule. A coolheaded football player made smarter decisions, Brown thought.

Soon, Brown earned the reputation among some in the media as a man of few words or opinions. "Jim is a quiet fellow," the Cleveland *Plain Dealer* wrote of Brown in his rookie season. "He seldom initiates conversation and he thinks before he answers."

In fact, Brown was anything but quiet. His opinions raged in side his head and, increasingly, in volatile conversations with several of the black players; but for now Brown allowed the belief that he was simply a brooding batterer stand, because perhaps the one thing Brown hated more than anything else was to be understood.

Browns practices were intense and water breaks were rare, so when the breaks did occur, players took in as much water as they could, knowing the next opportunity to take a drink might never come. Brown stayed away from ingesting water before and during games entirely. When the water breaks came, he would move to the side, standing alone, hands on his hips, waiting for the break to end.

Throughout Brown's varied athletic career he had absorbed the faulty reasoning from coaches and other players that drinking water could turn a speedy runner into a lumbering one. Water was seen not as a vital lubricant, but as an enemy that drained athleticism. "Water was not a regular part of workouts in those days," said Brown's high school coach, Ed Walsh. Since Brown was the ultimate self-motivator, he also avoided water because he hated the feeling of being fulfilled. He wanted to remain anxious and angry, and drinks of water improved his mood. So Brown would often go entire games and through hours of practice without consuming a single drop.

Brown enjoyed his mind games with the bruisers and assassins on opposing defenses—winning those games, in particular—and the enjoyable feeling that accompanies a swelling male ego after one man pummels another. He was infatuated with the violence of football.

Inside Brown, there was another force at work on the field. In the late 1950s, racial discrimination was a drastic factor in the life of every black American. Brown was no different. The daily indignities suffered even by a star fullback in professional football created a hardened film over Brown. His life thus far had been full of equal numbers of whites who had helped him and those who had hated him. The latter created scars on Brown as thick and jagged as his physical ones.

Brown's awareness of the reality of race and professional football grew steadily and stubbornly. On the field, coaches and fans wanted Brown to push the limits of human physiology by absorbing blows and hits that would cripple most. Off the field, blacks in the NFL—including even the biggest stars—were expected to be docile and quiet. They were not to discuss publicly the nation's tumultuous racial climate; if they did, they risked being banned from the sport. With Brown this contradiction was more evident than with any other player. Brown had the mental sturdiness to become the toughest player in the toughest sport, and the idea that he would be meek and without opinions away from the field was thoroughly unrealistic to him.

In a matter of just a few years, despite his newness to pro football, Brown would organize the black players on the Browns into a politically active group that was the most advanced and organized in all of sports. They were a group of rabble-rousing, women-chasing partyers whose influence and organizational skills would spread across the league from team to team. There was nothing in professional sports like what Brown had begun.

Like other black players, once he entered the league, Brown became aware of a mandate—unrecorded and not publicly acknowledged—among the NFL's owners. No more than ten blacks were allowed on a professional franchise. Owners and the NFL leadership planned the quotas to prevent blacks from dominating the sport and alienating the white fan base. Paul Brown was known as a man who did not care about the race of a player as long as he was a solid football athlete, which was a scandalously liberal attitude in those times. Yet not even Paul, one of the more powerful men in the NFL, could topple the stout forces of racism and segregation.

Teams went to diabolical means to enforce racial firewalls. It was not a coincidence that teams kept small, even numbers of black players on their rosters. "Most of the time blacks and whites were not allowed to room together in those days," said one current NFL official, familiar with the hiring practices of teams in the 1950s and 1960s. "Segregation and quotas were common. No one spoke about it. It was just done. If there was an even number of whites and blacks on the roster, then whites would be paired with whites," the official explained. "An odd number meant that whites would have to be paired with blacks and share rooms on the road. Owners tried to prevent that from happening in the 1950s."

If an injury kept a black player from traveling and so an odd number of blacks went on the road, instead of having a black player and a white player room together, teams purchased separate rooms, one for the black player and one for the white player. In other words, franchises paid extra money to keep the races apart.

Jim always despised final cut-down days. He'd walk around the locker room, looking at some of the black faces, knowing they would be gone in a matter of hours, not because they did not deserve to make the team, but because there were simply more blacks on the Browns than the quota allowed.

It was not just segregation and fear of a backlash from white fans that kept the numbers of blacks in the NFL to a minimum. Many NFL coaches and fans believed that blacks did not possess the intellect or vigor to play professional football. Jim's power and passion were also fueled by the desire to disprove that prevalent notion. Each yard he gained, each time he outsmarted a defense, was a sort of validation, not just for Brown, but for the other blacks inside the Cleveland locker room, and the growing number of black faces around the country that began to follow Brown's every magnificent run.

IN THE SUMMER of 1958, preceding Jim's second season, Paul Brown did as he had done for many years before: set the guidelines for standards and behavior in a blistering speech to the players. The team gathered at its Hiram training camp facility and dutifully listened to Paul address the team with the kind of tone usually reserved for a father speaking to his five-year-old son.

"We're going to be as good a football team as the class of people you are," Paul said. "We intend to have good people because they're the kind that win the big ones. If you're a drinker or a chaser, you'll weaken the team and we don't want you. I'm talking to the veterans as well as the rookies here today. If you're an older player and have reached the point where you can't concentrate on what I have to say, maybe you've reached the point where you ought to be looking for other work.

"If you think about football only when you step on the field, we'll try to peddle you," he continued. "You've got four months of this ahead of you, and for four and a half months I expect football to be the biggest thing in your life, as it is in mine. In this game, more men fail mentally than physically."

Paul paused for effect, hoping that last sentence would settle over the team like a thick blanket. Jim looked cautiously at the other players within his peripheral vision and noticed how their eyes were fixed intently on Paul. There was utter silence, yet Brown was stunned not so much by what Paul was saying, but by how his teammates were reacting. He knew from speaking to some of the veterans that they had heard this speech many times over, but they acted as if Paul were saying it for the first time. They were so afraid of Paul, so intimidated by him, Jim thought, that they feigned interest in a preseason speech they had heard many times before.

"Maybe you've read or heard that there are four or five jobs open on this team," Paul said. "I want to tell you right now that that isn't true. There are thirty-five jobs open. They're going to be won by the men who convince me and the other coaches that they're best qualified to fill them. I like to think that the Cleveland Browns are somewhat different from the average professional football team. I want to see some exuberance in your play, some sign that you play for the sheer joy of licking somebody.

"We've been in business thirteen years. In eleven of them we've won division championships," Paul continued. "In several others we've taken the whole pot. We're the Ben Hogans, the Joe Louises, the New York Yankees of our game, and that's the way we aim to keep it.

"At home and on the road we stay together," Paul went on. "On the nights before home games we go to a downtown hotel in Cleveland. We eat together, go to a movie as a group. It gives us a feeling of oneness that helps to make us a team and not just a collection of thirty-five football players."

Jim found this part of Paul's speech interesting, since Jim knew that the Browns did not truly stay "together." Black and white players sometimes did not share the same hotel rooms. Blacks sometimes drank from different water fountains than white players and ate in different restaurants. The togetherness of the Browns was part illusion.

"I expect you to watch your language, your dress, your deportment, and especially I expect you to be careful of the company you keep," Paul said. "That pleasant guy who invites you to dinner may be a gambler. Probably he doesn't intend to offer you a bribe. Maybe he isn't even after information. But he wants to be seen with you in public. I'm telling you to avoid him.

"Here's a rule," the speech continued. "In your rooms at ten, lights out at ten thirty. Occasionally the coaches make a bed check. For the player who sneaks out after the bed check there's an automatic fine of $500. And it sticks. I have had to levy many fines for violations of many rules, and I have never rescinded one for good subsequent behavior or meritorious performance.

"Here in Hiram we eat three meals a day together. Sports shirts are approved, but I don't want to see any player in the dining room in a T-shirt. I expect civilized table manners and table talk. There have been people who failed to make this team simply because they were obnoxious to eat with. We're determined to have a team of men who are willing to pay the price of success in football, and the price is high. If you approach this just as another job, another means to a payday, we don't want you. I want you to keep your wives out of football. Ask them not to talk football with other wives. I've seen it cause trouble."

Paul then concluded with words that were meant to convey compassion but were delivered with the sincerity of a grocery store clerk informing a customer of the price of a can of peas: "Before the season opens I'm going to have to tell some of you—many of you—that you won't make it. It's the part of my job that I like the least, but when the time comes, my good wishes will go with you. Now, let's get to work."

As the players and coaches separated into smaller groups, Paul's speech still ringing in their ears, Jim was uncertain of what to make of it, or of the reaction of his teammates. It struck him as cartoon-like, almost phony. "How could anyone buy this shit?" he thought. Brown was only in his second year in the league, but he was already showing significant signs of defiance and independent thinking, both of which were uncommon among most NFL players. His opinion of Paul would change swiftly and dramatically, shifting from respectful to contemptuous, as the men's relationship would become intensely chilly, hostile, even hateful, though rarely a cross word was exchanged between them. Jim's machismo and buoyancy and growing sense of racial pride were not the only factors at work in this metamorphosis. Also inside Brown's powerful and unbreak-able frame were choking insecurities, the kind that can make a big man small, insecurities fashioned by years of racism and the memo-ries of a young boy abandoned.

IN THE SPRING *of 1803 a small schooner sailed gently alongside the Georgia coast with seventy human beings sealed tightly inside its dark cargo hold.*

The vessel carried slavery-bound West Africans from a tribe called the Ibo. Historians believe their dangerous trip took them thousands of miles from Africa after their capture in 1802, to a Gulf of Guinea seaport, and eventually to Skidaway Island near Savannah, where two wealthy south-erners, who just five years earlier had helped to ratify a Georgia constitu-tion that prohibited the importation of slaves, purchased the Ibo for $500 each.

Once the ship reached shallower waters and the slaves were readied to be taken ashore, an Ibo leader urged others of his tribe to fight their cap-tors, and there was a bloody insurrection. During the fighting, ten of the Ibo walked off the boat, in unison, and subsequently drowned, preferring death to captivity.

That sad and stunning act of rebellion took place on St. Simons Island, Georgia, and would become lore and lasting legend there.

It was on this island, generations later, that James Nathaniel Brown was born. The day was February 17, 1936.

HE LOVED WOMEN and gambling and indulged in both to great extremes. He was the man who charmed much of an island, St. Simons Island, the man whose wife had no other choice but to leave, the man who could not turn his back on the dice and poker, but could on his own son. He was Swinton Brown.

Swinton was often called Sweet Sue. At six feet two inches and 225 pounds, he was a heavy, solidly built man, with a large smile and the eloquence and persuasive demeanor all good street hustlers possess. Sweet Sue despised the conventional, yet he still married, choosing a pretty dark-skinned woman named Theresa, who toiled in the homes of rich white families as a maid.

In his 1964 book *Off My Chest* Jim Brown wrote of his father:

People told me that Sue—his friends called him just plain Sue—was a huge man who had been a good football player in nearby Brunswick, Georgia, and had boxed professionally around the state. They also said he loved to dance and fancied himself a man about town. Everyone who told me about Sue spoke of him with affection, because he was, by all accounts, impossible to dislike. It just happened that he had a weakness for the dice and cards. Sue always figured that Lady Luck was due to smile on him, but she mostly turned her back. This was why the marriage broke up. My mother loved him but she just couldn't run a household on inside straights that didn't fill.

Sweet Sue left just several weeks after Brown was born, and it would be some time before the two would see each other again. It was a relationship that never materialized into one of father and son. Even Brown's mother, Theresa, temporarily abandoned Brown when Jim was a child.

St. Simons was a stunning paradise, full of tranquil beaches and pecan trees, but its allure could not stop history. Brown's parents both left Georgia for cities in the North, joining a stream of black Americans who departed the South for better job opportunities in other parts of the country, creating a massive relocation. In the 1930s and 1940s, some 77 percent of black Americans called the South their home, with 49 percent living in the rural South.

That would soon change. The Great Black Migration from cities in the southern countryside to the great metropolises of the West and North started with the mechanization of the cotton picker, which left millions of blacks looking for employment. They left the South in large numbers, 6.5 million doing so between 1910 and 1970, 5 million after 1940. When the migration ended, the South was only half black. It was one of the largest and swiftest mass internal movements of people in human history; the passage of the Italians or Irish from their countries to America pales in comparison.

Theresa and Sweet Sue were swept up in dreams of better opportunities. Brown's father abandoned him and never became a significant part of his son's life, while Theresa promised a young Brown that she would one day come back for him and they would be together in New York.

The departure of his parents at such a young age begat a lasting feeling of abandonment and insecurity that would haunt Brown for much of his life, affecting many of his personal and professional relationships, and shaping his views about women.

Brown was raised by his extended family, led by Nora, his great-grandmother, a strong, disciplined woman who would take a thin switch to Jimmy's backside after he sneaked into the house the back way after a forbidden night of roaming the island. Jimmy called her Mama, but he knew Nora was not his real mother. They lived with an aunt, Bertha, and a grandmother, Myrtle Powell, in a tiny house that had one floor and peeling white paint on the exterior, but was comfortable and sturdy. The legend of Jim Brown growing up in a dilapidated cabin, a story propagated by newspapers across Cleveland, was more fable than fact.

Many young blacks in the South during this time felt the sting of racism at an early age but did not fully comprehend its ugliness and impact until later. Brown played with young white kids almost as much as he did with black ones, and during much of his St. Simons childhood was unaware of the color lines. As his playgrounds expanded and shifted across various parts of the island, from the abandoned, centuries-old forts, from the ponds and the long, worn piers, to the segregated beaches, his racial awakening slowly began. He was allowed, sparingly, to play on the whites-only beaches because he served as a form of amusement for some of the vacationers from the larger cities in the East and South. Brown had elegant facial features, a disarming smile, and dark skin. No matter how fanciful his looks, that latter fact was the first piece of information whites noticed.

His natural mother, Theresa, kept her word, and sent for young Brown when he was eight. He had not seen Theresa since he was a toddler, and thoughts of a reunion energized Brown. As he left on the train for Great Neck, New York, he left behind what for much of his childhood had been his family. Mama, Grandma Myrtle, and Aunt Bertha remained on St. Simons. It would take decades for Brown's scattered memories of that place to coagulate into tangible ones about the ugliness of the bigotry he had encountered as a boy: the two-room shanty schoolhouse overcrowded with dark faces, blacks limited to mostly domestic work, and a host of other ignominies.

Brown would return to the island for summer visits after reuniting with Theresa in New York. One of his last visits was when Brown was an upperclassman at Syracuse University and the college football world was buzzing about his exploits and athleticism.

Brown wrote of that day:

The last time I visited St. Simons Island I had an experience that made me know I'd probably never return. I'd become, by then, a nationally known college football star. Mama was dead but I wanted to go home and visit aunt Bertha and grandmother Myrtle. When I got there Myrtle told me she was doing housework for a white family and that when she had mentioned to them that I was coming home the man of the house said to her, "Ask the boy to come over and visit a spell. I'd like to meet him."

I drove out to his house and knocked on the door. Myrtle's employer answered the door and stepped outside and shook my hand. "Well," he said. "I'm certainly glad to meet you, son. I've followed your career at Syracuse, and we're sure proud of you down here." He stood there in front of the door for quite a while, telling me how I'd done myself proud and telling me what a good worker Myrtle was. He had nothing but kind words. But I said to myself: "This is a lot of crap. He asks me to drive out here so he can shake my hand and tell me what a big man I am, but he doesn't invite me inside and offer me a seat. He's glad to meet me, but I'm not worthy of common courtesy." I was more saddened than angry. I said goodbye to my island in the sun, the wonderful place where I'd hung my crab basket from the pier and hunted buried treasure in the woods.

St. Simons was no longer mystical to Brown. He would indeed go back, but not for many, many years.

AS JIM BROWN began his unusual new life in Great Neck, Long Island, an undersized quarterback named Paul Brown was beginning his high school career in a small town called Massillon, Ohio.

Massillon and Canton are the places where professional football's first great rivalries and athletes were born. Jim Thorpe played for Canton, and names like Knute Rockne and Gus Dorais were on Massillon's roster when the two teams played each other in 1915. When Paul departed Norwalk, Ohio, for Massillon he began to ingest the game of football even at a young age. He wanted to be those players; he snuck into games to see his heroes. When he attended Washington High School in Massillon, which was commonly known as Massillon High School, Paul played high school quarterback and was a lean, feisty thrower with a big brain and a weak arm. When Paul was fourteen, he weighed just over 100 pounds; by high school, he was barely 150 pounds. Strength and athleticism were not what made him a solid passer. It was the way he absorbed information and carried himself that allowed Paul to be a fine passer and play college ball at Miami of Ohio (now called Miami University), where he followed another vertically challenged passer in five-foot-seven-inch Weeb Ewbank.

Being a professional player was not his destiny. Paul knew that. Coaching was his vocation. Paul knew that, too. When a head coaching position opened back at Massillon High in 1932, he jumped at the chance, and took the job at the ripe age of twenty-three. There was great skepticism about this upstart and his lack of experience. Would he be good enough to turn around a floundering but proud program that had won only two games the season before? But once the community and hard-core Massillon supporters met

Paul and heard his ideas, they could not build a bandwagon big enough.

What struck them was hearing Paul talk, not solely about building game plans and players, but about constructing an entire program, something no one else had mentioned. He wanted his players to have warm-up jackets. He wanted a better mascot. He wanted his players to have the best equipment.

Those boosters gave him their support. He did what he said he would, and more. The new Massillon coach asked a local psychologist to design one of the first psychological-testing programs for athletes and administered it to his high school players. The results of the test were combined with a player's grades and provided Paul with a more multidimensional profile of the player.

When Paul started to win immediately, he got more than praise. He gained power and control, rising to the title of athletic director. Eventually nothing happened at Massillon without Paul knowing. The lesson Paul learned even on the high school level was how one man and one man only must have the power over all football matters, or the team could quickly wither because of a leadership vacuum.

Paul's system on offense was not sophisticated or particularly inventive. The way he taught football was. In its pubescence, football was almost strictly visual. There was not the kind of extensive classroom studies that would become common in the sport only a short time later. Paul spent hours drawing plays on dusty, gritty blackboards. Players then took those plays and copied them into tiny spiral notebooks—and even the notebooks players utilized had to be approved by Paul. Those books became the team's playbooks; the practice of players actually studying for football the way they did for a history final had begun.

Massillon would become one of the most successful high school athletic programs in the history of the country. In nine years at

Massillon, Paul Brown coached his team to a record of 80 wins, 2 losses, and 8 ties. He won not because his athletes were better, but because they were more prepared. Paul also scouted opponents, which was almost unheard of for high school programs.

Most of all, Paul won because he demanded perfection and got it. He demanded that the only voice in the heads of players during practices and games be his. And it was. No player questioned him, no one doubted him, and no one inside the Massillon program ever spoke out publicly against him. No one said he was humorless or lacked personality. No one challenged his supreme authority.

Paul looked like the teacher he was. His hairline began to retreat before he turned thirty. He was not an imposing figure, with his average height and slim build, and a youngish face that usually, in the game of football during that period, would draw chuckles, not respect. He wore suits, often brown, with polished brown shoes, a brown fedora, a white shirt, and a nondescript tie; sometimes a white handkerchief sat in his jacket pocket.

Paul's looks were not intimidating, but his words and actions were. By 1942 he was coaching at famed Ohio State, and he initiated the construction of a near dynasty almost a decade before Woody Hayes and the Buckeyes would become synonymous with greatness. By that time, Paul had established a reputation as such a methodical and reliable winner that high school coaches across the state of Ohio funneled their talent to him more than to any other college coach. Some of those players, like guard Bill Willis and wideout Dante Lavelli, would go on with Paul to the Cleveland Browns.

At Ohio State, just like at Massillon, the rule of law was Paul. There was rarely screaming or rants from Paul, just insults or cutting remarks, and ruthless repercussions if his rules were broken. The qualities that Paul was later criticized for—that he was an automaton who cared little about the feelings of his players and only about his rules and the science of football—worked well as he took football from its dusty and disorganized beginnings into a more modernized era. Then, players did not question authority with regularity. They craved leadership and instruction. When Paul sometimes went too far with discipline, kicking players off the team whether they were all-Americans or third-stringers, no one questioned Paul's wisdom or fairness, because winning armored him. At Ohio State a former Massillon player named Charley Anderson broke the team curfew by creeping out the night before a game to party at a Columbus nightclub. Paul embarrassed Anderson by kicking him off the Buckeyes in front of the entire team. It was a stunning and cruel moment that no one within the Ohio State administration questioned. Whether he was tossing a captain off of one of his teams for getting into a fight with police or suspending a player for showing up to a team meeting just seconds late, Paul could be a cold and uncompromising coach. No one cared, because of the results. Ohio State won a national championship.

When Paul began building the Cleveland Browns—the *Chicago Daily Tribune* trumpeted his hiring as head coach with bold headlines and hype—he put together a collection of charter talent that included six future Hall of Famers. Some of these players were black. The rules of the All-America Football Conference and the NFL, the two competing professional football leagues, stated nothing specific about banning black athletes. Yet it was an unspoken rule, and from 1932, the date considered the beginning of the modern era of professional football, until 1946, no black players had participated in either league.

The idea of discriminating because of race was something that never occurred to Paul. It just seemed so damned illogical. "I want the best players," he once told team owner Mickey McBride, "period." Before Jackie Robinson risked his life to play baseball for the Brooklyn Dodgers, two young black men, fullback Marion Motley and guard Bill Willis, were playing for the Browns, and had been signed by Paul.

"I never considered football players black or white, nor did I keep or cut a player just because of his color," Paul once said. "In our first meeting before training camp every year, I told the players that they made our teams only if they were good enough. I didn't care about a man's color or his ancestry; I just wanted to win football games with the best people possible."

It is not that Paul would become close to his black players, or that he empathized with them or was particularly disgusted at the treatment of these men; he saw them as he did his white players: valuable tools to plug into his system.

Paul may not have cared about race, but he was not stupid. He knew much of the country did. He worried about the physical well-being of Motley and Willis, as well as the effect that being pioneers would have on their psyche and play (there was always a bottom line with Paul—performance). So in the summer of 1946, he quietly brought the two players into the Browns' training camp. While there was a violent reaction in some quarters of the nation, bringing them into camp, instead of introducing them to the public months earlier, softened the pressure.

Paul received criticism from owners and coaches who despised the idea of what he did. Paul simply ignored it. There were, however, some situations he could not ignore. When the Browns traveled to Miami that year to play the Seahawks, Paul asked both Motley and Willis to stay behind. A Florida state law prohibited any athletic competition between blacks and whites.

Paul timed his players in sprints. He devised the first playbook. He used messenger guards to send in plays. He dreamed up the draw play and the down-and-out pass pattern. He invented the face mask. He even tried out a CB radio in the quarterback's helmet. When football was a sport played mostly by large-bellied behemoths

who drank too much beer and smoked too many cigarettes, along came Paul, who administered psychological testing and classroom studying, increasing the professionalism of the sport dramatically. He hatched a nest of men who would become great coaches—Chuck Noll, Don Shula, Ara Parseghian.

Yet his greatest contribution to football may be the one he is least recognized for. Paul Brown's efforts led to the breaking of professional football's color line.

JIM BROWN ARRIVED in Great Neck, Long Island, a short time before his eighth birthday in 1943. His mother, Theresa, continued her work as a maid, this time with a wealthy family of Jewish descent named the Brockmans. Jim and Theresa were given a tiny room on one side of the house. This was his new home, quite a contrast to the wide-open space of St. Simons.

Great Neck was a place of substantial wealth and overwhelming poverty. Real estate professionals, oil tycoons, and executives prospering from the mushrooming automobile industry and the World War II economic boom began purchasing large homes in the city. Film actors and Broadway musical stars also came to Great Neck, creating a vivid social scene reminiscent of *The Great Gatsby*.

Jim and Theresa's home was humble, but they were better off than many of the other blacks in the area. Jim went to elementary school in Manhasset, where mom and son eventually moved, living in a ground-floor flat at 104 Lee Avenue in Manhasset Valley, nicknamed "the Valley" by local residents. As the wealthy of Long Island moved into the area and settled into the large houses and estates, a subculture of housekeepers, landscapers, and laborers grew just as fast. This group was initially composed of newly arrived Polish and Italian immigrants, but after the black migration, a large influx of blacks cleaned the houses and manicured the lawns of the wealthy. Conversely, the decaying neighborhoods of the Valley could be seen clearly from a heavily traveled highway nearby.

Jim's father remained mostly absent from his life. Sweet Sue moved from job to job, occasionally arriving at Jim's doorstep unannounced. Jim never loved his father, because Sweet Sue was not around enough to engender those kinds of feelings.

Without the stability of a solid family structure, and a father more interested in gambling than in his own son, Jim grew more rambunctious as he aged into a young teen. His mother was caring, and taught Jim to be meticulous about his appearance, but eighteen-hour workdays made her mostly unavailable to him. Jim practically raised himself, and the lesson he learned was that power and force were the rule of law on the street, not civilized behavior, and his fists were what gained him respect. Thus Jim's penchant for brawls with other kids did not stop after the move from St. Simons to Long Island. Theresa would send Jim to school wearing neat clothes and starched shirts that would promptly get dirtied when he fought the other kids in the neighborhood. When he was eleven and in seventh grade, a classmate called him a "dirty nigger." Brown cocked his arm back and, without saying a word, punched the kid in the face, knocking him to the ground. Several days later, the mother of the punched-out youngster phoned one of the teachers to wonder how someone her son's age could hit so hard, because her son was still incapacitated in bed several days after the punch.

Jim became recognized as one of the toughest in the Valley, pouncing on opponents and using quick punches before subduing them by throwing them to the ground and hitting them until someone stopped the fight, or until Jim decided he had bloodied his opponent enough.

Classes and schoolwork bored Jim. He was not an academic as he entered his young teens; he was a brawler, fighting often. He

joined with a group of other tough Valley kids who called themselves the Gaylords. The gaggle of kids was what could loosely be
considered a gang, though Jim's reputation as a gang member has
become remarkably embellished over the decades. Police reports
and news accounts from that time show little evidence of pervasive
and violent gang activity in Great Neck or Manhasset. They were
more like fight clubs than gangs.

Like Brown, most of the kids in the Gaylords had absent fathers.
Some lived with aunts and uncles because both parents had abandoned them. They all gravitated to the Gaylords because the group
represented the security that their family life never did. "We were a
group of ten to fifteen kids that didn't have fathers or families, so
we started the club for stability and safety," says the Reverend Ed
Corley, who grew up in the Valley with Brown and was a member
of the Gaylords. "It was an athletic social club. We got into fights,
we brawled, but there were no guns or knives.

"We would go to other neighborhoods, go to parties, try to pick
up girls," Corley says. "We'd fight other gangs. Sometimes we won;
sometimes we lost."

In between the brawls, they played football. Lots of football.
They proved their toughness to one another by playing on the Valley's side streets, littered with debris and broken glass. They played
with cut hands and broken lips, all the while blocking and tackling
on the blackened asphalt. They used these games as a test of manhood.

Jim had natural ability and was among the larger of the Gaylords, but he was among a group of skilled athletes, not the exception. "One of the reasons we were all good athletes is because we
were always running," Corley remembers. "We were either always
chasing other guys, trying to fight them, or we were being chased.
Running, running, running. I was always running."

In fact, one of the great misconceptions about Jim and his days growing up in the Valley is that he was the only great athlete to emerge from that group. Many of the Gaylords were as athletically gifted as Brown. "We did not realize the kind of athletic ability Jim had," Corley explains. "When Jim was around the black kids, he was exceptional, but a lot of us were exceptional. It wasn't until he started playing around the white players that he became better than everybody. I can't explain why. I think he wanted to prove to whites that he was just as good, if not better, than them. It was a chip there, to be honest. The sad truth is there were some men in our group that actually exceeded Jim Brown's abilities in football. That is true. It is just that they were forced down a different path. They ended up in jail or dead."

While Jim's gang exploits were more legend than actuality, the reality was that he was slipping into a more turbulent, fight-filled world. He was headed toward a life of delinquency and violence and possibly prison. It was a passageway many young black men, because of societal limitations and discrimination, were taking.

That trail would change after a succession of people noticed a raw athletic ability in Brown, despite seeing him play just snippets of sports. In junior high school Jim played on a choppy lacrosse field at Plandome Road Junior High School, not far from the Valley. His immersion in a sport invented by American Indians and played mostly by wealthy whites was almost by accident. While Jim's reputation in the community as a poor student and pseudo thug was firm, his physical skills were something few knew about.

Jim picked up a lacrosse stick out of curiosity. It was strange to him, this game. When he played it initially with other boys in school, running and scampering the way kids do, Jay Stranahan saw this large black boy, quicker than kids years older than he was, and stronger too. Jim moved gracefully with the stick, despite never having seen or held one before.

Stranahan knew lacrosse as well as anyone in the area. He

was a physical-education teacher who introduced the modern form of lacrosse to Long Island in the 1930s. He would help to create a legion of legendary players. The man players sometimes called "Coach Stranny" would bring his car packed with battered equipment and run practices on a parking lot until darkness sent everyone home.

Stranahan was selfish; he wanted Jim to play lacrosse because, like any coach, he craved superb athletes. Yet Stranahan saw something else. While other teachers and adults saw Jim as gloomy and quiet and often not in control of his temper, Stranahan saw a young man who was introspective and lacked a steady father figure. He was drawn to Jim and constantly reminded him of how good an athlete he was.

The message, delivered to Jim repeatedly over many months, finally got through. Jim was a constant presence on Plandome's athletic fields, playing lacrosse, basketball, and football. In some ways, football on a field with lines, as opposed to the Valley's gritty streets and trash cans, was almost as foreign to Jim as lacrosse was. He never played football on St. Simons, but he took to the sport and others with great ease. His natural athleticism was coupled with how he listened intently and respected his coaches, a shocking contradiction to the Brown that many people had come to know. On the streets, any perceived slight led to Jim using his fists. In sports, Jim discovered that physicality and anger, if controlled, could lead to the same reward that fighting did—the thrill of ruling over another man. The reward was winning. I can do all of this, he thought, and not end up in prison.

AS THE 1950s began, Jim Brown was blossoming, just beginning to comprehend the power of team athletics, and how he fit into that new world. Paul Brown was emerging as well, even if some of his

Cleveland players, under Paul for years now, were moaning about his ways, which they viewed as infantilizing.

When he insisted that his players purchase notebooks and replicate the plays he put up on the blackboard on those pages, there were always curious looks. The love/hate relationship Paul had with his players was beginning. When Paul hired a year-round coaching staff—the first coach to do so—he had the assistants break down film, and Paul would show the clips to his players. The team would sit in a small, dark classroom, the images flickering on a wall, and Paul would use the black-and-white pictures to demonstrate what went right and wrong. The film sessions were both instructional and painful, because no matter how well the Browns played, Paul discovered something wrong. A blocking technique was not quite right, or someone was out of position. A missed tackle was replayed over and over. Players worked hard in games just so they would not end up starring in the picture show.

Paul's teams in the All-America Football Conference were dominant, but they were also challenged by teams and stars from other franchises in the AAFC like Joe Perry of the San Francisco 49ers and Tom Landry of New York. This constant push-and-pull prepared the Browns for when the All-America shut down after four years and the Browns, Baltimore Colts, and 49ers merged with the powerful NFL in the 1950 season.

The dislike between the settled and visible NFL and the pipsqueak All-America conference was palpable. The NFL constantly ridiculed the AAFC as a tiny upstart that lacked the NFL's prestige. This slight was not forgotten by a proud and stubborn Paul, particularly when the supremely arrogant NFL, in a remarkable attempt to capitalize both on Paul's growing legend and on the intense animosity that had festered between the two leagues, scheduled a season-opening game in the initial week of the 1950 NFL season between Philadelphia and Cleveland.

The Eagles had just won the championship and were the talk of the sports world. By pitting the Browns against the Eagles, the NFL was hoping for a dominant Philadelphia victory that would embarrass Cleveland and make a statement that the AAFC was a laughingstock.

Paul emphasized to his players just what the NFL was trying to do. "The NFL wants you to lose this game," he told the Browns. "They want you to look foolish."

Paul spent the days before the contest constantly reminding the Browns about the disrespect the NFL was showing them. Playing the respect card was a tactic used by coaches going back decades before Paul (and has been used for decades since). Yet the truth is that Paul's attempt to manipulate his players' emotions was unnecessary. "When we played the Eagles in that first game I would say that there was never another team in the history of sports, anywhere in the world, that was as prepared, physically and emotionally, to play a ball game," said quarterback Otto Graham. "We would have played the Eagles for a keg of beer or a milk shake."

Paul's excessive attempts at controlling every aspect of his players' lives, from what they ate to where they stood on the field to what they read and what they said, was no more evident than before his game against the Eagles. In preparing for Philadelphia, Paul knew that the Eagles' defense would be vulnerable to his passing offense, which used schemes and stratagems not regularly seen before in the NFL, a league that focused almost strictly on a pounding ground game.

Philadelphia's defensive line was the most formidable in football, known for strangling most of the offenses it faced. It used an unusual five-man front, daring teams to pass. Paul dissected Philadelphia for days, staying awake for several nights at a time, and began to notice great gaps in that vaunted defensive front. First, he thought, the Browns had a significant speed advantage. "They're tough but slow," he told his assistant coaches. Paul envisioned a game plan that could spread out Philadelphia's defense, and his wide receivers and running backs would take advantage of the cracks by darting through them. Once the game began, Paul's strategy became clear to everyone except the Philadelphia coaching staff.

Paul first had the Cleveland offensive linemen spread several inches wider with each series as a way to thin the Eagles' front. This in effect created holes in the middle of the line that made it easier for the Browns to generate plays. The way to counter this sort of attack would have been for Philadelphia's line to simply stay put, but since they were unaware of what Cleveland was doing, the hulks from the Eagles followed the Cleveland linemen outward, centimeter by centimeter.

Otto Graham blistered Philadelphia. The Browns did something to the champion Eagles that no one had been able to do for some time: blow them out. The score was 35–10, and if it were not for some dubious penalty calls by game officials who Paul felt were favoring Philadelphia, the score could have been much worse.

The NFL had hoped to embarrass Paul; instead, the reverse happened. When the great upsets in sports are chronicled, this game is often dismissed or left out of the argument, yet it was one of the more stunning games in the history of the league. While Paul's accomplishments were known and respected by some, many of his techniques, as well as his coaching style, were dismissed by the stodgy NFL establishment as childish or even harebrained. His easy win over the Eagles changed all of that. Players who had tired of his insults and chilly nature and seemingly inane quizzes saw the rewards of what Paul was preaching. At a time when athletes did not voice or even think their own thoughts, the players got tired of Paul's deeply controlling processes; yet they endured them because with him they knew that winning would be the end result.

When Bert Bell, as inventive a commissioner as Paul was a head coach, publicly declared the Browns a great group of champions, it cemented Paul as a rising genius. "That was the most prepared team I have ever seen," Bell stated. When Paul heard those remarks he did not so much as smile, but he took Bell's comments as confirmation that his system was successful.

The only man not impressed with Paul and his upstart Browns was the coach of the Eagles, Greasy Neale, who prior to the contest had declared that the Browns were not a welcome addition to the NFL and the Eagles would make an example of them. Neale (who had been a Cincinnati Reds outfielder during the Black Sox scandal of 1919) was a braggart. He called Cleveland's tidy and impressive victory a fluke, pointing to how an injured Steve VanBuren, the quick six-foot-one, two-hundred-pound four-time rushing champion who would be inducted into the Hall of Fame, had not played. Most galling of all, Neale took a personal swipe at Paul's system, telling reporters it was all flash and no substance. "They're a basketball team, not a football club," Neale huffed.

Paul took mental notes of Neale's disrespect. A short time later, the two teams clashed once again. This time, VanBuren, just one year removed from a 1,000-yard season, played in the game. Instead of attacking Philadelphia through the air, Paul won using a bruising ground control offense, beating the Eagles, 13–7. Neale never publicly criticized Paul again.

Paul's relationship with his players consistently alternated between occasionally comforting and exceptionally demanding. After demolishing the Eagles in their stunning opener, the Browns continued to shake up the NFL by reaching the championship game against Los Angeles on Christmas Eve of 1950. Cleveland trailed by 1 point late in the second half and was about to take the lead, when Graham fumbled after a ferocious hit from behind just as he extended his throwing arm to make a pass. The football was recovered by Los Angeles. After the play Graham walked deliberately toward Brown and the sideline, angry because he might just have lost the game, while also wondering what Paul would say to him. Paul unexpectedly put his arm on Graham's shoulder and told the quarterback he would earn another chance to win the contest. "Don't worry, Ott," Paul said.

The relationship between Paul and Graham had been stressful throughout their tenure together, which began in the All-America Football Conference from 1946 to 1949 and continued with the NFL Browns for five years beginning in 1950. As Graham became more popular, Paul grew weary of Graham's fame overshadowing Paul's concept that no individual is larger than the team. Paul's pursuit of selfless, almost clonelike franchises, teams that were without stars, sometimes went to absurd levels.

"One thing Paul never wanted on his team was prima donnas," Graham once remembered. "One time I complained in practice that the center stepped on my foot, and Paul stopped practice, called everybody together in a big circle, and said, 'From this point on, I don't want anybody stepping on Graham's foot.' If I ever had thoughts about being a prima donna, that was the end of them.

"Paul felt that you had to make sacrifices for the team," Graham continued, "and there were times when I hated him for the things he would demand of us. All the while, though, he never raised his voice. If he was mad, all he had to do was look at you with those eyes of his. But he knew when to kick you in the rump, and when to pat you on the back. Against the Rams that time, after I fumbled the ball, I could have crawled into a hole if I'd found one. I felt miserable. But Paul said, 'Don't worry, Ott, we're gonna get 'em anyway.' And that meant a lot to me. So our defense held them, and we had a minute fifty to go 80 yards, and Lou Groza kicks the field goal and we win."

Paul's inventive systems and techniques, coupled with highly disciplined players who feared him, led to Cleveland playing for the

NFL title in each of its first six years in the league. The Browns won three of those games. What Paul did in taking his principles and ideas from Massillon to Ohio State to the NFL and not just winning, but dominating, was quite simply one of the greatest achievements any coach has ever accomplished in any sport, and would only be surpassed in the NFL by Vince Lombardi's dominance, and later Bill Belichick's establishing a dynasty in New England in a salary-capped league.

The Browns won games and championships with regularity, but Paul's methods became increasingly taxing on his players. The relationship with each of them would become tested and strained repeatedly, and none more than Paul's bond with the man who would become his star runner.

ED WALSH WAS on a scouting mission. He had hurriedly departed Manhasset High School for the short trip to Manhasset Valley Grade School. He sometimes hated these trips. There was a part of Walsh that was always uncomfortable with eyeing such young kids for their athletic potential. This time he was surveying the abilities of unusually tall twins who were supposedly two of the more gifted young athletes in the area.

Walsh entered the crowded gym and saw the twins as they darted up and down the basketball court during an intramural game. Yet Walsh's focus changed almost immediately from the twins on the court to another young boy playing in a different corner of the facility. At the time, the Manhasset coaches scouted all sports, no matter what they coached, looking for athletes, and something told Walsh he had just lucked into one of the more special ones. For over an hour, Walsh stared at the kid who glided and sped across the court. He moved like a dancer.

The twins became a memory. Walsh was transfixed.

He returned to Manhasset High the next day and immediately reported to the athletic director and another coach. "How'd the twins look?" Walsh was asked.

"I don't know," Walsh responded. "I barely saw them."

There was an uncomfortable moment of silence.

"But I did see someone else," Walsh said, "and he was this pudgy kid, a fifth-grader, gliding around the court. And you know what? He's going to be great."

Walsh's soft-spoken nature and diminutive size concealed a firm sense of confidence, particularly in his ability to judge even the youngest of athletes. In many ways Walsh was not a typical high school football coach. He refused to scream excessively at his players, and while it was not unusual for coaches then to push or even hit their athletes, Walsh shunned such aggressive techniques. The players listened to Walsh because he was an instructor and not a bully.

Off the field, Walsh often dressed in a smart suit and tie, even in the blistering humidity of a Long Island summer. On the turf, his 145-pound frame barely filled his shirts and shorts, revealing him to be all sinew and bone. Walsh's glasses made him look younger than he was.

Walsh had been hired to elevate Manhasset athletics. When he first met with the influential parents and business leaders, they told him Manhasset had not had an undefeated football season in twenty-two years, and they could not remember the last time they beat their chief rival, Garden City. "If you beat them," one parent told Walsh, "we'll elect you mayor."

Walsh thought there was talent in the area—great talent—but as he studied the school's football program, it became clear that the major issue was attitude. The teams lacked cohesiveness and closeness.

"There were a bunch of athletes, but there was no true team," Walsh explained. "The problem was many of the kids did not come from a structured background. Some came from broken homes with no father, or they had a mother and father who both worked in New York City all day and did not see the kids that much. Some of these kids were practically raising themselves. They needed structure and discipline."

One player who needed both was Jimmy Brown. After his early scouting trip to the grade school, Walsh raved to another football coach and the director of physical education about the pudgy player he had seen scrambling around the basketball court. What Walsh noticed was that Brown, in just the fifth grade, moved with a command of his body that most kids didn't possess until they were four or five years older.

Walsh stayed in touch with Brown in the coming months, and the more they spoke, the closer they grew. Walsh had uncovered Brown's reputation in the community as a part-time, ersatz gang member who liked to settle his differences with his fists. What Walsh saw was a quiet, confused, and respectful Brown who said "no sir" and "yes sir." He saw a kid starving for direction.

When Brown eventually began attending Manhasset High School, Walsh saw that he was not the kind of football player who relied strictly on the fact that he was faster and stronger than most kids. Brown had a work ethic unlike that of any other kid he had coached.

In order to improve Brown's already formidable quickness, Walsh instructed Brown to work on his starts, first by sprinting from a three-point stance after a verbal command, and then by using a sight reference, such as someone waving a hand. The idea was to increase Brown's explosiveness once he broke through the line.

Over one summer, after his ninth-grade year, Brown followed Walsh's instructions, sometimes running those sprints two or three dozens times in a few hours.

At the beginning of each day during the football season, Walsh directed his secretarial assistant to post details about the impending practice on a bulletin board inside the school. Brown would see the list of drills and instruction; during his lunch break, he would practice them alone. Walsh noticed the increasingly less pudgy kid moving and shaking with no one else around. Brown would do the same thing after practice on the street outside of his home.

It is too simplistic to state that Walsh began to serve as the father figure absent from Brown's life. Walsh represented something more basic: stability. Brown had never experienced its powerful effects before. Their relationship began as strictly one of coach and player, but quickly grew into something more poignant. Brown loved football, but he cared equally that people loved and cared about him, and one of those people was Walsh.

Brown's intense spats with his mother over her dating often led Theresa to throw Brown out of the home. Brown was not unlike many young men who were the products of a divorce and went through the uncomfortable period of watching their mothers go out with men who were not their fathers.

There was also the uncomfortable fact, as Walsh says, that while Brown lived with his mother in one home, his father lived in another home that was down the street, almost diagonally, from where Theresa and Jim lived. Theresa and her husband had divorced, and Jim's father was not around much, but when he did decide to make an appearance, mother and father fought viciously.

"They would fight in one part of the room," Walsh remembers, "and Jim would just sit there in another part of the room and not say a peep."

If Brown did not spend those hours or sometimes days away from the household at a girlfriend's, he was visiting the home of Walsh, who would often convince Brown not to do anything rash.

"Just stay here until you calm down," Walsh would tell him.

Whether Walsh was purchasing Brown a jacket and nice slacks because Theresa could not afford to, or putting Brown up for the night after an argument with her, Brown never believed there was any element of insincerity to Walsh's gestures. Brown lowered his formidable guard around Walsh and rarely questioned or challenged him. This step in itself was remarkable, as Brown tended to confront and query almost anyone. He once questioned Grandma Myrtle about why, as a black woman, she hung a white Jesus on the wall of her St. Simons Island cottage.

Because of the color of his skin, many of the white men and women on St. Simons either ignored Brown or despised him, much like the rest of America in the 1940s and 1950s. Blacks were either a necessary evil, needed to clean their houses or cook their food, or a plague to be contained. Brown sensed none of that with Walsh, who could not fathom or tolerate racial ugliness.

"There was prejudice in communities outside of Manhasset, but inside Manhasset, at the high school especially, the teachers did not tolerate it," says Walsh. "I can't explain why our community was somewhat different. It just was. I tried to treat a lot of these kids like they were my sons. I didn't care what color they were."

Walsh was part of a Manhasset community that was almost a racial oddity in 1950s America. While blacks were indeed segregated, cooped up in the Valley, the level of racial hostility toward them, particularly when compared with other communities, was rare, a few incidents aside.

The primary reason? Sports. If a black kid was an excellent athlete and a productive student, he was allowed to mix within Manhasset's upper crust free of discrimination. With few repercussions, many of the black athletes openly and frequently dated white girls, according to black athletes who played sports in Manhasset during that time period. Mixed-race dating was not just a rarity in midcentury America. It was a crime. In the 1950s, marrying someone of a different race was a felony in thirty states. Emmett Till was murdered by white thugs after they said he whistled at a white girl.

But the peaceable relations between the races ended at the Manhasset town limits. During games in nearby Long Island communities, the young black athletes were subjected to racial taunts and threats of violence.

"Many of the coaches in Manhasset were ahead of their time," says Ed Corley, Jim's former teammate. "We'd go to play games in other cities outside of Manhasset and that was when you heard the racial stuff—'nigger this and nigger that. You're gonna die, nigger.' Coach Walsh would just say: 'Ignore it and play football. You're going to get them back by winning.' That was the best way to approach it, and we did."

The young black boy and the older, bespectacled white football coach, from drastically different backgrounds, had accomplished peace easily. Jim Brown and Ed Walsh had reached a point in their relationship where race was mostly irrelevant.

"You niggers might as well go home right now."

Manhasset was playing its nemesis, Garden City High School, and the slurs were abundant.

"You ain't coming through this hole, nigger."

The players on Manhasset, black and white, ignored the ugly words coming from more than a few defensive players on the Garden City team. They had heard them before. They were armored against them. They blocked them out. They believed in what Walsh had said many times, that winning was the ultimate revenge. No, they were not worried about Garden City. They were worried about Jimmy Brown.

Brown had been stuffed for much of the game and had become extremely irritated. Late in the contest, he walked back to the huddle and glared fiercely at his offensive linemen and blocking back. Some of the Manhasset players had seen this look before and knew that something was coming.

"If you guys don't start blocking for me," Brown said, "I'm going to kick all of your asses. I'm going to climb over your backs. Stop playing like fucking sissies. Start blocking."

Brown talked in a perilous monotone. He did not scream, he just talked, matter-of-factly, knowing his menacing looks were more than enough. Everyone in that huddle knew Brown could and would physically overpower him. Brown would intimidate with glares and words and, if needed, fists.

Soon after Brown's threats, the holes opened wide, and as Brown began mastering the Garden City defense—galloping over them as he had threatened to do to his own offense—the racial taunts died down. Brown had literally beaten the epithets out of them. It was not unusual for these kinds of games against Garden City. Walsh remembers one season when each time Jim carried the football, a Garden City player punched him in the gut. Jim was infuriated, and it took Walsh's calming presence to prevent Brown from striking back. He kept his temper under control and even got a modicum of revenge. The player doing most of the punching played, like Jim, both running back and defense. When the offender carried the ball, Jim, from his linebacker spot, tackled him so hard, he drove the player into a fence located several feet from the sideline.

Brown would at times single-handedly demolish his rival. In his final game against them, in Garden City's last drive of the contest, Brown made seven tackles in eleven plays.

Walsh used Brown in three main ways, all of which played to Brown's different strengths—speed, power, and athleticism. Manhasset's end-around play allowed Brown to use his speed to get to the outside. The dive play used his increasing power. Walsh also had a number of passes thrown to Brown after he bolted out of the backfield. Manhasset had never had an offensive player with that kind of versatility.

By his sophomore year at Manhasset, Brown had sprouted to six feet tall and weighed a solid 174 pounds. That season, after being inserted into the starting lineup by Walsh, he averaged 7.4 yards a carry. One year later, he had gained an inch in height and 20 pounds. He averaged just over 15 yards a carry. One year after that, in his senior year at Manhasset, he weighed over 200 pounds. He was no longer a pudge; he was formidable. He became larger than other kids, but his most significant advantage was his speed, which was the main reason Brown averaged 14.9 yards a carry his senior season, despite having two defenders assigned to stop him each game, usually a linebacker and a safety.

Brown played football, basketball, and lacrosse at Manhasset and dominated each one because no high school athlete could compete with his combination of strength and quickness.

He controlled the football field, crushing tacklers or running around them. In basketball, he once scored 53 points on a Tuesday, setting a state record, and 55 on a Friday, breaking his own mark. "He had these huge, soft hands," Walsh remembered. Yet it was on the lacrosse field that his skill was perhaps most evident. Brown was a middle fielder, a position that emphasizes agility. When Brown ran, no player could stay with him, and during the brief moments of physical contact, he overpowered opponents. Quickly, news of Brown's abilities on the lacrosse field began to spread across the state, attracting college coaches, who came to see firsthand the young player who was already being called one of the best lacrosse players in the country. After one coach scouted Brown, spending the entire game frantically taking notes as Brown scored five goals, the coach pulled Walsh aside and made a startling proclamation about Brown: "He is better than anybody on our college team and better than anybody we coached against."

As fierce as Brown was on the field, he was more determined to do something that he had never been quite as good at: schoolwork. It would be an understatement to say that Brown didn't take his studies seriously before crossing paths with Walsh. It is not that Brown did not possess the mental faculties to become a solid student—he had them in abundance—it is that Brown did not care about his education. The most pertinent reason was that the turmoil in Brown's home life blocked his ability to focus on schoolwork. Jim was still upset about his mother's dating as well as the fights between her and his father.

Walsh managed to get Jim to work through the home issues and concentrate on studying as well as sports. Walsh knew it was only a matter of time before colleges wooed Brown to play sports, and if that happened, Brown needed to have the grades to get into those schools. So he repeatedly stressed to Brown the importance of his schoolwork, and since Brown always paid heed to Walsh—the diminutive teacher would be one of only a handful of people in Brown's life he would consistently listen to—Brown began capitalizing on what was a naturally large intellect.

Brown played up to five sports, earning thirteen varsity letters, being so good at them all that he was usually the best player at Manhasset—quite possibly in the entire state—at each of them. One spring he briefly switched from lacrosse to baseball just to see how well he would do, playing first base and pitching. Baseball scouts saw so much potential in Brown that the New York Yankees offered him a minor-league contract. He declined.

When Brown entered a national decathlon championship in bustling Atlantic City, New Jersey, doing so with almost no training or practice, few at Manhasset were surprised by the startling outcome. Brown was forced to borrow a pair of track shoes before the meet because his had been pilfered. His previous use of a shot put and discus had been almost nonexistent. He had never even tried some of the events. Brown finished in tenth place.

Despite working with his body incessantly, Brown and his brain sustained a strong B average. Manhasset teachers learned that Brown had a sharp mind and picked things up quickly. Soon, Walsh no longer needed to pester Brown about maintaining good grades.

Brown was popular among most of the 1,100 Manhasset students, who discovered that behind a sometimes daunting glare and quiet personality was a serious student. He was elected chief justice of a student court empowered by the teaching staff to hand out disciplinary action to the Manhasset students accused of violating school rules. The gritty part of Brown, the street brawler, had never been eradicated, however. Some of his Manhasset teammates and fellow students felt Brown was an intimidator who bullied them. What would become a lifelong battle inside Brown—between the Brown who craved acceptance from friends and loved ones and the Brown who wanted to dominate them—had begun. "Some kids called Jim a bully," said Corley. "I personally never saw him go out of his way to do that, but I was also aware that other kids felt he did. I could rely on Jim. He was a great friend who never stabbed me in the back. But he also had a hair-trigger temper. If you riled him or opposed him, he could get very, very angry. The trick was knowing what angered him and not doing anything to trigger that anger."

Brown wanted to control every conversation or physical confrontation. When away from the stability-generating personality of Walsh, Brown enjoyed a good brawl, and he rarely lost. One of the few times he did came against the Green brothers—Joe, Robert, and Charles. For some time the Greens had wanted to fight Brown, but as a testament to just how much Brown had grown physically, they wanted to fight him three on one. Brown pushed to fight one brother at a time. For months this sort of awkward negotiation continued until the oldest Green agreed to fight Brown. Brown lost a bloody altercation. It was considered big news at Manhasset High.

Brown's loss to the Green brother was about the only thing that had gone awry for him once his athletic career began to skyrocket him to national prominence. By the time he would leave Manhasset, Brown would average 14.9 yards a carry in football, lead the school to its first undefeated season in almost three decades, and score 38 points a game in basketball, a sport in which he could easily have been a professional. Brown handled the ball with the ease of a point guard and used his power to score inside against taller opponents.

It was abundantly clear to Walsh that Brown's next step was to become a college athlete. The problem was getting Brown to focus on one primary sport, since Brown liked the challenge of playing many of them. Walsh approached him one day after practice. "So, what do you want to do when you grow up?" Walsh smiled. Brown thought for a few seconds and stated: "I want to play football."

Walsh nodded. It was the sport he thought Brown should focus on, but Walsh wanted Brown to make that decision. Still, Walsh was surprised by the firmness of Brown's response. "Why football?" he asked. Brown replied: "Because everything I've tried in my life, I've done my best and developed to a certain point and then run into a racial barrier."

Walsh had come to expect that kind of mature statement from Brown, but Brown's words also seemed odd. Brown had faced almost no discrimination from any coach or player in any sport at Manhasset. What Brown was saying was something he had also told friends. He had long felt that a black running back had greater potential to progress further in that sport than in any other—perhaps the degrading effects of racism would be lessened. The validity of such a thought may have been questionable, but it was what Brown believed.

By the end of his senior season at Manhasset, in 1953, Brown had received scholarship offers from more than forty colleges, and was courted by the Ivy League. In some cases Brown was illegally offered hundreds of dollars in cash by schools (a large sum of money at the time, particularly to a young Brown who was the son of a maid) to attend their programs, but he declined. Brown had a brutish and rough side, but he was also remarkably honest. The thought of a school cheating to acquire Brown was offensive to him. "I ain't no slave to be bought," he said at the time.

Brown trusted Walsh to sift through the numerous offers, and it seemed at one point that Brown was headed to Ohio State to play for the legendary Woody Hayes. The Buckeyes were the premier choice in Walsh's mind because he wanted Brown to star in the Big Ten, the most competitive conference in the nation. Brown was excited and appreciated Walsh's efforts, but he was also concerned about the prospect of moving a great distance to the Midwest. Brown had a comfortable base on which to fall back upon and wanted to stay close to Manhasset.

Then Kenneth Molloy, a Manhasset resident who had closely followed Brown's high school career, introduced the teenager to another option. Molloy was a graduate of Syracuse University and had been an all-American lacrosse player, and like so many others in Manhasset he found Brown to be a charming and dedicated kid. Molloy was also a gifted lawyer who would later become a state supreme court judge. He was well known throughout Long Island's sports community as a kind man who sincerely wanted to help less fortunate athletes find the financial means to afford college.

The Syracuse football program was a far cry from the powerhouses of the Big Ten; it was, in fact, a program that lacked prestige. In upstate New York the athletic program trailed those of schools like Colgate and Cornell. In 1953 Syracuse played in the Orange Bowl and was pounded 61–6 by Alabama. But Molloy eloquently convinced Brown that Syracuse was an up-and-coming force, one that would soon reckon with Ohio State.

That was a stretch; what Molloy did next was an even bigger one. He met with Brown in the summer of 1953 and informed him that he had the power to grant Brown an athletic scholarship if he selected Syracuse. Brown was ecstatic and told Molloy that Syracuse was his choice. What Molloy did not reveal was that no such scholarship for Brown existed. In fact, the Syracuse coaching staff at the time had never scouted Brown and did not want black players on the team.

Molloy never informed Brown of his true predicament, knowing that if Brown became aware that the coaches did not want him, Brown would never attend the university. Molloy was relying on his prediction: once Brown arrived at Syracuse and began playing, the coaches would see his ability and instantly grant him a scholarship. Molloy's actions seemed odd to some. Why was he working so hard to put Brown into a university that was not the best place for him, at least on the surface? There is no question that a portion of Molloy's motives was selfish. He envisioned Brown leading Syracuse to national prominence. Yet Molloy sincerely believed that Syracuse would shape Brown into not only a spectacular football player but also an even better person. Molloy was hopeful and charming, but he was also terribly naive and perhaps too idealistic.

Molloy moved forward despite the obvious warning signs. He initiated a citywide fund-raiser to pay for Brown's tuition and expenses. He penned a dramatic letter to community leaders that would forever alter Brown's life. It read:

You were undoubtedly one of those who felt pretty proud of Jimmy Brown and his athletic record at Manhasset High School. When he finished last June, he was probably Nassau County's outstanding athlete of all time.

There was good reason for our pride in this fine young American—and there will be more. But we need your help.

That is, Jimmy Brown needs it. Here is the situation: Jimmy recently matriculated at Syracuse University. When he did this, he relied upon the assurance of certain residents of Manhasset that they would contribute toward his expenses there. Frankly, Jimmy and his family cannot handle that, for it will come to about $1,000 for this semester.

Given this chance, however, Jimmy will, we are convinced, give us in Manhasset ample reason to continue our confidence in him as an athlete and as a representative of all that is fine in young American manhood. Several of us have joined to see what can be done to give Jimmy Brown his big chance. We think this will be one of Manhasset's soundest investments.

We think, too, that you may feel the same way about this or you would not have gotten this letter. If you agree, please send us your check to the order of Arthur H. Wright—as generous as you can make it—in the enclosed envelope.

Sincerely yours,

Kenneth D. Molloy

The letter was typical of someone from Manhasset. It stressed to leaders that Brown was an exemplary American—not an exemplary *black* American. It illustrated just how much Brown had enchanted many of Manhasset's leaders.

The letter also contained another Molloy fib. When Molloy wrote that Brown had declared he would attend Syracuse based on the promises that a number of Manhasset residents would contribute to paying for his expenses, this was false. Brown had no idea.

Molloy's plea led to funds pouring in from some forty men across the Manhasset community. A coalition of bankers, doctors, gas station owners, and others all contributed. The unity and goodwill of the people from Manhasset as well as Syracuse lacrosse coach Roy Simmons—who had heard of Brown and had become a fan of his—was met equally by the nastiness and racism of some members from the Syracuse coaching staff. "My father went to the head football coach and played up Jim," remembers Simmons's son, Roy, a former teammate of Brown's. "The coach told my father, 'Not interested. He's colored.' "

There was one undeniable fact. Despite being the most talented athlete Syracuse had ever seen, the school was not quite ready for someone like Brown.

When Brown arrived on the Syracuse campus in the fall of 1953, the country was still buzzing about a book by Ralph Ellison called *Invisible Man*. A review of it appeared in the *Nation* magazine. "This novel is a soaring and exalted record of a Negro's journey through contemporary America in search of success, companionship, and, finally, himself," began the review, written by Irving Howe; "like all our fictions devoted to the idea of experience, it moves from province to city, from naive faith to disenchantment."

Before Brown arrived at Syracuse, making that similar shift from a buoyant personality to a soul disillusioned with an America outside the province of Manhasset, there was a tall, good-natured Syracuse quarterback named Avatus Stone.

Stone was recruited to Syracuse at the dawn of the emergence of the school's flirtation with black athletes. Stone was a stunning physical specimen who was instantly the fastest player on the Syracuse team and could throw the football more than 60 yards. He grasped the offense quickly, was extremely well liked by many of the players, and earned significant playing time not long after he arrived. (The university has little biographical information on Stone.)

Stone was black. Therefore, he was despised by many of the white men on the coaching staff, who recruited him only because his talent was so impressive that he was impossible to turn away. Stone was not allowed to room or to eat with the team. He was popular with many of the students and dated several of the white coeds, angering the coaches even more, who told him to stop. Stone didn't. In fact, some of his girlfriends would gather on the sidelines, singing to him as he practiced. Or so the legend goes.

When coeds were not pursuing Stone, he was subjected to raw and blistering racism: notes threatening that he would be lynched if he did not quit the team were posted on his dormitory door, and one coach referred to him as "Nigger Stone," according to a person familiar with Stone's history there.

Stone eventually tired of the brutal treatment. In August of 1952, prior to the start of one practice and after an intense argument with one of the Syracuse coaches in which he says he was called several racial slurs (rumors that Stone actually punched a coach could not be confirmed or refuted, and Syracuse University officials said they could not find Stone's surviving relatives), Stone abruptly quit the team and signed with the Canadian Football League. Instead of acknowledging its wicked treatment of Stone, the coaching staff instead blamed Stone for leaving, and his departure only reinforced the coaches' opinion that black athletes could not be trusted.

When Ben Schwartzwalder and Walsh spoke, the conversation exemplified the racial politics of the time. The Syracuse football coach told Walsh: "I'm not prejudiced, but I never want another colored person on my team at Syracuse. Never again. They are too much trouble." Walsh, without a bit of prejudice in his tiny body, wanted to strangle Schwartzwalder, but he stayed calm and listened. Schwartzwalder outlined a plan in which Brown could play football at the school. It involved ten rules, the first of which was that Brown could not date white women. "I was at first shocked into silence," Walsh says now.

Some of the other rules were that Brown could not leave his dorm room after a certain time, was not allowed to eat with the team, and was not allowed to live with the team, Walsh remembered.

"He is not doing any of that," Walsh responded to Schwartzwalder; "that's just not right. That's inhuman."

"Walsh and my father were outraged by how Jim was treated," says Roy Simmons Jr. "But I think they and Molloy genuinely thought that Syracuse was the best place for Jim."

Brown went, completely unaware of the ten commandments, and that he had an army of guardian angels composed of Walsh, Molloy, Simmons, and others watching over him. Brown followed Stone just a short time after Stone headed to Canada, entering Syracuse innocent and wide-eyed, expecting that the coaching staff desired him and that he would be treated as fairly as he was by the people running Manhasset athletics.

Brown was treated almost as coolly as Stone had been. He was also just as alone. That fact never became more apparent than inside the cramped team meeting room, where players with crew cuts sat almost shoulder to shoulder, staring forward, listening to barking coaches, with Brown's one dark profile alone among a sea of white faces.

Few of the coaches or players on the freshman football team, on which Brown was the only black participant, spoke to Brown at first. When they did, it was only to offer a vague warning that he should never duplicate the behavior of Stone. "Don't be like him," said the freshman football coach, Lester Dye. Schwartzwalder echoed the same sentiments. No other player was given this warning, and Brown realized he was being told this only because Stone had been black and Brown was black.

"It seemed to me that everything was upside-down at Syracuse," Brown wrote. "In high school I had known nothing but fair treatment. Now I had advanced to the world of higher education and I felt that I had promptly been viewed as a potential trouble-maker and threat to Caucasian women. Naturally enough, I got my back up. I bristled. I hadn't come to Syracuse to be treated like an enemy in the ranks."

Most of the football team roomed on one part of the campus, while Brown lived in a corner of the Syracuse campus called Sky-top. The area was indeed sky-high, perched atop a large hill more than a mile from campus. The Skytop apartments, barracks-like buildings erected quickly to accommodate the influx of World War II veterans at Syracuse on the GI Bill, were a far cry from the places the other football players lived. Brown often hitched rides to classes and practices with sympathetic students.

Brown took this treatment as a sign of the school attempting to humiliate him. How true that was is uncertain. Syracuse historical documents show that many walk-on football players lived at Sky-top, and once Brown made the team he moved to Callendale, a complex where other football players lived, across from Manley Field House.

While there are questions about just how discriminatory Brown's living arrangements were, what is not in dispute is that many of the coaches despised him because of his race. Unaware that he was not a scholarship athlete, Brown plodded on, becoming increasingly angry and bitter about his treatment, yet refusing to lash out. While facing double standards and hostility, he was mostly poised; despite a few fits of anger and rebellion, he displayed a ma-turity few people his age possess.

It was at Syracuse where Brown demonstrated perhaps his most heroic moments. It was also there where Brown's legendary tough-ness and mental resolve were honed. He cycled painfully from pride and defiance through self-doubt and bitterness. Once, tired of being ignored by the coaches, he simply lay down on a corner of the practice field alone, hands and legs wide apart the way a kid prepares to make a snow angel, and did not move for several minutes. Some of the varsity coaches glared at Brown, and probably thought: This is what happens when you trust *them*.

As resilient as Brown was, he was not immune from breakdowns. He became close to Roy Simmons Sr. because Simmons showed patience and understanding, and the two would sometimes talk for hours. "When Jim felt alone or out of place," Roy Jr. recalled, "he went to my father. They became close."

"Roy Simmons is the greatest man I have ever known," Brown would say years later. "Roy treated me so well during my first season in football that I went out for lacrosse purely because of my affection for him. He's the kind of guy you never want to let down. He was the reason I stayed in school."

Several times, Brown angrily stormed off the practice field and into the locker room. Simmons Sr. would enter, and see Brown packing his things, ready to leave campus. Simmons talked Brown out of it each time.

When a small contingent of Manhasset supporters and Syracuse alumni traveled to the campus to investigate what was happening to Brown, they were told that the only way Brown would make the team was as a defensive lineman. Another coach suggested that Brown should become the team's punter. Jim Brown. Punter.

Meanwhile, Brown also eventually tried out for the freshman basketball team. Despite being one of the great scorers in Long Island history, he was benched initially and then allowed to play as a reserve, where he averaged a double double in his first year. Track soon followed.

The dual emotions of resentment and accomplishment Brown felt fueled a sense of strength and confidence, and he emerged from an understandably withdrawn shell to become the stunning athlete that his Manhasset friends knew was always there. Brown's handling of the bigotry at Syracuse enabled him to deal with any broken bones and bruises that would later mark his unparalleled NFL career. "No pain on the football field," Brown once told Walsh, "can match the pain of discrimination."

No matter how much the Syracuse coaches attempted to bench Brown or to move him from running back to defensive end or linebacker, Brown's talent was so superior to every other player's that it became impossible to bury him at the bottom of the lineup or ignore him. Molloy's lobbying of a stubborn Syracuse football staff, as well as Brown's resilience, eventually worked, and the school gave Brown a scholarship. When he arrived at camp in his second year, Schwartzwalder had listed Brown as the fifth-string back, a stunning insult. Still, with his resolve returned, Brown did whatever the coaching staff requested, and the work ethic that had made him legendary at Manhasset reawakened. Almost daily, Schwartzwalder ordered his players, in groups of six, to climb hand over hand up a twenty-foot-long rope, which was tethered to a series of metal loops. They climbed and grunted and struggled, wearing their shoulder pads and white practice uniforms, and try as they did, few ever climbed as fast as Jim, who rarely lost one of those battles. During grueling postpractice gallops that were up to a mile long, Brown never finished lower than second. He eventually worked his way to the second string.

It took a remarkable turn of events for the greatest college athlete in history to break the starting lineup of a Syracuse football team that was one of the more mediocre in the nation. When an injury to a back ahead of Brown forced Schwartzwalder to insert him into the starting lineup, Brown fumbled on his first carry, and was immediately taken out of the game. Later that season, another rash of injuries at Brown's position again forced a reluctant Schwartzwalder to put Brown in the lineup, this time against the

University of Illinois. He was spectacular, once running an end around running play to the right—just like at Manhasset—for a 20-yard gain and damaging the shoulder of tackler J. C. Caroline, an all-American, in the process. Still, another fumble, this one on special teams, sent Brown back to the bench. At every turn, the Syracuse coaches, despite growing fan support, attempted to bury Brown on the depth chart, punishing him for the tiniest of mistakes.

Amazingly, it was not until Brown had played almost two years at Syracuse that his football career began to thrive. Even then it happened by accident. It was the week of the sixth game, this time against Cornell University, and Sam Alexander, ahead of Brown on the depth chart despite constantly being injured, hurt his ankle several days before the contest. Rather than simply insert Brown into the lineup, the coaches switched the right halfback to left and moved the second-string right halfback into the starting lineup. There was no greater indication of just how much the coaches despised Brown than their shuffling the starting lineup to keep Brown out of it.

The plan could do little to anticipate the violence of the sport. Just minutes into the game, one of the backs inserted ahead of Brown, Arthur Troilo, suffered a severely sprained ankle. Syracuse had no choice but to give Brown significant playing time. As he had done so many times at Manhasset, it took just one play for Brown to change the game. This one was a 54-yard score up the middle of the Cornell defense. Brown rushed for a total of 151 yards that game.

Brown's on-field accomplishments, no matter how explosive or telling, could do little to stop some Syracuse coaches and players from seeing anything but his race, and the comparisons between Brown and the black man who had played on the team before him, Avatus Stone, agonizingly continued. The week following the Cornell game, and just several minutes before Syracuse played rival Colgate, quarterback Mickey Rich approached Brown and attempted to deliver what Rich likely thought was some sort of pregame rallying speech. "You're not like Stone," he told Brown, according to the runner's account in his autobiography, "and you've got a chance to show them you're not."

Brown was stunned. He nodded to Rich and then quietly walked away. Frustrated and angry, Brown almost single-handedly dominated Colgate, rushing for two touchdowns, and his second straight 100-yard game.

Brown had equal trouble convincing Syracuse's basketball coaches to start him, as the staff allowed no more than one black player to start for the team. Despite spending much of his sophomore season as the sixth man, he finished the year as the team's number two scorer and leading rebounder. In one of Syracuse's track meets, he scored a startling 28 points, almost the track equivalent of hitting for the cycle in baseball.

It seemed that no matter what Brown did, carrying a football or cradling a lacrosse stick or leaping the high-jump pole—or even drilling for the local ROTC detachment—nothing impressed the football coaches. During the season-opening game against the University of Pittsburgh in 1955, Brown was stopped for one of the few times in his history as a starting running back. After that game, he was moved back to second string, and angrily left the practice field, again, preparing to quit.

Brown decided to stay at Syracuse only after a number of Manhasset friends and coaches pleaded for him to do so. "A bunch of us told him, 'The Jimmy Brown we know is no quitter,' " Walsh said.

The following afternoon, Brown returned to practice, perhaps as angry as he had ever been. In one of the bloodier days of practice in the history of Syracuse football, Brown as the second-team running back wrecked the starting defense by scoring four touchdowns in just five plays. Syracuse players on the defense suffered from an assortment of aches after Brown's rampage through the defense, including bloody noses, bone bruises, and mild concussions.

Brown was inserted back into the starting lineup after that practice and never left it again.

Syracuse's Archbold Stadium resembled a Roman coliseum; it was a gray concrete monstrosity, 670 feet long and 475 feet wide, and included a garish archway. It was the center of Syracuse athletics.

The lacrosse field was a short jog from Archbold, and if there was one thing the lacrosse athletes had become used to seeing, it was Brown, slowly walking between the various fields, crossing in and out of Archbold more than anyone else.

Unlike some of the football coaches, who did not want Brown and looked for every reason to bury him, the lacrosse staff had no such feelings. Schwartzwalder was built like a fire hydrant and possessed a sarcastic, acid temperament. A World War II veteran who had taken part in the Normandy invasion, Schwartzwalder was a no-nonsense coach some players called "the general" behind his back.

Roy Simmons Sr. was different. Instead of wanting robotic players who would never question his orders, he desired intelligent freethinkers. Instead of screaming at his players and threatening them, he was seen as a benevolent grandfather who was more the teacher and less the foulmouthed drill instructor.

Simmons did not care about Brown's race. He had recruited players from all walks of life, and the only thing that mattered to the coach was ability. One player was from the nearby Onondaga Indian Nation. There were players from many corners of the Northeast and beyond, and when Brown arrived he joined a mature group of young men that, for the most part, couldn't have cared less about his skin color.

That in itself was quite an achievement. Lacrosse may have

been invented by American Indians, but the sport had been adopted by the white upper class. College students attending Harvard, Yale, Dartmouth, and other elite Ivy League programs picked up the sport because they could find an athletic niche without being large, fast, or especially athletic, three things needed for sports like football or basketball.

Brown was all three. He shattered the notion that young men not athletically gifted enough to play other sports were the ones who took up lacrosse. What was a preppy, restricted sport in which the players wore buttoned-down oxford shirts underneath their jerseys evolved overnight into a slick, athletic sport when Brown played it.

The first time some members from the lacrosse squad saw Brown, they were stunned. None of them had seen a body quite like his before. "His physique resembled that of a Greek god with dark skin," said John Burger, who played lacrosse with Brown at Syracuse.

When the team would take a shower after practice, some teammates could not help but stare at Brown as he entered and departed the shower area.

Brown's size and speed differential was drastically more evident in lacrosse than it was in football. The heftiest players were often 170 or 180 pounds, while according to media reports, Brown was six foot two and weighed 235 pounds by his junior year at Syracuse, bigger than he would be once he joined Cleveland. Brown utilized this combination ruthlessly, speeding by opponents, or running them over when required. It is believed that Brown's fast hands allowed him to win every face-off in which he participated. (A face-off starts the game at each period and after each goal, with two opponents facing each other in the middle of the field, and after the ball is dropped between them they use their sticks and bodies to joust for control of it.) There were moments when the team was stunned as Brown broke into the open field and outran everyone near him. The few times someone did attempt to pull Brown to the ground, he used his left arm as a battering ram. Opponents literally hung from it, attempting to trip Brown up, looking like eight-year-olds trying to take down their dad.

Most football players who attempted to play lacrosse were athletic but had difficulty handling the stick. Brown shot the ball underhanded, right-handed, and left-handed with equal skill and made goals by flinging the ball over his shoulder as well. The country became aware of Brown's skills when he scored five goals in the North-South all-star game, which included the nation's best players.

Brown's movement was always fluid, and in some ways he was a conservative player, which is ironic, since Brown scored 30 goals his junior year and in 1957, his senior season, made all-American with 43 goals and 21 assists, while also participating in football and track. Schwartzwalder once replied, when asked about Brown's speed: he runs as fast as he needs to. It was not unusual for Brown to lightly jog or even stand casually as the action went on nearby. Then, suddenly, he would explode, as if he were a launched projectile, his quickness and physicality shocking opposing teams. "He saved his energy for when it was needed," teammate Burger explained.

Roy Simmons Jr. played with Brown when Brown was a senior and Simmons was a junior. Brown was such a target of other teams that he opened up the offense, allowing others to score. He was also a target in a different sort of way. "He was always called racial slurs by opponents," remembers Simmons. "It was constant, every game." Brown may have been called a "nigger" dozens, if not hundreds, of times by opposing players throughout his Syracuse lacrosse career. Brown usually responded to the racial taunts in one way: "The more someone called him a disgusting racial name," says Simmons, "the more he scored. He punished teams that used that stuff by embarrassing them on the field."

The way Brown was regarded by the Syracuse lacrosse players differed sharply from how he was treated by the Syracuse football team. No one brought up the name Avatus Stone. He was not shifted in and out of the starting lineup. The players actually admired Brown for what he did on and off the field. "First of all, no one cared about his race and no one said anything to him about it," says Burger, "because he could beat you up inside out if you did. But also we liked him. He was a nice guy and a great talent. We also admired how successful he was with the ladies."

By his senior year at Syracuse, few on campus dated more than Brown. "I've never seen anything like it," says Burger. "The girls just flocked to him." The players giggled at the success Brown had with the coeds, but Brown's smile and charm did not work solely with the women on the Syracuse campus. Brown had stayed in contact with a girlfriend back in Long Island, and their romance, which had begun in high school in Manhasset, with Brown at one point living with the girl and her parents in their home, continued for years, ending in the woman's becoming pregnant with Brown's first child, a daughter named Karen. It was in these early years that the vast contradictions in Brown's life started to crystallize. No one was braver or tougher on the field, and even fewer were more selfless or loyal; yet Brown sometimes treated women close to him much differently. After his girlfriend gave birth to their daughter, Brown declined to help raise her, deciding that becoming a father would injure his athletic career. Brown remained almost absent from his daughter's life—as well as from the lives of some of the other children he would father later—for many years.

Brown's senior year on Syracuse's athletic fields was spent racking up the single greatest athletic collegiate season ever seen. It remains unmatched to this day. It's likely that nothing like it will ever happen again. Nothing like it could happen again.

In some ways, Brown's year began at the end, on November 17, 1956, a cold and windy day inside Archbold Stadium, the day that Syracuse played Colgate. In the stands was Governor W. Averell Harriman, an accomplished diplomat who once served as ambassador to the Soviet Union. Harriman had heard of Brown and believed it was time to see what the fuss was about.

That week, Syracuse players held a team meeting and decided that they would attempt to obliterate Colgate as a way to impress some of the bowl committees. Brown's stunning day truly began just about halfway through the first quarter, with Syracuse already ahead by two touchdowns. Quarterback Chuck Zimmerman called the play in the huddle and punctuated it by saying: "They can't stop you, Jimmy." Brown took the handoff and raced toward the right sideline. Within seconds he was downfield, beyond the reach of outstretched Colgate defenders, who were clutching and grabbing, but touching only air. Brown demonstrated the kind of powerful acceleration he had shown so many times before, both in practice and in games, but this touchdown run, which covered 50 yards, was something different. It was as if Brown had outdone Brown, which until this day had seemed impossible.

After the long blast, Brown was huffing, but he did not take a break. He lined up to kick the extra point. It was just wide. Brown was the kicker because no one could do it as well as he did, and in those days players often pulled double duty.

There were almost forty thousand people watching the game, and some who attended it would later state that it was one of the single most memorable days of their lives. Syracuse would win 61–7, and Brown would score six touchdowns and attempt seven extra points. He finished with 197 yards rushing, ending the year with 986, a new school record. At halftime a jovial press box announcer exclaimed: "The score is now Brown 27, Colgate 7."

A small number of professional football assistant coaches and scouts watching the game still remained unconvinced about Brown's skills, saying his dramatic day was because Syracuse was playing against a drastically outmanned Colgate team. Some in the NFL were determined to dislike Brown for a variety of reasons and would have been convinced only if he had donned a cape and flown over Archbold Stadium at Mach speed. Others in professional football knew better. They had been watching Brown closely for some time and had taken copious notes on all of his performances. They remembered one of his better games earlier in the year, against Maryland, in which he scampered for 154 yards, more than the entire Maryland squad. When Brown's forehead was gashed and the blood seeped into his eye, quarterback Zimmerman, concerned about Brown's vision, asked if he was still able to carry the ball. "I can carry the ball all right," Brown replied. "I just can't see where I'm going." Indeed, an increasing number of professional teams were quickly falling in lust with Brown. The Cleveland organization was one of them.

The Browns were remarkably thorough in their examination of the runner, and one of the things they loved about Brown was his versatility. This was evident in Brown's final lacrosse game. That warm May morning was the same day as the track meet against Colgate, with Syracuse winning the track event by 13 points, the exact point total that Brown accumulated while participating in three events.

Brown's explosion in the track meet was never supposed to happen. The Syracuse track coach, Bob Grieve, approached the lacrosse coach, the legendary Roy Simmons Sr., and asked for a favor. "Can I have Jimmy for just one event?" Grieve asked. "The high jump?" He assured Simmons that the best Colgate jumper could barely clear five feet and that Brown would be back soon, ready for lacrosse. That was the intent, but something unusual occurred.

At the end of the track meet Brown raced into the dressing

room to change uniforms for the lacrosse contest against Army. Brown quickly put on his slim shoulder pads and had picked up his stick, when one of the Syracuse student managers breathlessly ran into the room. "Jimmy, we need you back at the track," he said.

Colgate had pulled to within just a few points of Syracuse, and the Orangemen needed Brown to secure the win. He removed his pads, put his track uniform back on, and returned to the track, where he won the discus and placed second in the javelin throw. Brown then made the short jog back to the locker room, partially changed uniforms once again, and headed to the lacrosse field. It all happened so quickly that Brown did not have time to change out of his track shorts into the ones he used for lacrosse. Brown led Syracuse to an 8–6 victory—he had one goal and three assists—and a 10–0 season, the first unbeaten mark in lacrosse for the school since 1922.

It turns out Brown had been sufficiently motivated for that wondrous afternoon. At the end of lacrosse practice the day before, Brown had gotten into a heated fight. While trying to break it up, Simmons Sr. got hit in the back of the head by accident. Half of the team stopped dead in their tracks, wondering how Simmons would react. "That's enough practice for now," he said. Simmons knew Brown and the team had been properly agitated and irked and were ready to play.

Just 7,500 people saw what Brown did that day. Some of them, after the lacrosse game, clamored for his autograph. He retreated into the locker room for several hours waiting for the crowd to disperse. When Brown emerged, Archbold Stadium was completely empty. There are several different versions of what happened next (even Brown has told the story differently). The most reliable comes from a discussion with the late Val Pinchbeck, the former sports information director for Syracuse, who years ago told the author what he saw on that remarkable day. Pinchbeck witnessed Brown leave the Syracuse locker room alone carrying only a small, dark duffel bag, and watched him slowly walk up to the top row of the stadium. Brown then turned around and stared at the empty concrete structure for almost two minutes before suddenly waving good-bye to the stadium, turning back around, and exiting. It was one of his rare public displays of emotion.

Brown's accomplishments at Syracuse were arresting, but, ironically, they would not be properly understood and quantified until decades later. "You have to remember that in the 1950s, Jim Brown was big, but he was not the household name he should have been, and would be all these years later," says Ernie Accorsi, a longtime NFL executive and football historian. "There was a bias against football played on the East Coast, and Brown was caught up in that."

Chuck Howley, the Dallas Cowboys great who played against Brown when Howley was at West Virginia, remembers Brown being the toughest runner he ever faced. "When I played him in college, I rode his back the entire game," Howley says. "His sense of balance was remarkable. He was the best runner in the country, but because he played at Syracuse he didn't get the publicity that he should have."

Syracuse didn't tower over the competition in football, to say the least. The media focused on the powers in the Midwest. Football played in the eastern portion of the country was seen as of lower caliber. People outside of Syracuse noticed what Brown did, but the public paid less attention to him than to other Heisman Trophy favorites. Names like Johnny Majors at Tennessee, Tommy McDonald from Oklahoma, and Paul Hornung from Notre Dame were more on the minds of sportswriters and fans. Race was also a factor when it came to notoriety. Brown was fifth in the Heisman voting his senior season, garnering the most votes on ballots in the East. Yet he was fifth in the South and received no top five votes in the West, Southwest, or Midwest.

The country got its first extensive look at Brown when Syracuse played Texas Christian University in the Cotton Bowl on January 1, 1957. After accepting the Cotton Bowl bid, Syracuse did something that shocked Brown. The city of Dallas, the site of the game, was like many cities in the South: it was segregated. When teams with black athletes traveled to southern cities, black players were often forbidden from staying in the same hotels as their white counterparts. Blacks would practice with their teammates, and then stay with a host black family once their time on the field concluded. The situation was often devastating to the morale of the segregated athlete.

Syracuse took a different approach. The team decided to risk having Brown stay with them in a hotel about fifteen miles outside of Dallas.

(A similar scene would occur just a short time later when another black, star running back Ernie Davis, followed Brown to Syracuse. Brown had helped to recruit Davis and warned the first black man to win the Heisman that his every move would be examined. Davis had been told directly by some of the white Syracuse coaches to conduct himself carefully around the white students. He led Syracuse to an unbeaten regular season in 1959, and the team again traveled to Dallas to play in the Cotton Bowl, this time against perennial power University of Texas. John Brown—no relation to Jim—was the only other black player on the team. He said in a 2003 interview about that game: "We arrived at the Melrose Hotel in the city, and Ernie and I were immediately escorted around the lobby to a room with two cots behind the kitchen. That is where we were to sleep. They also said they knew we were going to have team meetings in the upper floors of the hotel where the rest of the team was staying, but we were told to stay off the elevators so we wouldn't offend any of the white guests."

Davis handled the indignities with strength and class. Jim

Brown said of Davis in a *Sports Illustrated* interview in 1989: "The greatest thing about Ernie Davis is that white people liked him and black people liked him. And I liked him, too, because I never thought of him as an Uncle Tom. I thought of him as a certain kind of spirited individual, a true kind of spirit who had the ability to rise above things and deal more with the universe, so that white people would forget their racism with him and black people would never think he was acquiescing to white people. Usually, you either line up on one side or the other. So Ernie Davis transcended racism. That was his essence. That was his greatness.")

Syracuse's previous bowl appearance was against Alabama in 1953; Syracuse was obliterated by 55 points. The game against TCU was sharply different: this time the school had Brown. After trailing 14–0, Syracuse handed the ball to Brown, who scored two quick touchdowns of 2 and 4 yards (and followed the touchdowns with two successful point-after attempts).

"Brown appears to be a driven ball carrier rather than a nifty one despite his speed," wrote one January 2, 1957, newspaper account. "He ran into and over people instead of slipping by them. When he was drafted, the Browns' staff thought of him as a possible fullback but the TV screen showed him as a straight-up runner, which is not the mark of a power fullback. The real power boys who move leaning forward will usually fall for an extra couple of yards after they are hit; the straight-up runners usually bounce back."

The contradiction in watching such a large, fearsome athlete then line up and daintily toe in an extra point added to the curiosity of the reported several million people watching the game on television. Brown would score again, but have a critical extra point blocked. Syracuse lost the game by that point. Brown finished with 132 yards and scored 21 of the team's 27 points, had twenty-six carries, threw two passes (one was completed and one was intercepted), performed the kickoffs, and had one kick return, which he took for 45 yards. He was named the game's most valuable player.

By the time Brown had departed Syracuse, he had redefined what it meant to be an athlete. He single-handedly put the Syracuse football program on the map. He was an all-American in that sport and in lacrosse, where he led the school to its first unbeaten season in more than three decades. He ran track and played basketball. He remains the only person to be inducted into the Halls of Fame for professional football, college football, and lacrosse. He never took his athletic gifts for granted—he constantly worked at getting better and was likely the best combination of intellect and physical ability ever to play college sports.

"Every other college athlete was compared to Jim Brown after Jim Brown," said Accorsi, "and it will always be that way."

The evolution went beyond what he did on the field. At Syracuse, Brown traversed the tenuous tightrope that is race by maintaining pride in his ethnicity while also befriending whites. As one of the few black men on a predominantly white campus, he felt the pull of total assimilation, but he never compromised, never sold out. Such a thing is at times impossibly difficult.

That does not mean Brown did not emerge from Syracuse a far different young man than when he arrived on campus as a starkly naive Manhasset kid mostly unaware of the extreme racial hostility and double standards that existed in America. Brown had been touched by racism before Syracuse, just not singed. His treatment by some members of the Syracuse coaching staff and others at the school, as if he were some sort of black pestilence, had changed Brown. It would take years for Brown to forgive Syracuse for his treatment, and he did not completely reconcile with the school until the late 1980s. Some fifty years after he carried Syracuse sports to prominence, the university, in the spring of 2005, announced two athletic scholarships, for football and lacrosse, in

Brown's name. That half-century delay speaks to how damaged the Brown-Syracuse relationship was.

His Syracuse experience caused Brown to undergo a sort of social awakening, just as the decade of social awakening was beginning. He became intensely interested in and affected by the plight of blacks fighting for basic freedoms in the South, as well as the stark poverty that left much of black America in financial straits. Almost overnight, he became more independent, more determined, more aloof. And more angry.

"I think once he left Manhasset he became disenchanted with how things were in the rest of the country," said his childhood friend Ed Corley. "I think he became angry with how blacks were treated. He was different after Syracuse. I think he wanted to be a great football player, but I think he also wanted to change society. He was going to do whatever it took to make things better for his people."

1960

"THE NEGRO CLARK GABLE"

No one had seen this kind of black man in professional football before. He didn't kowtow to whites. He didn't care what they thought. Many black athletes in that time were afraid of whites. Not Jim. He'd tell a white man "fuck you" the same way he would anyone else, and then he'd dare you to do something about it. People thought he was arrogant but he was also incredibly brave.

—**A friend** of Jim Brown's

I do not crave the white man's approval; I crave only the rights I'm entitled to as a human being. The acceptance of the Negro in sports is really an insignificant development that warms the heart of the Negro less than it does that of the white man, who salves his troubled conscience by telling himself, "Isn't it wonderful that Negroes and whites are out there playing together?"

—**Jim Brown** in 1964

The morning of the first day Jim arrived at Browns camp in Hiram, Ohio, came after he had driven for most of the night, some seven hours, in a convertible, from the Chicago area, the site of the college all-star game. When he got to training camp, Jim was not tired, but he was still irritated. Curly Lambeau, the coach of the 1957 all-star team who would become one of football's more historic personas after starting the Green Bay Packers, had basically buried Jim on the roster, relegating him mostly to special teams. It was a moment remarkably similar to Jim's early days at Syracuse. He had once again been treated poorly by a head coach, despite being one of the most gifted athletes in the group.

Otto Graham was an assistant coach for the all-star game under Lambeau, and within the first few days of practice, Graham approached Jim and told him: "You will never make it in the NFL."

"Otto would change and become a different person later in his life, I believe," said one black Hall of Fame player who knew Graham and asked not to be identified. "But Otto told a number of

black players they would be no good. He told me that. He told Gale
Sayers that. He told several other black players the same thing, and
a bunch of the black players he told that would end up in the Hall
of Fame." In 1964 Graham would go even further, claiming at a Pro
Football Hall of Fame luncheon that "the Browns won't win anything as long as [Jim] Brown is there."

With an effort, Jim put the ugly all-star game experience behind him. Even though he had arrived at the complex at four in the
morning on no sleep, he was still energized. The moment had hit
him. He was a professional football player.

The players on the Browns were as curious about Jim as he was
about them. They had heard of this supposedly fearsome and hardy
runner and had watched him on television in the all-star game.
What Jim did off the field had also caught their attention. Jim was
the first player in professional football to use an agent—an extremely controversial decision at the time. Players in the NFL feared
using representation because it was commonplace for owners to
refuse to negotiate with any player who attempted to use an agent,
and even trade a player who hinted at utilizing one. Jim hired his
longtime supporter from Manhasset, Ken Molloy, to handle his
contract with Paul Brown. When the several days of discussions
between Molloy and Paul concluded, it was decided that Brown
would earn a base salary of $12,000 and a signing bonus of $3,000. It
was the most money any Browns rookie had ever been paid up to
that point.

The Browns were a collection of gritty, tough stars, many of
whom had played for Paul for some time. They knew Paul's system
and what to expect from Paul himself, and in the summer of 1957
they began to pull Jim aside, one on one, informing Jim of what
life was like under Paul, whom some called "the Man." One of
those players who initially approached Jim was Lenny Ford, the all-
American from the University of Michigan. Ford symbolized the

stoutness of the Browns. In his first season as a professional, against the Chicago Cardinals, Ford suffered a broken nose, two cheekbone fractures, and three lost teeth when Chicago fullback Pat Harder elbowed him. It took plastic surgery to repair Ford's face. He returned later in the season wearing a specially fitted mask for protection. Ford was so intimidating as a defender that Cleveland shifted its defense from a six-man front to a four-man line so the defense could better take advantage of Ford's pass-rushing skills.

On one of the first days of training camp, Ford spoke to Jim, and what Ford said was stunning to a man who was quickly becoming numb to what seemed like a series of eye-opening experiences. As Brown recounted in his 1964 book, Ford told him: "First, when you're running through plays in practice, always run twenty yards downfield. Don't just run through the hole and then jog a few steps and flip the ball back. The man doesn't like that. Run hard for twenty yards, even if you feel silly. He likes to see that."

Ford paused, and looked harder at Brown, attempting to emphasize what was coming next. "Secondly, keep your mouth shut when he speaks to you. When he tells you how to run a play, run it the way he tells you. If you have an idea for improving the play, keep it to yourself. Suggestions make the man mad. If you're pretty sure you can make more ground by changing the play, change it in the *game*. Don't change it in practice. Run it your way in the game and hope it works, and if it does, don't say anything. Just make your yardage and act like it was a mistake."

Jim was taken aback by Ford's warnings. To Jim, it sounded as if the team feared Paul so much they would rather deceive him than level with him. "Also," finished Ford, "don't start any conversations with the man. Don't initiate anything. You see something wrong, let it go. He does all the talking here."

Jim was perplexed. His initial talks with Paul showed no controlling aspects in Paul's nature. Paul was smiling and approving in his dealings with Jim as the summer practice months turned into preseason games. In the second game, against the Pittsburgh Steelers, Jim scored a touchdown from 40 yards out in the third quarter after outrunning the entire Steelers secondary. Paul pulled Jim out of the game, waving for Jim to stand next to him.

"You're my fullback," Paul said. Then Paul casually moved away from Jim down the sideline.

Jim would consider that moment one of the greatest of his career. Paul Brown wanted *him*. Jim at first thought he and Paul would share the kind of umbilical closeness Jim had shared with Walsh and the coaches back at Manhasset. Jim did not understand why the players feared and at times hated Paul. Just a short time later, Jim and Paul would become quiet enemies, two men that reviled each other, but rarely spoke a cross word about each other in public.

The relationship between Paul and Jim should not have been one made in dysfunctional hell. Paul had courageously signed black players when to do so was socially unacceptable, possibly even dangerous, and Jim initially saw Paul as a white man stemming from the same genetic mold as Walsh, Molloy, and Simmons, men who had been beneficial to his life and career, not hurtful.

The core of Jim and Paul's problems was not just a changing football league, but a shifting society. Paul could not deal with an America that was changing so quickly. Jim was a child of that change. The country's emphasis on individual rights and freedoms began trickling down to football. But individuality was contrary to Paul's beliefs. A young Jim was maturing into an activist who refused to bend to Paul's will, and Paul declined to change the ways that had made him the most successful coach in football.

"Jim was not going to score touchdowns and get beat up physically and then stay quiet and say nothing once the game was over," said former Cleveland teammate Bobby Mitchell. "He found the notion offensive that he was supposed to be this quiet brute. Jim was anything but quiet. Jim was opinionated. Under Paul, players were not supposed to be opinionated. You were supposed to just shut up and play."

JIM'S EMERGENCE AS a leader on the team occurred deliberately, game by game, run by run. Veteran Browns players who were not easily impressed were taken aback by what they saw Jim do. In the ninth game of his rookie year Jim ran the ball thirty-one times. It was a pounding, brutal day, with Jim once getting smashed so hard that his helmet cracked slightly and bounced off his head. His performance began to turn heads in the league, and inside the Browns locker room the respect for Brown was growing exponentially.

No player in the long tenure of the NFL had risen to such a position of leaguewide dominance as rapidly as Brown. The players' references to Jim as "rook" were now replaced by "Hey, Jimmy." He was named Rookie of the Year in 1957. The more he played, the more reverence he gained in the eyes of players and the more he was able to intimidate some of his opponents. Before games, he would taunt his defenders by stretching and jogging directly in front of their sideline. "Imagine before a game seeing that big, giant, fast runner," said teammate John Wooten. "You couldn't help but be awed."

By the late 1950s, Jim was not just influential, he was one of the most powerful men inside the Browns organization, particularly among the black players. By training camp of 1958, the Cleveland dining room looked drastically different than it had in 1956. Now, the black players sat on one side of the dining hall while the white players sat on the other side. Before Jim, the team was somewhat intermixed, and race was a topic rarely publicly broached.

Privately was another matter. Black players on the Browns

were, for all intents and purposes, segregated, reflecting society at large. On the road, blacks roomed with other blacks. Paul kept their numbers artificially low so a team with more black players wouldn't offend white fans. "In some ways we were second-class citizens in the NFL," said Bobby Mitchell. Paul was not alone among coaches and the leagues' owners in this practice.

What Jim decided to do was something that had been discussed by previous blacks on the Cleveland team but never enacted. Jim organized. He inspired black players to brook no discrimination—from the Browns or anyone else—and always to carry themselves professionally in public. The black Browns players were women-chasing partygoers, but only behind closed doors. When the newspapermen interviewed them, they were serious and polite. None of this was by accident; it was Jim's well-designed plan. None of the black players in the league were as determined to improve their status as the Browns were. It was a groundbreaking phenomenon that to this day remains unappreciated and underreported.

"I always talk about Jim in terms of power and I mean power of the mind," said Mitchell in a rare interview. "In terms of community and social issues, he was far ahead of his time. Brown's message was, 'I'm a man. Don't disrespect me.' Black players in the NFL were not saying that then. As black players were signed by the Browns, their attitude changed overnight, they became more proud and defiant. That was Jim. We set the tone across the league for all black players."

Paul was initially shocked and then angered by how his Browns were changing. Despite controlling every aspect of the organization, from who was drafted to what went into or came out of the mouths of his players—no curses, no cigarettes—Paul was helpless to stop the growing racial pride in his black players that Jim had stirred. There were no outright acts of defiance to the coaching staff. There was simply increased unity. There was also little clowning or jiving around whites. Though the black Browns remained good teammates to their white counterparts, there was an increased sense of division in the locker room.

Paul approached Jim one day in the dining room. Paul's face was reddish with anger. "Don't do this," he told Jim. "You're hurting your team and I don't see any purpose in segregating our dining room."

Jim remained firm, and the differences between Paul and Jim would only become wider and more ingrained. When a stunning talent from the University of Illinois named Bobby Mitchell joined the team in 1958, the divide between Jim and Paul would become irreparable.

BOBBY MITCHELL WAS in love.

In 1958 he married his college darling, Gwen. His marriage was perhaps the biggest factor in propelling Mitchell to a career in professional football, a career that might be the most underrated ever.

At the University of Illinois, Mitchell was known more for his achievements on the track than on the football field. Despite being one of the fastest athletes college football has ever seen, Mitchell wanted to stick with track as the 1958 NFL draft approached. "I just was not into pro football," he said. "I knew very little about it."

What Mitchell knew was running. At Illinois he set a world record for the indoor hurdles and dominated several other events. Mitchell was told repeatedly that in the upcoming 1960 Olympics, he would be a gold medalist. That is what he set his sights upon. Then marriage changed his priorities. Now with a family to support, Mitchell had no choice but to enter the draft.

Despite having dramatic quickness, the Jim Brown–like ability to shift directions suddenly, and an eerie aptitude for making even the most sure-handed tacklers grab nothing but the tail end of his jersey, Mitchell was not drafted until the seventh round. When Paul thoroughly examined Mitchell's football background, he dismissed rumors that Mitchell was a fumbler. Paul selected Mitchell thinking he would be a speedy counter to Jim's punishing style.

When Mitchell arrived at the Browns' camp in Hiram and walked into the dressing room, the first person to greet him was Lou Groza. Then a group of other Browns walked up to him and shook his hand, welcoming him to the team. A smiling Mitchell was in awe.

Jim was next. He folded his large hands around Mitchell's. Before even saying hello, Jim told him: "I have never seen a guy cut like that without touching the ground."

"When I first saw Jim I was shocked at his physical size," said Mitchell. "I didn't realize he was built like that. Jim was as quick as most halfbacks, but he played fullback. He was such a smart player, too."

Mitchell himself was no dummy. He learned Paul's offense in six or seven days, taking full advantage of the fact that Cleveland ran a system similar to Illinois's. Yet as bright as Mitchell was, he was also a genuinely good-natured and naive man, which in the cutthroat world of the late 1950s NFL could be a dangerous combination.

Mitchell had no idea that he was soon to be in the middle of what was an ego-driven, racially tinged power struggle between Jim and Paul. The two players would remain lifelong friends—"No one respects Jim more than I do," said Mitchell—yet they were in many ways complete opposites. Mitchell was at times timid and reserved. He was also fabulously in love with his new bride, and the idea of leaving her at home while he chased other women was offensive to him. Jim was increasingly a partyer, whose stable of women was multiplying. When Paul made them roommates, other differences began to emerge as well. Their arguments were constant and rough; Jim would get so angry sometimes—because

Mitchell would not succumb to his reasoning—that teammates around them often wondered if the two men would come to blows.

Once the two friends came perilously close to doing just that. In the locker room prior to a game Jim and Mitchell got into a heated argument about who was the most beautiful woman in the world. Mitchell thought it was Jacqueline Kennedy. That selection infuriated Jim only because Mitchell's choice did not agree with his, and Jim thought it was impossible that Kennedy was the prettiest woman on the entire planet. Other Browns players thought Mitchell was right; that only made Jim madder.

Jim told Mitchell that if he did not change his mind and agree with him, he was going to physically harm Mitchell. Mitchell was befuddled: why was Jim so angry over something so trivial? The answer was not so complicated. Jim was testing Mitchell's resolve: not a new Jim trick—he had done it with other players before. Jim also did not want to lose face.

The argument and threats continued during pregame warm-ups, and the entire team watched closely as Jim seemed on the verge of a violent blowup. Jim cursed and glared at Mitchell as the team stretched and jogged, and teammates peered. Mitchell had no intention of fighting Jim. "I'm not taking on Jim Brown," Mitchell says now. He knew he could not win, and if a fight did erupt, Paul would blame him, not Jim, so he appealed to Jim to put the entire argument behind them. Just minutes before the game, Jim did, telling Mitchell that the episode was forgotten.

Moments like that illustrated the brutish side of Jim, and they were not isolated. There were other arguments between the friends that almost ended with Jim attacking Mitchell. At one point, Jim went to Paul and demanded that he be assigned a white roommate instead of the black Mitchell. Paul informed Jim that the only way such a switch would occur was if the new roommate agreed. Jim soon dropped the matter.

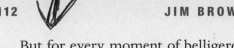

But for every moment of belligerence, there were many more featuring Jim's leadership and compassion. Jim was the first on the team and maybe in the sport to use his power for the betterment of other players and not just himself. Just a few years after his arrival in Cleveland, he was the undisputed leader of the Browns, and his power and influence were beginning to equal even Paul's. He put new players—particularly the black players—at ease by deciphering some of Paul's dicta or telling other players to back off if they were treating the new guys poorly.

When Mitchell came to the Browns, he was remarkably confident, clearly at ease with himself, a rarity for a rookie. He had a tremendous preseason his rookie year, and soon Paul was using him heavily on punt and kickoff returns, capitalizing on his speed. At the start of one practice Mitchell and running back Leroy Bolden were both setting up to return kicks when Bolden moved close to Mitchell and attempted to elbow him to the side. "Get out of the way," Bolden told Mitchell. "I'm returning these kicks. I don't like you anyway because you're trying to take my job." Jim later told Mitchell not to worry about the confrontation.

Nothing fazed Mitchell, and that relaxed manner irked Paul. "I changed slightly after Bolden said that to me," Mitchell explained. "It made me think of football for the first time as a job and not something I simply enjoyed. But I was still having fun. Paul hated that. He wanted everything to be serious."

Toward the end of the 1958 preseason, as the battle for starting halfback between Mitchell and Bolden heated up, Paul called Mitchell into his office. "Do you really want to play pro football?" Paul asked. "You're not committing yourself to me." Mitchell was stunned. Did Paul not see the big plays he was making in practice? "I love playing football and I love playing it here," he told Paul.

"I'll tell you what I'm going to do," Paul said next. "I'm going to take you on this trip to play the Rams and we'll see what happens. I'm just not convinced you can play in this league."

A confused Mitchell went to Jim. The same man who had once threatened to beat him to a pulp now played the role of friend, consoler, and translator. "You'll be great, you'll be fine," Jim informed him. "Paul is just trying to see if you are tough enough."

Before the game against the Los Angeles Rams, Bolden had run for 113 yards against Detroit. Against the Rams, Mitchell started, and he dashed for 114 yards in the first half alone. As they walked to the locker room, Paul approached Mitchell. "You've shown me more than enough," Paul told him.

Jim later told Mitchell: "Told you that you'd be okay."

JIM AND MITCHELL'S friendship deepened, despite regular bitter arguments. What they did on the field was stirring. The first half of the 1958 season saw the Browns win five of their initial six games, with Jim leading the league in rushing and Mitchell being second. Each was averaging 7 yards a carry.

They were so comfortable together that their chemistry on the field became electric. Each knew what the other was going to do. A busted play against the Chicago Cardinals led to an impromptu pitch from Mitchell to Jim, who was standing alone in the backfield. Jim took the ball, broke through the traffic at the line of scrimmage, and ran for a 41-yard score.

Jim virtually owed Mitchell the fact that he ran for so many touchdowns. Mitchell would often break a long run and then get pushed out of bounds inside the 5-yard line. Then Paul would call Jim's number to punch the football in. After scoring, Jim would smile at Mitchell: "Thanks, Bobby."

The relationship between Paul, Jim, and Mitchell would end up a terrific mess. The reason remains a source of confusion and mystery. Jim felt it was because Paul didn't want two highly visible black stars on the Browns. "If an NFL coach has ever dominated a city, it was Paul Brown in Cleveland," wrote Jim in his second autobiography. "I think Paul was jealous that Bobby and I were stealing all the press in his town. I also think Paul was looking for a reason to bench Bobby. He was hard on Bobby from the day Bobby arrived, even rougher than he was on most guys. When Bobby showed without any doubt he could play, Paul put him in the starting lineup, but he continued to make every practice a drag for him. Ultimately, I think Paul became uncomfortable having two black stars on the 1958 Cleveland Browns. That thinking certainly would not be unusual in other cities, and I believe that's what happened in Cleveland." Then addressing Mitchell's three fumbles in one game against the New York Giants, Jim wrote: "I think Paul used the moment to return our team to the status quo, meaning one black star was plenty."

Paul felt that he had to trade Mitchell because Jim disliked the attention Mitchell was receiving. There was something else. Paul despised the increasing amount of partying and womanizing Jim was doing. Paul intervened in one training camp when a father and two of his sons, all of them possessing guns, intended to attack Jim because they thought Jim had been sleeping with the father's teenage daughter. When one of the Cleveland players found out about the planned trap, he informed Paul, who then instructed one of the assistant coaches to warn Jim. The attack never happened.

Mitchell probably has the most accurate and truthful account of why the situation turned so hostile so quickly. "When you have two egos like Paul and Jim, it is not going to work out," Mitchell says. "To Paul I became the reason why Jim was a problem. If Jim showed up to the bus late, it was my fault. If something went wrong, it was my fault. I became Paul's whipping boy. He couldn't go after Jim, so he came after me."

Coach Paul Brown congratulates rookie fullback Jim after he scored four touchdowns against the L.A. Rams, setting a new record of 237 yards rushing, November 1957. Jim's relationship with Brown started warmly but quickly cooled. Paul would later come to believe that Jim caused the team to divide along racial lines. *(© Bettmann/CORBIS)*

Johnny Unitas, Vice President Richard Nixon, and Jim Brown at the annual Touchdown Awards Dinner in Washington, 1959, where Unitas and Brown tied for Pro Player of the Year. *(AP Photo/Charles Gorry)*

Jim Brown, playing in his last lacrosse game at Syracuse University, 1957. Just before face-off, Brown had competed in a track meet and only managed to get into his lacrosse jersey—but not his lacrosse shorts. Brown is regarded as the best lacrosse player ever. As much as he loved the sport, he went pro with his passion, football, instead. *(AP Photo/Syracuse University Handout)*

Brown never missed a game or a practice, despite severe injuries. He played hard because it was in his nature—and because he knew that without him, Cleveland would have little chance of winning. Here, he rounds at right end after receiving a pass in the second quarter. The Browns would go on to beat the Dallas Cowboys, 48–7, October 16, 1960. *(AP Photo)*

Brown with his twins, Kevin and Kim, at their Ohio home, 1961. Brown did not believe in demonstrating physical affection toward his children; many of his sons and daughters have spoken of their father's distant nature and the years they were not a true part of his life.
(© Bettmann/CORBIS)

Brown often sat alone at halftime or in practice, thinking out plays, gathering his thoughts, and getting over his fear. He had decided that being poised but quiet was better for a football player than acting gregarious and chatty. Moodiness was as much a part of Brown's pathology as was his power and speed, but some of what he did was contrived. He wanted people to believe he was imbalanced. This reputation, Brown knew, would work to his advantage.
(Cleveland Press Collection)

Jim Brown took a break from filming *Rio Conchos,* his first film, to visit Elvis Presley on the set of his own film, *Roustabout.* When *Rio Conchos* premiered in 1964, those in attendance witnessed the beginning of a Hollywood leading man and the creation of a brave, new action hero. The combination of gigantic football star and movie actor took Brown to a new level of fame. There was more money, more power, more women, and more trouble. *(© Bettmann/ CORBIS)*

Brown did not simply go to football practice or games and then go home. He purposely used the clout accumulated from his years of football stardom to try to enact social awareness and change. Brown was not going to be solely one of the great athletes of his generation, but one of the more distinguished men as well. *(Cleveland Press Collection)*

Brown built an impressive media empire in the 1960s. He was a sports commentator and a newspaper columnist and began a closed-circuit business to broadcast boxing matches. Brown's radio shows and columns offered some insight into Brown's psyche—mainly his fearlessness in addressing almost any topic. *(Cleveland Press Collection)*

Brown, with caddy Nick Zinni, June 1965. Brown was able to morph his skills to excel at whatever sport he was playing. In his first try at golf, Brown shot in the upper 80s. He scored a 77 in his fifth attempt. Once, frustrated at shanking the golf ball, Jim practiced so long and hard, he wore the skin off one of his fingers. *(Cleveland Press Collection)*

Brenda Ayres, eighteen, accused Brown of striking her in the face, and Brown was charged with assault and battery. The trial opened a public door into Brown's personal life, and whispers about his womanizing grew louder. Here, Brown eyes his accuser as she is escorted from the courtroom. *(Cleveland Press Collection)*

Brown and his wife, Sue, who had testified on his behalf, smile at the "not guilty" verdict in the Ayres trial. Several years later, apparently weary of Brown's increasing distance from her and their three children, his flings, and an even bigger controversy involving another woman, Sue filed for divorce, citing gross neglect. *(Cleveland Press Collection)*

The owner of a championship ring and twenty NFL records, Brown is the only athlete in the College Football, Pro Football, and Lacrosse Halls of Fame. In 1965 he allowed a photographer into his home, who captured him with his numerous trophies. One year later, he would retire from football, giving up his life as an athlete forever. *(Cleveland Press Collection)*

In October 1965, Brown almost single-handedly destroyed the Giants, leading to the New York *Daily News* headline: "Browns Rip Giants, 38–14; Jim Runs, Catches, Hurls." Cleveland's victory over New York symbolized the end of the Giants' reign over the Browns. That same day, Jimmy Brown announced that he would retire after one more season. *(Cleveland Press Collection)*

Brown joins Muhammad Ali for a morning jog, May 1966. The men's bond was simple: both were athletic freaks in their sport and dedicated to bettering the lives of the poor and underrepresented. They were both also remarkably fearless. (© Bettmann/CORBIS)

Muhammad Ali visited Brown on the film set of *The Dirty Dozen* in Bedfordshire, England, 1966. Brown was proud that he portrayed realistic black men in his movies, not just Uncle Toms. Brown said, "I feel so good that Negroes are finally starting to play roles that other Negroes, watching, will feel proud of, and respond to, and identify with, and feel *real* about." *From left:* Brown, Rahaman Ali, Clint Walker, and Ali. *(AP Photo)*

Cleveland Browns owner Art Modell holds up Jim Brown's soon-to-be-retired number 32 jersey, 1967. The two men's close relationship caused several problems for the team. *(© Bettmann/CORBIS)*

Brown gathered many of the country's top black athletes in Cleveland for what was called a Muhammad Ali draft summit. Ali's decision to forgo the draft turned him into one of the most controversial athletes in the nation. *Front row, left to right:* Bill Russell, Ali, Brown, Lew Alcindor; *back row:* Carl Stokes, Walter Beach, Bobby Mitchell, Sid Williams, Curtis McClinton, Willie Davis, Jim Shorter, and John Wooten. *(© Bettmann/CORBIS)*

Brown with Giants middle linebacker Sam Huff, 1967. Huff and Brown were considered enemies, but there was mutual admiration that would last throughout their NFL careers and beyond. Their battles led to several exaggerated tales told by Huff on the banquet circuit, one of which was repeated in *Time* magazine. *(Cleveland Press Collection)*

Brown in Cleveland in 1968, before the premier of his movie *The Split*. Brown's handsome looks and athletic build turned him into the first black action-movie star. He was a revolutionary presence, particularly to black film audiences, who for the first time saw someone on the screen who seemed more like them. *(Cleveland Press Collection)*

Before Brown, a black man was not allowed to be sexual on the big screen. In this scene from the film *100 Rifles,* Raquel Welch willingly submits to Brown moments after struggling with him. The love scenes in the film remain one of the more significant turning points in cinematic history, because they show interracial kissing. (© *Bettmann/CORBIS*)

Brown arriving in a sheriff's bus at Beverly Hills Municipal Court, 1969. He was arrested earlier in the day for ramming his car into another man's vehicle. Brown was later acquitted of all charges, but he would spend time behind bars throughout the 1970s, 1980s, and, 1990s. (© *Bettmann/CORBIS*)

In 1971, Brown was inducted into the Pro Football Hall of Fame with other legends. *Standing, left to right:* Vince Lombardi Jr. (holding the bust of his father), Frank Kinard, Bill Hewitt (his bust held by his daughter), Brown; *sitting:* Andy Robustelli, Y. A. Tittle, and Norm Van Brocklin. *(© Bettmann/CORBIS)*

In 1985, Brown pleaded innocent to three counts of rape and sexual battery. Johnnie Cochran (seen here with Brown before the arraignment) ultimately succeeded in having the charges tossed out of court. A decade later, O. J. Simpson, another number 32, would use Cochran to get off a murder rap. (© Bettmann/CORBIS)

Facing misdemeanor charges stemming from an incident in which he allegedly threatened to kill his twenty-five-year-old wife, Monique, Brown appeared with his wife on *Larry King Live* in a massive public relations counterattack. In that interview Monique claimed that PMS led her to fabricate the abuse allegation. (© Reuters/CORBIS)

Brown was treated by some members of the Syracuse coaching staff, and others at the school, as if he was some sort of plague; he did not fully reconcile with the school until the 1980s. In 2005, Syracuse announced two new scholarships—for football and lacrosse—in honor of Brown, and retired his number 44 jersey. *(AP Photo/Kevin Rivoli)*

There was no better example than what occurred once after a game. Paul was notoriously crazed about players being on time for the team bus; being tardy was akin to treason. In one instance because Jim was speaking to someone on the telephone, he and Bobby headed to the team bus late. When they got within several feet of the bus, Paul came storming off of it, approaching them both in a huff. Bobby and Jim were standing right next to each other, but Paul did not approach Jim, who was the reason for the tardiness; he went directly to Mitchell. "Bobby," Paul said, "who do you think you are? You are not better than this football team."

"Paul used me as a way to deal with Jim Brown," Mitchell says.

Mitchell's talent was among the best professional football has ever seen, yet he never fully blended in with the Browns. Against Philadelphia in one game, he returned a kickoff 98 yards for a score and then returned a Philadelphia punt 68 yards for a touchdown. Still, no matter what he did, Paul never fully appreciated him.

The Cleveland press played up the fact that Jim was the battering ram to Mitchell's rapid attack. The increased press Mitchell was receiving irked Jim, but it did not disrupt their friendship. "Jim and I argued, but as far as on the field," says Mitchell, "there was never a problem. He didn't care about me getting the football. We had a nice competition."

Mitchell is right: Paul desired to control Jim but could not. He considered trading Jim, but Jim was too talented, too crucial to the franchise. Paul never forgot the November 1, 1959, Browns game versus the Baltimore Colts. It was billed as Jim Brown against John Unitas—the Legs versus the Arm. Brown finished with five touchdown runs and Unitas four touchdown passes as the Browns won 38–31. After the game Brown visited the Colts' locker room. Weeb Ewbank, a former assistant under Paul and now the head coach of the Colts, broke away from a pack of reporters once he spotted Jim. "We knew you were a great runner," Ewbank said, shaking Jim's hand, "but you're even better than we thought." Paul enjoyed that victory more than some of the others because he always felt Ewbank's departure to Baltimore from Cleveland was disloyal, and beating him was the sweetest revenge. When the Browns landed in Cleveland there were more than a thousand fans waiting for them at the airport; some of them chanted Jim's name in unison.

Each time Paul thought of discharging Jim, the running back would amaze Paul with another ground-gaining run, whether it was for 6 inches or 60 yards. There was grudging respect spiced with intense dislike. The same could be said for Jim's feelings about Paul, except with heavier doses of both emotions. When Cleveland played its key rival, the Giants, in New York, a kick to Jim's head would put further stress on Jim and Paul's already strained affiliation.

Jim was smashed in the head after a Giants defender kicked him early in the game. In all likelihood, Jim had a severe concussion. Barely staying conscious, he rose slowly, as he had done so many times before, except this day was different. He could recognize nothing except the faces of his teammates. Jim realized that he failed to remember the plays or his responsibilities, and he asked quarterback Milt Plum for help. Plum then told Jim where to go. "Go right there, in that hole," Plum said. When Plum realized just how damaged Jim was, particularly after a rare Jim fumble, Plum called a time-out, and Paul removed Jim from the game. Doctors looked Jim over and instructed Paul that he needed to sit out the second quarter.

At halftime, Jim sat alone in a corner of the locker room. There was little he could remember. Jim was both angry and alarmed. When Paul approached Jim and informed him that another injured player had gotten right back into the game, Jim was incensed. He returned to the game furious with Paul.

Sam Huff, the great middle linebacker for the Giants, told Jim during the game that Paul was both pitiless and crazy to leave Jim in the contest. Afterward, Huff blasted Paul in the New York newspapers for being cruel. (Huff would later write an apology to the Browns coach.)

But Jim would never apologize, never give an inch to Paul. And the pair's relationship only worsened when Paul decided to trade Mitchell after the fumbles in the New York game. That decision would turn out to be one of the few personnel mistakes the great coach ever made. Since he coveted another Syracuse running back, Ernie Davis, Paul contacted the owners of the first pick of the 1962 draft, the Washington Redskins. Unlike Paul, the owner of the Washington team, George Preston Marshall, fought to keep black players off the team. But after moving the Redskins into a government-owned building, Marshall was forced by federal authorities to comply with laws that prohibited discrimination on property owned by the government. The stubborn Marshall finally relented and traded with Cleveland for Mitchell. With fresh first-round picks in hand, Paul was going to draft Davis, the first black Heisman Trophy winner, a runner who wore Jim Brown's number 44 at Syracuse. Davis, who practiced with the Browns but never played, died in his sleep from leukemia in 1963, before his Browns career ever began.

(Jim had grown extremely fond of Davis and was emotionally stirred by his death. He made a point to attend the funeral for Davis, as did the entire Syracuse and Cleveland Browns football coaching staffs. The funeral led to an interesting moment. After Davis's casket was lowered into the ground, Jim, Paul, Roy Simmons Sr., and Ben Schwartzwalder were walking slightly ahead of a group of Cleveland players and others. They were all departing the cemetery when Jim announced to his teammates: "I want all of you to meet my favorite coach of all time." Schwartzwalder stopped and turned, thinking Jim was going to introduce him. "Simmy, come here and meet my friends," Jim exclaimed, speaking to Simmons. It was no accident that Jim had made that pronouncement loudly, in front of Paul and Schwartzwalder, two men he did not get along with.)

When Jim first heard of the Davis trade, he was concerned Paul was going to ship him off the way he had Mitchell. He nervously went into Paul's office the day news of the Davis trade broke. "Am I still on the team?" Jim asked.

Paul informed Jim that he thought the offense would run better with not just one but two fast, big runners, and no trade was coming. That was mostly true. Privately, the Browns coaching staff, many of whom were irritated with what they wrongly thought was Jim's lazy approach to practices, wanted Davis just in case the time did come to trade Jim.

Mitchell had been serving in the army, playing in his games on weekend passes. At the time of his trade to Washington, he had no exposure to the newspapers or radio and thus had no idea he had been traded. When he left his base and arrived at the Browns complex, one of the first people to greet him was Jim. "I wanted you to know I had nothing to do with this," Jim told him.

"What are you talking about?" Mitchell responded.

Paul had never told Mitchell about the trade. "Paul said that he sent a letter to me, but I never got it," Mitchell says. "You would think there was a record of something like that. The first thing I told my wife was—and we had just built a house in Cleveland six months earlier—this is the last time someone was ever going to make that big a decision about my life. From that point on, I was going to make the decisions."

Once he left Jim's planet-sized shadow, Mitchell demonstrated that his skills were as formidable as any offensive talent to play football. When Mitchell was inducted into the Hall of Fame in 1983 he had amassed more than 14,000 total yards, a number that was bettered by only Jim and O. J. Simpson. Still, it had taken considerable lobbying by Jim and others to get Mitchell into the Hall. For many years, mainly because of a low-key personality that abhorred self-promotion, he was the cloaked candidate, the forgotten superstar, and in some ways, he remains that way.

"My years with Jim were some of the most rewarding of my life," Mitchell says. "I appreciate his friendship. We're still close now. I also think that it is true I was overshadowed in some ways when we played together. Don't think I am not aware that people don't consider me among the best when they talk about the great runners and receivers. I am aware, and I can't say that it does not bother me."

THE STORY GOES like this. Jim was playing the Giants and his nemesis, Sam Huff, when the hulking but quick Huff jammed Jim at the line of scrimmage, wrapped him up, and tossed him to the ground. As Jim lay there, Huff towered over him and shouted, "Look at you, Brown. You stink." Later in the game, Jim broke through a Huff tackle and ran for a 50-yard touchdown. Jim turned and hollered at Huff: "How do I smell from here?"

When Jim appeared on the cover of *Time,* Huff repeated the anecdote to the magazine. It was a juicy story. It was also apparently false. Huff had made the entire thing up while speaking about Jim on the banquet circuit, Brown maintains.

Stories about Brown indeed sprouted quickly. During a 1963 radio interview, a former Philadelphia Eagles public relations director, Ed Hogan, told the story of Brown's encounter with Eagles player Tom Brookshier three years earlier during what was a presidential election year. It took four Eagles to tackle Brown after a 30-yard run. Brookshier got up and shook his head. "You always do that after tackling Brown. This is to make sure you still have a head. I asked Jimmy then who he was voting for in the election. He

said he didn't know and asked me who I was voting for. 'Kennedy,' "
Brookshier said. After the election, when the Browns played the
Eagles again, and again Brookshier and a group of Eagles tackled
Brown, he got up, turned to Brookshier, and said, "Your boy Ken-
nedy did all right." Just how true this and similar yarns about Brown
are remains, all these years later, in question.

The tall tales were an indication of how much Jim's power and
presence had grown. In the 1960s the NFL continued its growth
from a mom-and-pop league to a powerful entity, and Jim was one
of its most visible players. In a way, as he had done with Cleveland
so many times, Jim had taken the NFL on his broad shoulders and,
along with a handful of other stars, was carrying the league to
greatness.

With Mitchell now traded there was no other runner in Cleveland to grab any headlines away from Jim. Or plays for that matter.
He became the certified leader of the offense and its fulcrum, at
times to the dismay of Paul. Jim proved to be as skilled a negotiator
as Paul—another irritating point for the head coach. In the early
spring of 1960, as Jim and his representatives were privately lobbying Paul for a new contract, Jim was publicly talking about possibly leaving football for a boxing career. Suddenly, the Cleveland
papers were filled with rumors that there was a 50 percent chance
Jim might leave football for a two-year, $150,000 fight deal. Jim did
nothing to stop these rumors; in fact he fueled them. "I haven't
signed for next season and unless it is for what I think it ought to be,
I'll quit," he told reporters. "The coaches in professional football
seem to think there is a limit on salaries. I don't. I think a player
ought to be paid according to the improvement he shows from one
season to the next."

Jim was doing what he always does: pushing the boundaries
and testing his opponent, even if that opponent was his own head
coach. He knew that owners could and should pay players far more

money than they were earning, and he was going to be the person who pried open the safe.

Paul was incensed. He knew Jim's boxing threat was a negotiating ploy, but the city was abuzz about the possibility, and fans were becoming increasingly edgy. Besides, if anyone was capable of following through on such a threat, it was Jim. Paul was all too familiar with Jim's athletic prowess and ability to morph his skills to excel at whatever sport he was playing. Just one year earlier, Paul had been taken aback when he learned that Jim, in his first try at golf, shot in the upper 80s. His fifth attempt saw Jim score a 77. Once, frustrated at shanking the golf ball, Jim practiced so long and hard, he wore the skin off one of his fingers.

Paul hated doing business through the media. But he had no choice but to ensure that Jim re-signed with the club. In June of 1960, Jim signed a two-year contract extension with the Browns that made him the highest-paid player in football, earning a salary of just over $30,000. The money was a far cry from Paul's days in the All-America Football Conference, when a lineman received $25 a game.

Jim built his clout with his legs and smarts on the football field first and foremost. In 1961 Paul decided to use Jim sparingly in the preseason as the league expanded the schedule from twelve to fourteen games. The strategy worked. In Brown's final game that year he rushed twenty-four times for 101 yards, accruing just enough to beat out Jim Taylor of the Green Bay Packers for what was Brown's fifth straight rushing title. Jim totaled 1,407 yards on the season, his highest since 1958.

Around the NFL, he was now known as the toughest, most unstoppable weapon in the sport. It had reached the point where defensive players remembered their one-on-one tackles of Brown because they were so rare. "I remember playing him in Cleveland," said Dallas linebacker Chuck Howley, the first defender to be named a Super

Bowl MVP. "There was this one play that he won't remember, but I will never forget. He was running an end sweep, and for once he was just a little off balance, just for a second. That allowed me to catch up, and I was able to grab him from behind. It was the one time I tackled him one-on-one. Those are the things you remember about playing Jim Brown. The times you could tackle him alone. Usually, it took a gang of guys to get him down."

"You always hear people say how great he was, and he was a great player," said Hall of Famer Len Dawson. "But what made him special was his durability. I played with him in Cleveland for two years and I never saw him once in the training room. He stayed away because he didn't want people to think he was weak, and he would just fight through pain. I mean, he never got his ankles taped. He could be aloof, yeah, but he was the best."

Tough, yes, and remarkably moody. Former teammates recall how they never knew which Brown would make an appearance on that particular day. They tell stories of Brown scoring a touchdown and then going to the end of the bench to sit alone. In a 1968 *Playboy* interview with journalist Alex Haley, Brown responded to accusations that he was indeed cold and distant to teammates.

I know you've heard that I was supposed to have a reputation for being distant, aloof and hard to get along with, especially in football seasons, most especially close to game time. Well, maybe I was. Maybe I was rude to people and had very little to say to anybody. The reason is that I was focused mentally on that coming game. I was concentrating, visualizing things that I knew could happen and what I would do if it went this way or that way. I knew I had it working right when I started seeing plays in my mind almost like I was watching television. I'd see my own line in front of me, the guards, the halfbacks, the quarterbacks, and then the other team over there—especially big Roger Brown and Alex Karras, two of the best tackles in football. Both of them are quick, agile, smart, fast and big, and they like to hit *hard*. Notice I don't just say they hit hard, but they *like* to hit hard— that's mental; that's positive thinking, see? I'd walk around in the locker room, seeing Roger Brown in my mind—for some reason, not his face or hands or shoulders, but those thighs of his. Massive thighs, like some huge frog. I always envision Roger hopping up in the air, jumping over blocks— all 300 pounds of him. And Alex Karras—in pro football, he's just a little cat, just 250 pounds, but he's built like a stump, with a boxer's sneering mouth. I hear him growling; he actually growls when he's charging.

Positive thinking again, see? Anyway, I'd be watching them mentally across the line and sizing up the moves they might make against me. I'd see plays running and things happening—see myself starting a run and having to make spur-of-the-moment changes of strategy and direction. Every play I ever ran, I had already run a thousand in my mind. Right now, I can see a sweep run. I'm starting—my first three steps are very fast. Then I'm drifting, to let my guard in front of me get into position. There he is; now others are throwing their blocks; my guard is blocking their halfback to the outside. Now I accelerate and I shoot through the gap. That outside linebacker is my greatest danger now. I can see the order in which the tacklers are going to come. I'm looking for that end first, or maybe that outside linebacker, since no one could get to him right away. I see myself making all kinds of instantaneous adjustments, step by step, through their secondary—and then into the clear and all the way for a TD. Do you see what I mean? You get a jump on the game when you visualize beforehand not only the regular plays you run but also the hundred and one other things that might happen unexpectedly. So when you're in the actual game, whatever happens, you've already seen it in your mind and plotted your countermoves—instantly and instinctively.

Each football accomplishment was also purposely punctuated by a public statement or appearance. Everyone wanted to speak to him, to be close to him. No one was exempt from desiring to be in his presence, not the many women who courted him, not even American presidents. In December of 1963, after beating Washington, Jim and teammate Frank Ryan, the Browns quarterback, were invited to the White House by President Lyndon B. Johnson. Jim walked into the meeting with Johnson dressed impeccably in a dark suit and tightly knotted tie. When Johnson shook hands with Jim, the president noticed the bruises and cuts on Jim's hands. "I guess that's the sign of a great runner," Johnson told him.

When they went to talk, the president sat in his famous rocking chair, leaning forward, speaking closely to Jim. Ryan was the quarterback, but Jim was the star. It was Jim whom Johnson truly wanted to see. When the three men spoke, Johnson stressed that high-profile athletes could indeed make a difference in the lives of young people.

"It's up to people like us to make this country a better place to live," Johnson said. Brown nodded in agreement. It was a sentiment that he strongly shared. He had already begun living his life that way.

After a few conversations about football and the Browns, Jim and Ryan departed, but before they did, Johnson handed them two cigarette lighters. When Jim and Ryan both remarked that neither smoked, Johnson replied, "You can have them on hand for guests." The lighters had the seal of the vice president's office.

In 1961 the three most noticeable and powerful people on the

Browns were Jim, Paul, and the new owner, Art Modell. Paul had first met Modell at the team hotel a year earlier, following the Browns' last game in New York. Modell was handsome and funny and delivered one-liners that put people at ease. He was also young and cocky. At just thirty-six years old, he had become a significant success at an advertising agency in New York. "I loved the NFL," said Modell. "I wanted to be around football."

Modell and Paul's relationship was destined to be problematic. Paul was the conservative, brilliant, extremely controlling lifelong football coach. Modell was the cool, smart, rich ad man who was used to getting his way and knew little about the sport other than what he heard on the radio and read in the papers.

Cleveland was suspicious of the New Yorker Modell, but his clout was enhanced when, shortly after purchasing the Browns for almost $4 million in 1961, he was a key part of the NFL signing a multiyear television deal with CBS.

Paul was convinced that his rights and duties would remain intact under Modell. Those beliefs were reinforced when he signed a ten-year contract extension that included his right to purchase some ten shares of the Browns a year, a $7,500 expense account that Paul could use any way he chose, and an annual salary of more than $80,000. As far as Paul was concerned, he was still in control, and though he would grow intensely suspicious of Modell, Paul had no idea how wrong he was.

In the early 1960s, which would become Paul's final years, Jim had become accustomed to seeing a familiar sight: the New York Giants showing dazzling clairvoyance by guessing the Browns' next play.

The Giants worked together as a robust team; they were as intellectual as they were violent on the field. They studied Paul's system intently, and during their fervid rivalry with the Giants, no team comprehended the Browns' offensive system better than the Giants.

In fact, in many ways, by 1962 Paul had become a victim of his own decades-long brilliance. Teams led by brash young coaches like Vince Lombardi in Green Bay and Allie Sherman in New York had stolen Paul's messenger system—using players to send in the plays—and improved upon it. They did so by being more flexible. The newer breed of coaches allowed their quarterbacks to make changes in the huddle or at the line of scrimmage.

Paul's techniques were becoming outdated because by now defenses were changing their alignments after the offense got set. Since the unyielding Paul declined to let his quarterbacks audible out of a set play, teams that played the Browns simply shifted out of their initial defense into another one, which made it difficult for the Cleveland offense to run a successful play. There were actually instances in which the Browns would purposely change plays without telling Paul, and then claim the change was a result of miscommunication from the messenger. In effect, the Browns players were committing infrequent but significant acts of mutiny.

Mitchell remembers an incident prior to his departure from Cleveland to Washington. Following a long run, Mitchell jogged back to the huddle winded. The messenger trotted up to the players with the call: an outside run for Mitchell. Noticing that Mitchell could barely breath, Jim told Mitchell to switch positions with him, so on that play, Jim played running back and Mitchell played fullback. Jim took the play designed for Mitchell and burst for a touchdown.

The Giants became experts at taking advantage of Paul's refusal to adapt to the newer NFL. Andy Robustelli, the frenetic Giants defensive end who played in eight championship games, would irritate the players by calling out the play that the messenger had just sent in. "It's 32 Trap, isn't it! You know I'm right!" he would scream. The Browns were annoyed because Robustelli was often correct, and the defense would shift right into the proper holes, stuffing Jim.

At the end of the 1962 season the Browns finished 7–6–1. They had not won a division title since 1957. Many of Paul's players remained intensely loyal to him, but a group of others, led by Jim, grew increasingly frustrated.

Jim's relationship with Paul had never been worse. Jim's relationship with Modell was totally different. Modell urged Jim to have his own radio show, and Jim gladly accepted, sometimes using the show to criticize Paul's play calling and messenger system, further widening the rift between the two men. Over a period of months, Modell had created such a close relationship with many of the team's stars that Paul felt Modell was undermining his authority. Paul became infuriated when he learned that Modell had been taking the players and team leaders out to expensive dinners and Cleveland nightspots. Often, the players would complain to Modell about Paul, sometimes for hours, and Modell would reciprocate, openly wondering to the players if the game had passed Paul by.

During a game against Washington, Modell sat in the press box and railed against Paul's play calling, doing so in front of the writers, who promptly informed Paul. In another game, a loss against the Giants at Yankee Stadium, Modell blasted Paul for his play calling in the final seconds. Modell chastised Paul in full view of several players.

No other owner had done anything like that to Paul Brown. Ever.

It was clear that the insertion of a volatile and opinionated Modell into what was already a flammable mix created a major problem, mainly because Modell appeared to take sides, courting Jim, and then seemed to use Jim to assist in publicly undermining Paul. Modell publicly referred to Jim as his "senior partner," which elevated Jim to a level that put the runner far above other players, and perhaps above even Paul. That latter possibility became evident when Paul and his staff started seriously discussing trading Jim.

Once he heard the news, Jim went to Modell and convinced the owner to insert a no-trade clause into his contract. Paul was infuriated.

Though later Jim and Modell's close relationship would crumble (and then revive decades later), in 1962 they formed what at the time was an unusual partnership, since player and owner were rarely so close. While it is unfair to say that Jim and Modell plotted the demise of Paul, it is also blithely silly to believe that both men did not want Paul gone. They both worked, at least to some extent, to get him out of Cleveland.

The inevitable occurred on a chilly December day in 1962, the same month that Jim and Johnny Unitas appeared on the cover of *Sport* magazine, which asked the question "Who's More Important, the Passer or Runner?" In Cleveland, the answer became apparent when Jim and a group of about six offensive veterans, including the man who had become one of Jim's closest friends, offensive lineman John Wooten, decided to plead for the coach to open up the offense. They were going to meet either at Paul's house or at the team hotel at next week's final game in San Francisco. Modell heard about the planned meeting from an official in the team's public relations department and called it off. After hearing from Jim and others that if Paul would not change his ways, several key players would publicly demand a trade, Modell used the ugly situation to make a final decision. He was going to fire Paul.

Jim played much of his and Paul's final year together with a painful wrist, just one of many seasons in which Jim fought through serious pain. In the last game, against New York, Paul rewarded Jim for fighting through the discomfort with a game ball. Jim awkwardly accepted it, smiling slightly, something that Paul felt was odd.

Jim's strange reaction was because he knew Paul was gone as coach of the team.

Soon after that game, on a Monday, Modell called Paul into his office and informed him: "I've made a decision. You have to step down as coach and general manager." Then Modell informed Paul of the reason why: "The Browns will never be mine as long as you're here." That is what Paul's version is anyway.

Years later, Modell made his case. "Don't portray me as a backstabber," Modell says. "I did not run him out of town; that's not fair. I think it was a case where things had run their course."

The autobiography *PB: The Paul Brown Story* was published in 1979, before Paul's death, and remains one of the preeminent books about professional football, albeit one of the least known. It offers insight into the best coaching mind the game has seen. In the book, however, Paul spends considerable time excoriating Jim as a selfish, troubled man. The comments about Jim reflect their relationship. In one breath, Paul says he had no hard feelings about him, but later he attacks the running back's character and motives. The things Paul says about Jim are both fair and inaccurate, honest and deceptive. Jim did not always behave admirably in his dealings with Paul. Jim's issues of insecurity manifested themselves in numerous ways in his dealings with the coach. Jim was as controlling and egotistical as Paul was.

What Paul leaves out of his book is his own accountability for the problems between these two great and narcissistic men. In many ways Jim represented the changing persona of not just the black athlete, but any professional athlete: more outspoken, more demanding of his rights. Paul arose at a time when the athlete was docile and predictable and said, "Yes sir." Paul never adapted to the changing men in a changing sport and society.

However, Paul saves some of his most biting criticism for Modell. "During the two years between his coming to the Browns and my dismissal, I lived through a period of almost constant intrigue," Paul wrote. "Player was set against player; the loyalty of my coaching staff was questioned, and attempts made to find out which ones were 'Paul Brown men'; public criticism of my coaching was encouraged among the players and steadfastly carried on by management through the media; discipline and control were torn apart by flagrant disregard for team rules; and the team itself was subjected to unfair and overwhelming pressures when the ownership twice guaranteed the public it would win the championship."

Paul also stated: "Art was not a football person. I resented his lack of background in the football world and did not respect his knowledge, and I probably showed it many times, not helping the situation any. As we continued, however, I saw he was eroding my position with the result that I could not be successful and carry out my responsibilities. The player-coach relationship became progressively more intolerable, to the point where I was no longer able to call the shots, no longer in position to demand from all of our players all the things which make or break a successful football team. That had never happened to me before in all my years in football."

According to Paul's autobiography, twelve hours after Modell dismissed Paul, a cardboard box appeared on the former coach's front porch. Inside were the contents of his office—including the pictures of his family. He was not to go near the Browns offices again. That was at least the way Paul saw it. Modell denies this story. The actual truth about how the relationship ended will never be known for certain.

"AFTER READING THE initial installments of Jim Brown's first literary effort," began a letter to the Cleveland *Plain Dealer* from one of its readers, "there is something I would like to get 'Off My Chest.'

As a writer, Jim has fumbled the ball. So far, his series has been nothing but a lot of cry-baby stuff unbecoming of one of the greatest athletes of all time. If these are truly his feelings about his former coach, they should be kept to himself. Everyone has his faults and Paul Brown is no exception. Unfortunately, making some enemies is a part of the price that one pays for achieving real greatness. However, the lasting memory of Paul in Cleveland will not be the tarnished image painted by Jim Brown, but instead the unequalled brilliance that truly made us the city of champions."

Not long after Paul's firing, Jim made the trip to Los Angeles for the January 13, 1963, Pro Bowl at Memorial Coliseum. Brown approached the game highly motivated. His old coach, Paul, had publicly declared that Jim's lower rushing numbers for the season were possibly due to a loss of desire, a statement that irritated the runner because Paul knew that Jim's badly hurt wrist was the main culprit. Jim decided to put the motivation talk to rest, and he burst for a new Pro Bowl rushing record with 144 yards on seventeen carries. He was voted the game's Most Valuable Player. "I don't know when I've had a better all-around game," Jim told writers after the contest. "And maybe I've convinced some people I'm not through. I knew in my heart I wasn't. You can't play 100 percent when you're hurt. Perhaps I've proved it to some others, too."

Paul's departure left Jim as the undisputed leader of the Browns franchise, and his Pro Bowl game erased any thought that he had lost either his flare for greatness or his tendency to speak his mind. He was now more powerful, in many ways, than Modell, the owner. Jim had also become a bigger target. Modell took most of the blame for Paul's firing, with more than three hundred phone calls jamming the team's switchboard in several hours following the city's coaching hero getting the ax. However, Jim was not absolved of blame. Fans became increasingly wary of Jim's growing power.

No black man in the NFL had ever possessed the kind of visibility Jim did, and few fans knew what to make of it. Some whites were cautious, at best, while others fumed.

When Jim wrote a powerful and remarkably doctrinaire auto-biography in 1964 called *Off My Chest,* it caused a furor in the sports world, especially in Cleveland. Jim angered many Clevelanders equally with a one-two punch of controversy: he ripped Paul for his aloofness and stated openly that the game had passed him by, which was blasphemy. There were elements of truth in both of Brown's assertions, of course, but no one had stated them so bluntly in a book. The book also offered direct and controversial views about race and talked openly about how players cheated on Paul Brown's intelligence tests.

To say that Jim broke new ground with his memoir is an un-derstatement. NFL players were not yet penning these kinds of books, which explains the media fury that detonated after excerpts were published in various magazines and Cleveland newspapers. Some in the media compared the revelations to other great contro-versies of the day. Cleveland columnist Howard Preston wrote: "The fullback hero, a proud man, downgrades himself by admit-ting he cheated purposely on tests given the squad by the head coach, Paul Brown, whom he disliked intensely. His excuse was that everybody did it; that the tests were impractical, purposeless in his opinion. So he deliberately cheated, used 'gyp sheets' to crib the right answers. There went another hero. Oh, it has been a bad few weeks for the American dream. The greatest football runner in the country cheated on tests; the head of the FBI screamed at the Su-preme Court and at a minority leader (Martin Luther King, Jr.) who had just won a world-prized award. We Americans, no matter what we claim, are hero worshippers and if something isn't done soon to stop this sort of cannibalism, we won't have much left to look up to but Dr. Casey and Lawrence Welk."

Jim's words were bold and possibly belligerent, but they were also truthful. He wrote about his appreciation for the Muslims, something that was startlingly controversial. He described a scene where a small, young white girl who was a fan wanted to kiss him on the cheek, but Jim declined, knowing that he would "look up and find that all the smiling adult faces have been replaced by frozen faces."

"The first thing the white man must understand is the depth of our protest," Jim wrote. "Does he realize that the Black Muslim's basic attitude toward whites is shared by almost 99 percent of the Negro population?" He later wrote: "I am skeptical of white men because even the best of them want me to be patient, to turn the other cheek until God knows when."

Some of the writers who followed the Cleveland team applauded Brown for his frankness. There remained a notion, however, that despite the revelations in the book, few people outside of a handful of close friends and family knew much about Brown other than that he was outspoken and talented. It was in this moment, after the publication of his book, that Brown was first described in the media as angry and brooding.

"It isn't easy to know the real Jim Brown," wrote Cleveland *Plain Dealer* columnist Charles Heaton in September of 1964. "During his eight years with the team he's been courteous and for the most part friendly, but we never seemed to penetrate his armor. The fact that the usually pleasant exterior housed an angry young man has been no secret for those close to the football club. We're sure this anger goes back even further [than] that December afternoon in 1956 when we first met him at the Concourse Plaza Hotel in New York City. Brown was the team's first draft choice after a brilliant windup year at Syracuse University. He had come to New York to see Paul Brown and watch the Browns finish their road season against the Giants. We were more interested in muscles and shoulders than probing the psyche that day. We did note, however, that Jim was quiet and slow to smile. . . .

"Brown quickly became the star of the team and its highest paid performer. He won the respect of his teammates but not their affection. And this was not because Jim Brown's skin was a different color from some of the others. Marion Motley and a string of other Negro athletes on the Browns had been warmly regarded. It was the same with most of the reporters who followed the team. Jim seemed to have his guard up whether the discussion concerned the fullback or the kids at home. And we must confess that for the most part we never felt completely at ease with this rather reserved man."

Brown could indeed be aloof and difficult with teammates. Sometimes they loved Brown, sometimes many of them despised him, but they always respected him. What many white reporters did not completely comprehend was that Brown was advocating not just for black teammates, but for blacks in general. He was addressing the socioeconomic concerns of his people, doing what Brown had done for some time: using his power and clout not solely to improve his situation, but to correct the predicaments of others.

The book was talked about in every Cleveland bar, restaurant, and barbershop where blacks gathered. While whites reacted curiously or irately, many blacks privately nodded in agreement. Others thought what Brown wrote about race was not so unusual.

One headline over a story by a black author read: "Why the Excitement over Jim Brown?" He referred to Brown as "a safe Negro" and declared that many of Brown's statements about racism did not shock blacks, since they knew all too well the sting of discrimination. In other words, what Brown was saying was nothing new to them.

Many white Cleveland fans were outraged. Some phoned the team complex to complain vehemently (though the number of calls to the complex's switchboard was not as great as the number of protests that swamped the operators when Paul Brown was dismissed). Some threatened to cancel their season tickets. Others phoned newspaper reporters at their offices and cursed into the phone. There were many letters to the various Cleveland newspapers.

"Just what is it that Jim Brown wants to get off his chest?" asked another reader in a letter to the editor. "Is it appreciation, or is it thinly veiled resentment of all the sincere whites who went out of their way to help him become what he is? He is paid a high price for doing a good job: This does not make him a hero to be idolized for services beyond the call of duty. His next book should be entitled 'How I Became a Prima Donna with the Help of My Teammates,' or 'They Made Me What I Am Today,' or 'The Chip on My Shoulder.'"

When contents of the book were revealed publicly Brown did not back down one inch from his published comments. On September 22, 1964, following the team's normal Tuesday work session in which they dutifully watched game film, Brown and Wooten, who was Brown's road roommate, and defensive end Bill Glass went for a light jog around the facility. Brown could see the gathering group of writers waiting for him to finish. He knew what was coming.

"Some people may not like what I have to say," Brown told reporters; "that doesn't matter to me. The things had to be said. As far as football goes, it won't make any difference. If I can produce it won't matter. And if I can't then it doesn't matter, either."

Brown loved to argue. He constantly debated and prodded his teammates, so when he began the publicity for his book and engaged in spirited discussions with media members, he was rarely frazzled. On television, in particular, Brown was highly skilled. Despite his physical toughness and the way his muscles practically broke through his tightly fitting starched shirts and pressed suits, Brown was soft-spoken, well-mannered but also powerful. In many instances he possessed a more extensive vocabulary and a brighter intellect than his interviewers.

This paradox was apparent when Brown was interviewed on *The Mike Douglas Show*. Brown was cool and reasoned as he was questioned by the host and by movie star June Allyson. Squeezed between the two petite people, Brown politely answered questions tossed his way about his book, including many about whether he was a Muslim. When he was asked about the Muslims, there was almost a breathless, panicked tone to the query. Brown looked at Douglas, his large hands clasped. "The Black Muslims are not terrorists," he told Douglas. "They are a religion. They believe Negroes should help Negroes. They believe in neatness and cleanliness, and they hold their women in high esteem."

Later in the interview, Brown looked at Allyson, almost nodding in her direction, stating that blacks live each day under strain. "We have to be aware of so many things. For instance, the way we might look at a person like June Allyson." The white actress smiled slightly uncomfortably, then turned the tables.

"Do you hate white people?" she asked him.

"No," he responded. "It's hard for me to envision hating an entire group."

Brown deserved accolades for staying calm during a sometimes excruciatingly condescending interview. But there was something else. Just before Brown went on the air, a telephone call came into the show's control room. The executive producer, Forrest L. Fraser, answered the phone. A woman was on the line. She began speaking about an article Brown had written in a sports magazine that had run excerpts from his book.

"I am from [an] organization in New York City," the woman said. "If Brown says today what he said in that article, we'll bomb his home." She then hung up.

Fraser was certain he had heard the woman correctly, but he did not know the name of the organization and thought the call was possibly a fake. Agitated nonetheless, Fraser cleared the line and telephoned the police immediately. Then he nervously approached Brown and told him what had happened.

"Do you still want to go on?" Fraser asked.

"It's all right," Brown said. "I'll still go on."

Brown's book launched what would become an impressive media empire. He began writing an occasional column for the Cleveland *Plain Dealer* called "Jim Brown Says." A photo next to one column showed the always sharply dressed Brown, wearing a long-sleeve shirt under a dark vest, on the telephone, sitting in front of a typewriter. "What type of person is this new heavyweight boxing champion—Cassius Clay?" began the newspaper's promotion of Brown's column. "Are the sports writers accurate in calling him a loud-mouthed braggart, referring to him as Gaseous Cassius and the Louisville Lip? Is there another side to this handsome young man who defeated Sonny Liston last Tuesday? You'll get all the answers from Jim Brown in Sunday's *Plain Dealer*. The Browns' great fullback was at ringside in Miami last Tuesday night as a radio commentator. Jim was with Clay before and after the upset victory. He has the facts right from the mouth of the champion. This is only the beginning. No. 32 will be a regular contributor to the Sunday *Plain Dealer* sports pages. His column will cover a wide range of topics including, of course, professional football."

One of Brown's columns ran in the *Plain Dealer* on May 10, 1964, and offers some insight into Brown's psyche—mostly, his fearlessness in addressing almost any topic. He begins the column with an introduction to his life on the banquet circuit, with fans peppering him with questions. Then Brown wrote about some of those questions and how he answered them, beginning with the question of his contract status.

"No, I haven't signed for 1964 but I have had some preliminary talks with Art Modell," Brown wrote in his column. "I'm not prepared to name a figure for publication but I do want what I call a baseball-type pay check. I mean that top players in football should be compensated in line with the baseball stars. I've talked these things over with Y. A. Tittle of the New York Giants and he agrees. So does Johnny Unitas of Baltimore. I should add that I've never had any contract problems with the Browns. And I'm not anticipating any this time." A football player asking to be paid the same money as a baseball star was considered aggressive, if not unreasonable, thinking.

There were moments when Brown used the media as a platform to further his activist causes. There were as many instances when Brown went on his radio or television shows or the banquet circuit to talk about a Browns trade or personnel move or anything he fancied. During a Cleveland Touchdown Club luncheon at the Pick-Carter Hotel, Brown told an enthralled crowd that after his playing days were concluded, he would consider coaching. "I've had thoughts about many jobs," he told the crowd. "I'm keeping an open mind. If anyone shows interest in me as a coach I certainly would consider the opportunity." When Cleveland tackle Floyd Peters was traded to Detroit for running back Ken Webb, an irritated Brown responded on a television show: "Detroit got the best of it. Peters is a good tackle. I don't know much about this Webb. I hope they do better the next time." A short time later, after speaking with coach Blanton Collier, a slightly embarrassed Brown told reporters: "I am more enlightened about Webb now. Understand things better after talking to Blanton. I guess Webb has been an underrated player."

Jim Brown spoke on the radio and appeared on television frequently, not just in Cleveland, but nationally. He offered boxing commentary on some of the bigger fights of the day and did soft drink commercials ringside between rounds of the February 1964 Cassius Clay–Sonny Liston fight.

Boxing became a sport that Brown followed closely, particularly after a budding friendship with Clay—two outspoken, resilient men—grew stronger. Clay and Brown's bond was simple: both men were athletic freaks in their sport and dedicated to bettering the lives of the poor and underrepresented. They were both also remarkably fearless.

Brown was so infatuated with boxing that he purchased stock in a fight promotion company called Main Bout Inc. The company began rather auspiciously. In 1965 Brown went to Toronto, Canada, to do color commentary for a televised boxing broadcast that featured a fight between WBA heavyweight champ Ernie Terrell and George Chuvalo. Brown enjoyed Toronto, which to him was a spellbinding, open-minded city. He walked the streets and enjoyed the nightlife. While there Brown encountered an attorney named Bob Arum, who would later become a legend in the sport. The two men went out to eat one night, and their conversation was intense and sparked a number of ideas and thoughts. Arum felt that in the near future the best challenger for Terrell would be Cassius Clay and told Brown so. Brown agreed. "Clay has no idea the kind of money he could make," an incredulous Arum told Brown. "If only someone could talk to the guy."

"I can talk to him," Brown replied to Arum. That is how Main Bout began, with two men talking.

The company purchased the Cleveland closed-circuit rights to the Clay-Terrell match. Brown had organized a group of black businessman, many of them former or current Browns like friend Wooten, to handle the distribution rights in Cleveland and other cities. After Clay declined to enter the armed forces draft, some of these exhibitors told Brown that they were being asked not to show the fight to protest Clay's criticism of the government's role in Vietnam. Brown suspected the real reason some distributors declined to show the fight was because Main Bout was composed mostly of black men; they did not want Brown's group to share in the large amount of money to be made from the highly publicized bout. Brown took his concerns to Adam Clayton Powell Jr., a Democratic congressman from New York, who promised to look into the matter. The end result was that little changed. Yet, again, Brown made history, as Main Bout was the first company composed of blacks to finance and run a major sports television broadcast.

Brown's face and words were appearing in newspapers in Cleveland almost daily. In public, his message rarely changed. During one press conference, seated before a bank of microphones and surrounded by some of Cleveland's most determined civil rights activists and social workers, as well as football teammates, Brown spoke to the media about a new youth center opening in one of the city's toughest neighborhoods as a response to recent riots in Cleveland's poorest districts.

"The circumstances which prompted last summer's Hough riots have remained," Brown told reporters. "If anything, the situation in the ghetto is worse because of the failure of the administration to keep its promises. It's up to the Negro and white leaders alike to stop calling each other names on the floor of city council and in plush downtown offices and get out into the ghetto and talk to the people."

Brown followed his own advice. He went into the roughest Cleveland neighborhoods almost daily, talking to gang members, the poor, the alienated. The most threatening, toughest criminal never challenged Brown. He was too respected and thoroughly trusted. He invested his own money in social programs and youth centers.

Brown not only worked to change the attitudes of Cleveland's blacks, but as the decade of social change continued, expanded his presence and message nationally. Brown's concern was that blacks were becoming so resentful and bitter about the racism they faced that they were refusing to better themselves. His significance was different and, in some ways, more grounded than other sports he-roes who were sending similar social messages, like Cassius Clay. Brown was more hands-on, more grassroots, than any other ath-lete, because he started organizations that funneled money directly into the pockets of the black poor and black entrepreneurs.

Not every black leader was convinced by Brown's message—or by Brown himself. Some of the city's leaders—black and white—felt his words were too radical and angry. Harvey Russell, the black vice president of Pepsi-Cola, met with Brown several times. While Russell would donate significant money to Brown's causes, he some-times walked away from his conversations and dealings with Brown dispirited and disappointed. "In some respects, Jim seems to be a rebel without a cause," Russell said publicly at the time, "an angry young man unclear about what angers him. He is an extremely complex person."

Such a reaction was not entirely incorrect. Some of that response to Brown was due in part to Brown's inability to lose an argument; it is not in his character to consistently see the other side, and to some, this made him appear angry or bitter. When newspaper columnists or television commentators chastised Brown, he did not hesitate to fire back. Sportswriter Charles Heaton wrote a critical piece sug-gesting that Brown's association with Clay would endanger Brown's causes, especially Brown's new project, the Negro Industrial Eco-nomic Union, which pushed for more black-owned businesses, and Brown responded to the article with a passionate retort.

"Cassius and I are friends, but he has never tried to influence me toward the Muslim religion," Brown told the writer. "I'd be less of a man if I tried to run away from him now. Clay's initial comments about the draft were just about what any fellow might think if he's pulled away from a job. He simply said them publicly. . . . The NIEU is a beautiful thing. I'd hate to see anyone trying to destroy it. I believe in this with all my heart. It can open up many doors for the Negro people. All I'm asking is that the truth about it be told. There are no secrets. I'm in touch with the young Negro people. They are not satisfied with some of the present, older leadership. I feel I'm better able to communicate with them. They want something dynamic to follow."

The chief symbol of Brown's activist leanings was the Negro Industrial Economic Union. The idea first came to Brown several years before its actual inception, when he was in Los Angeles attending a basketball all-star game. Several young black men and women approached him, asking him if he was interested in a start-up fashion magazine. Before Brown could decide to make a financial investment, the magazine collapsed after a handful of issues.

That magazine's demise crystallized in Brown's mind the economic plight of blacks. While many people had helped Brown evolve into the greatest football player of all time, his meteoric rise was due mostly to his own stern will, work ethic, and innate physical abilities. In his mind, he was a self-made, independent man, and he believed self-sufficiency was the key to saving his people.

Brown began organizing. He started with his teammates, asking for their thoughts and, eventually, their financial contributions. Many athletes aggressively jumped on board. One reason was that they wanted to take part in the struggle for civil rights, since practices and games—and to some degree great fear—prevented them from participating in the dangerous and life-threatening sit-ins that were taking place across the South and other parts of the country.

In some ways, the Browns were isolated from the racial turmoil affecting Cleveland and the rest of the country. When the team would go on the road to play games, the wives and girlfriends of the players would congregate at one home, often rotating, to socialize, and when the players returned, the women would go to the airport to meet the players, and many members of the team—both black and white—would return to the selected home to have a few drinks and some food. When the team played in Dallas, they stayed at the Ramada Inn near Love Field because it was the only hotel in the area that would accept all of their players. Most teams that traveled to Dallas had the white players stay at a posh hotel downtown while the black players roomed with generous black families. "The Browns were a little different from some other football teams," says Wooten. "The black and white players had great respect for each other. We had white players from Mississippi and Alabama and you never heard 'nigger this' or 'nigger that.' "

The Browns were not without their racial controversies, however. Wooten recalls how, after a 6–0 start in 1963, players began to wonder why one player was starting over another, and the disputes started to take on racial overtones. Why is that black guy playing over me? thought some of the white players. Suddenly, black and white players segregated themselves on the team buses. The divide almost crushed the team when offensive lineman Dick Schafrath was named Most Valuable Player of the Browns; although he'd also been named the league's MVP, his choice as the Browns' MVP was seen by black Cleveland players as a disgraceful affront. It took an intervention by coach Blanton Collier to stop what might have erupted into an ugly racial dispute. "By 1964, there were no racial problems on the Browns," says Wooten.

That was not the case across the country. Black Browns players as well as players across football and sports increasingly became angry at what was happening in society and looked for ways to join the fight. For Wooten, there was a moment that crystallized everything. A socially conscious and smart offensive lineman who would go on after his playing days to a decades-long career in football, Wooten saw something one afternoon in Cleveland that made him as irate as he had ever been. Wooten, like many players, was forced to seek employment in the off-season. "We had real jobs in the off-season," he says. Wooten taught in junior high school. One day he headed to Cleveland's board of education offices. Outside, a group of blacks was protesting the city's segregated schools. Just as Wooten arrived, so did the police, who began dragging the protesters away by their heels into police cars and beating them, even the women.

"I saw the whole thing and I was so angry," Wooten remembers. "But if I went over there to help, the whole thing would have broken out into an ugly fight.

"The athletes needed to do something to get involved in the struggle," Wooten says. "The Black Economic Union was that vehicle. Jim was the catalyst, but a lot of athletes became involved. Bill Russell, Wilt Chamberlain, Bobby Mitchell, Willie Davis, and a number of others."

The group first opened an office at East 105th Street and Euclid Avenue in downtown Cleveland; then, using the muscle and clout of NFL players, like Mitchell in Washington, and of other athletes, like Russell of the Boston Celtics, dozens of NIEU offices opened around the country, many in NFL cities. Some of Cleveland's top black lawyers and businessmen joined the venture.

The basic principle was simple: When a potentially black-owned business could not receive funding from traditional means, such as white-owned banks, the NIEU would either provide those monies, or arrange backing from an institution that could.

While there is great dispute about just how successful the organization was, few high-profile black athletes had tried anything like this before. Jackie Robinson, the groundbreaking baseball player, had opened his own bank, providing millions of dollars in loans to businesses in Harlem and other locations. Brown's attempts were larger in scope, and much more politically risky.

When he again met with the Cleveland press to discuss the new organization, Brown was serious, rarely smiling. "Of course we athletes are interested in civil rights," Brown told reporters. "But we're not interested in participating in the picketing, the sit-ins, the singing, the marching, and the kneeling. We're not interested in being nationalists. We don't want to go around shooting.

"What is the real basis for the Negroes' problem?" Brown continued. "It's economics. As athletes we feel like this is the area we can help in. We can do this, we think, by getting the Negroes to help themselves." He added: "We have been consumers. Not producers. If we could provide dollars to allow Negroes to become producers—to publish magazines, to run factories—there wouldn't be the need now for a poverty program, where people wait around for handouts. Instead of a Negro owning one little grocery store or some tiny record shop, maybe he could own a big one. Or several. What he would need is the financial backing."

At various points in the 1960s, there was no bigger name than Brown's. He was a star athlete, an entrepreneur, and a civil rights leader, and even Hollywood was beginning to notice his impressive build and handsome looks.

It was around this time that the FBI began its campaigns of disinformation and spying against Jim Brown.

"One of the first things we did, unfortunately, was listen in on a number of his telephone conversations," says a former FBI official who claims to have firsthand knowledge of the bureau's eavesdropping on Brown. "Personal, professional, everything. Conversations with his wife, his girlfriends, the Browns organization. We looked for anything we could use against him when the time came."

The former agent says that when Brown and his staff left the East 105th Street office of the Negro Industrial Economic Union, at least two agents would wait several hours, until the streets were dark and empty, then slip inside and examine various documents to uncover financial and other information about the group.

In some instances, agents closely followed Brown around the

city, the former official says. Agents even followed Brown to the motel rooms that a small group of players rented, where they would bring their mistresses and girlfriends. Agents took photographs of Brown and other players entering different locations with their various women.

Brown wrote about one of the gathering places, saying, "In Cleveland, the black guys rented a house, called it 'Headquarters.' Good times, brother. We used to throw a party for our main girlfriends. Those were the chicks we loved or liked a lot, who we'd hang out with when we felt elegant or romantic, the same chicks we'd hide like a motherfucker when we'd have a freak party. For the main girlfriend party, we invited our main girlfriends to Headquarters. The men all wore tuxedos, the women long evening gowns. Everyone arrived by limo. We ate fine food. Danced real slow. Had a ball."

The agent says that the name of every player who went into that house was recorded. Physical descriptions of the women who attended the parties were noted as well. The FBI assembled a file with the names and addresses of various Brown girlfriends, the agent claimed.

At Brown's home, the agent says, they went through his garbage, searching for information: bank statements, notes, bills. "It was all about finding any embarrassing information we could."

The agent estimates that the FBI spied on Brown for at least five years, beginning in the early to mid-1960s, and expanded its spying on various acquaintances of Brown, mostly NFL players. The bureau also investigated many of the chapters of the Negro Industrial Economic Union, the agent claims, sending infiltrators to steal financial and other data, as the organization spread deliberately and impressively across the country.

Some of the FBI's activities involving Brown were dutifully recorded by the agents themselves and forwarded to more central offices. At least some of those reports are in a centralized location at the FBI's headquarters in Washington, D.C. Brown has a copy of his file now, in fact. Yet records and evidence of some of the dirtier deeds were destroyed, the agent says, except for a handful of pictures of Brown alone or Brown with women that some agents involved retained.

"Souvenirs," the agent says. "No one ever believed what we did would ever become public. So some agents kept things. It was a way of saying, 'I got this on Jim Brown.'"

"Basically the FBI report Jim possesses," says the agent, "doesn't contain shit. It has nothing about what we did, because what we did wasn't put in that kind of file."

Where are the documents and proof of what you did? the agent is asked. "Kept by the agents themselves or later destroyed," he replies.

It took decades for the bureau to admit—and the public to realize—just how much the FBI violated the civil rights of thousands of people, including, the agent says, many black athletes from that time. By law, Brown's complete file is supposed to be available only to him; then after his death the file becomes public. Yet, even though he has his file, Brown is probably unaware of the scope of the FBI's stalking, because much of the proof of what the agency did was destroyed or hidden, if the agent is to be believed.

The FBI spied on Martin Luther King Jr., treating him like a criminal. In the 1960s, the FBI set wiretaps in his home, his office, and his hotel rooms, and inside the phones of close friends. King's file was thousands of pages long and contained reports from field agents who shadowed King wherever he went. Other activists were spied upon as well as part of the FBI's counterintelligence program called COINTELPRO.

One of them was Beatles singer John Lennon, who morphed from worldwide singing sensation into one of the symbols of the counterculture 1960s and then, apparently, into an enemy of America. According to declassified FBI memos obtained by historian Jon Wiener, the government spied on Lennon and Yoko Ono and even attended some of Lennon's concerts. Then, for over a decade, the government fought against the release of documents that would have fully disclosed what the FBI did. It took a successful lawsuit from Wiener and the ACLU to finally force the government to turn over the papers.

Brown of course was not the momentous figure King was, or the worldwide artist that was Lennon, but it is not difficult to believe that if J. Edgar Hoover conspired against King and other powerful civil rights leaders, it would be a short leap for him to order politically active athletes to be shadowed as well. The agent says that is exactly what happened, in what was an organized and orchestrated effort not as extensive as, but not so different from, COINTELPRO.

The FBI did send the author the file of the late Wilt Chamberlain, and while much of it is blacked out, it is still instructive. Chamberlain's file contains details about a confrontation Chamberlain had prior to boarding an airplane flight (and copies of newspaper articles about the incident), as well as accusations that he bet on NBA games. This is the part of the file that is heavily blacked out.

"As you know, the fact that players bet on a game or games in which they are involved, does not in itself constitute a violation of the Sports Bribery statute," states one part of Chamberlain's file, dated November of 1966; "the Bureau, however, desires to be furnished any information concerning wagering activity on the part of those engaged in professional sports. As you know, it is extremely important that the Bureau be advised in the event information is received indicating that an individual or individuals in any way offered a bribe in connection with the outcome of a particular athletic contest."

The agent believes that the FBI either concocted or exaggerated accusations against black athletes as a way of diminishing their popularity and any potential political clout their athleticism may have generated. He says that an athlete's main source of currency is not his education or money, but his appeal. The bureau believed that if athletes like Chamberlain, Brown, and Ali ever used that currency to the fullest, they could threaten that era's existing power structure.

The detail and size of the investigations and spying on Chamberlain alone are striking. Agents in Miami, Las Vegas, Boston, Baltimore, New Orleans, New Haven, Philadelphia, and New York took part in the perverse look at Chamberlain's life. The coldheartedness and lack of moral conscience with which the FBI went about spying on these men is alarming, even all these years later.

The full FBI file on Brown is likely more detailed and extensive than the one it accumulated on Chamberlain, who was not nearly the controversial figure Brown became.

The documents obtained by the author do not prove or disprove what the agent states, except to show the tenacity of the bureau against a St. Louis chapter of Brown's organization. Besides the photos, including the one of Brown and Raquel Welch posing together, the file still contains a story written about Brown that deals extensively with Brown's thoughts about race.

"As I have said, his race, and the fact he was with white women at times, was a big factor behind the FBI trying to injure him and hurt him," says the former agent. "His political views were another obvious factor, but race was the biggest factor. The attitude was always sort of, 'This black bastard is too big for his britches.' "

When the FBI struck at Brown's business, it did so anonymously, the agent says. As the Negro Industrial Economic Union started,

Brown and the organizers began soliciting local and national corporations for financial backing. Brown was successful in his bid for funding, eventually earning a seven-figure grant from the Ford Foundation.

Yet a disinformation campaign by the FBI may have hurt Brown's efforts to get even more money from other businesses. Once the agents became aware of Brown and his group's efforts to gain grants from companies, the former agent says, they would telephone some of the companies just hours or days after Brown's group contacted them, doing so anonymously, and claim that Brown was a Communist or a member of the Nation of Islam. If the agents did not phone anonymously, they wrote anonymous letters. The agent claims that companies considering loaning or giving money to Brown would then refuse to do so and give Brown a false reason why they could not. What the FBI claimed was, of course, a total lie. The agent maintains that such phone calls were made dozens of times. He offers no proof of this allegation, and media reports from that time contain no stories of companies pledging support and then abruptly canceling it.

While the agent admits that his actions and those of other agents were indeed despicable, he also says he had no choice. "If you refused to do this, you had no future in the FBI, and then they would do things to you that we were doing to Brown."

One thing particularly haunts the agent all these decades later, he says: during the holiday season one year, they followed Brown to a shopping area, where Brown was with his wife, Sue, and the Brown children. The agents photographed the children.

"When you start doing these things to kids," the agent explains, "finally your conscience kicks in."

It took kids to finally elicit pangs of guilt? he is asked.

"We committed disgraceful acts," the agent says now. "We

treated him like a criminal when he was actually doing great things. The government should apologize to Jim Brown. The FBI should. I should."

The irony of the FBI spying on Brown is that the secretive and paranoid Nixon administration worked with Brown's union, according to Dean Kotlowski, a history professor who in 1998 wrote an analysis for several publications of minority business growth under the Nixon administration called "Black Power—Nixon Style: The Nixon Administration and Minority Business Enterprise."

Kotlowski wrote: "In January 1973, Jim Brown, the former football player who had backed the president's reelection, applied for a $327,000 . . . grant to finance his Black Economic Union (BEU). Brown's organization had received a $100,000 grant the previous year and, according to Tod Hullin, a (Nixon) aide, it had 'accomplished absolutely nothing.' " Nevertheless, Hullin prepared an option paper on whether or not to raise BEU's stipend to $250,000 for 1973. "Any increase would be blatantly political," Hullin admitted, with embarrassing candor, because an "increase in funding is not justified on the merits." The BEU was given the grant for $250,000, Kotlowski said.

While the effectiveness of Brown's group can be debated, the paradox of the government's actions cannot. About the same time the Nixon administration was handing over a quarter million dollars to further Brown's group, the FBI was spying on the organization, and possibly sabotaging it. Now that is what you call typical government efficiency.

As Brown entered a riveting period of American history in what was the most riveting period of his life—and perhaps the most personally and professionally volatile—the FBI was secretly by his side, gleefully documenting his troubles, both major and minor, with newspaper clippings and reports. In part of the FBI's file that the author was able to acquire, there were two copied newspaper articles about a minor traffic stop involving Brown. On a Thursday in September 1961, Brown was traveling at night on Euclid Avenue and Cornell Road when a police officer stopped Brown as he drove his 1960 Ford Thunderbird convertible with a malfunctioning right headlight, according to the article. The officer stated that Brown was driving without a license and he was cited for the incident. The following day a judge dismissed the charges after Brown produced the license.

It was stunningly minute stuff, but the FBI still gathered such information. "Anything that was negative about him, we collected," the agent says. "It didn't matter how insignificant it was."

The agent says that when the FBI later learned that a thief had broken into Brown's Thunderbird, which was parked inside Brown's garage, and stolen Brown's golf bag and spare tire by shattering the lock on the trunk, the FBI considered anonymously leaking to the press and community leaders that Brown had concocted the robbery as part of some sort of insurance scam. They never followed through on the idea, the agent says. Why?

"We didn't think anyone would believe he would do something like that," is the former agent's reply.

"A part of me felt like shit, but a part of me believed the bureau's bullshit about radicals," the former agent says. "Looking back, it was simply the color of his skin that made him seem dangerous. He was trying to better his race and we did nothing but hurt him, or try to, because all he did was speak the truth."

Brown spoke constantly about the bettering of the black race, and apparently that made the FBI nervous. In his second book Brown gives a sample of the things he was saying in the 1950s and 1960s, before any other NFL player, and almost any other professional athlete.

I've never seen any white American who didn't want to make some money. Even the racist, if he can make enough money, will deal with black folks. You can go into the baddest black neighborhoods in America, you'll fine white entrepreneurs, risking their lives to make that green. Money is America's God. The stock market crashed, there were men jumping out of windows. Black leaders need to push that capitalist message. Even a man as great as Dr. King, who moved the nation and did effect change, did not quite understand economics and political clout. . . .

I loved Dr. King . . . but near the end I think he lost his way. . . . It isn't about integration, it's about discrimination. Nobody wants to live by anyone because they're white, or black. They just don't want to be kicked in the ass. In fact, a lot of people said so-called integration was the worst thing that ever happened to blacks. We became dispersed into the general economy, rather than having an economy of our own that could flourish, and then become a very powerful part of the general economy. That's what the Koreans and the Jews and the Japanese did. They kept their monies among themselves, poured it back into their own communities. They fixed up their stores, cleaned up their neighborhoods. Now they're an integral part of the economy, meaning they have political clout. Our monies, on the other hand, went to other merchants, other races. Our monies went largely to brand-name products. Blacks are the best consumers in the world.

If what Brown and others desired had come to fruition, and blacks had become far more financially independent than they were, it could have threatened the power structure of that period. A financially independent black population was considered a radical thought by some elements in the government.

THIS GREAT THREAT to democracy, this danger to the American way of life, was once in such pain that he could barely bend down to tie his shoes before games. Brown's wrist was so injured it was limp.

To say that Brown played through tremendous pain is akin to saying that football is a rugged game. In Brown's time football was uncivilized. For all of Brown's statistical accomplishments and galloping runs, his pain threshold, and mental ability to play through pain, set him apart from all runners in history.

One of the few people Brown spoke to about his wrist was Wooten. "Woot," Brown explained, "if my leg was broken, then I couldn't play. But I can play with this."

Showing weakness: it was something that Brown was convinced was as destructive as any hit by the hardest linebacker.

In 1963, Brown played the entire season on a broken toe. Modell found out about the injury and went to Brown alone, with no one around.

"I want you to see a doctor," Modell told him.

"I know it's broken, Art," Brown responded. "I don't need a doctor to tell me that."

"He was unbelievably tough," Modell recalls. "He was not going to take himself out of a game or practice." And he refused to take painkilling medication.

That season, despite terrible pain in his foot, Brown set the NFL's rushing record with 1,863 yards. He did it in just fourteen games.

By now, everyone in professional football knew Brown was special. What they were also digesting was his toughness and physicality. Word circulated around the various NFL locker rooms, far more than in earlier years, that Brown was not just fast and powerful. He was coarse, cement-coated, difficult to bring down, and he inflicted as much punishment on the tackler as the tackler would ever hope to administer to Brown.

In the book about the 1964 championship Browns called *When All the World Was Browns Town*, written by Terry Pluto almost a decade ago, two players recalled what it was like watching him play and trying to tackle him. They are noted because they are two of the better quotes spoken about the runner's physical style of play.

"The man's hands—huge," says Leroy Kelly, a former Brown. "He'd carry that football in one hand, run while holding it out from his body as if it were a loaf of bread. But when you got a look at those hands, you saw that they were all scarred and bruised." One of the biggest reasons why Brown sometimes declined to shake people's hands was because his were often mangled and painful. They were often so cut that he had a difficult time gripping a doorknob. President Lyndon Johnson also noticed how cut up Jim's hands were when the two met at the White House.

"We didn't wear gloves back then like they do now," Kelly continues. "His hands took a beating from hitting all the helmets and being stepped on with those cleats. Yet somehow, those fingers were strong enough to hold the ball."

"When I was with Detroit, I tried to tackle Jim Brown," says former Cleveland player Bill Glass. "He had that ball out in one arm. As I closed in on him, he took his free arm and dropped it straight down on my helmet. He bashed me with his forearm, and it was like being hit with a lead pipe. I mean it, visualize a long, straight lead pipe. No bend in the elbow. He just dropped it down on your head. I've never seen a running back do that before or since. It gave you a headache. Some of the biggest, toughest guys in the NFL got pretty scared when they saw Jim swinging that arm of his. Jim Brown could knock you senseless."

"I think toward the beginning of Brown's career, there was awe," says Ernie Accorsi. "As his career went on, there was intimidation. Jim Brown scared people with his style of play."

Brown was not solely a brutish gladiator, though that was definitely a part of his repertoire. Brown's runs were also part science and strategy, as Brown formulated an intense and intricate system of running that focused on details that were being noticed by teammates, opponents, and a few members of the press. A Brown run typically began in a three-point stance, his right toe lined up neatly on an imaginary line behind his left heel. When Brown fired out of his stance he absorbed the handoff with both palms up, and then immediately tucked the ball away inside his left arm while simultaneously freeing his other arm, readying it to be used as a bludgeon.

Brown's methodology was not typical of how fullbacks operated. Most covered the football with both hands and, as they approached the line of scrimmage, lowered their head and hit the pile of bodies like a mountain goat attacking a rival. Brown was different. He was a fullback in position only. "He had that halfback mentality," says Wooten. "He wanted to attack a defense not only with physical power, but with smarts and speed. No fullback was nearly as fast as Jim."

The scientific approach Brown took to running did not cease once he hit the open field. When a defender came at Brown's midsection or legs, Brown would first dip his shoulder, garnering momentum, then propel it forward into the tackler's chest or midsection. That was followed by Brown's forearm. If a tackler went high, Brown used his shoulder as a sort of deflector shield, glancing off, leaving the tackler grabbing for air. Unlike with other fullbacks, jumps and spins were a part of Brown's running. He had the agility to do almost any move, almost like a point guard with pads. The fear of being embarrassed by a slick Brown contortion or burst produced almost as much loathing as being run over by him.

At the beginning of the 1963 season, Cleveland was a far different ball club than what Brown had seen during those first days when he arrived at the Browns' camp years ago fresh from Syracuse. The team was rife with veterans, with a coach in Blanton Collier who was far more quiet and democratic with the players than the man he replaced, Paul Brown. They were an interesting and studious mix of stars and grunts, free agents and longtime Browns.

During his impressive 1963 year, Brown perhaps more than any player wanted to see Collier succeed, since—fairly or unfairly—it was Brown who was perceived to have been the leader of the rebellion against Paul. On a Tuesday before the September 1963 season opener, the team met and raucously decided they were going to win the game for Collier. Brown was mostly quiet—he is just not the screamer type—but his presence loomed large, as it always did.

A tense locker room minutes before the opener curiously led to an offensive explosion by Cleveland. Though he refused to admit it to teammates and the press, Brown ran with the conviction of a man who seemed to want to prove that this team could win without Paul. He ran for rushing touchdowns on a muddy, sloppy field, two being 80 yards or more. Against a reeling Washington team with Bobby Mitchell on it, Cleveland rolled up 543 yards of total offense, with Brown accounting for 362 of them.

On one play, a sweep to the left, three Washington defenders converged to tackle Brown. He lowered his shoulder and dragged all three men 14 yards before they finally brought him down. The run was talked about in Cleveland bars and homes all week.

Collier's plan was to do something that Paul Brown feared in his final years—he unleashed the offense and took the shackles of Jim.

Paul Brown had begun to cut back on the power sweeps, especially to the right side of the field, which Jim had enjoyed so much, because they allowed Brown to use his speed and power, since he would drop his shoulders and accelerate or run over defenders. Once Collier took over, he tossed in all the power sweeps Brown could handle. In the final exhibition game of 1964 Brown took one of those sweeps, broke left, and scored his second of two touchdowns of the afternoon.

By the third regular-season game of the championship season, the media began to notice a major shift in the way the Browns ran the offense. Writer Charles Heaton noted in one of his columns: "The age of democracy has come to the Browns." Players actually changed plays sent in to them from the sidelines, something akin to treason under Paul Brown.

And the system was working. Everyone was ecstatic—even owner Modell, who fretted at times over what were considered lower-than-expected attendance numbers. The Cleveland *Plain Dealer* reported how a running play for Brown was called the "Modell burst" by the players; it caused Modell to burst with excitement after Brown scored.

The first game against the Giants that year, at midseason, led to what was a low-key headline in the *Plain Dealer* that appeared on October 26, 1964: "Browns Rout Giants, 42–20." (The following year Brown almost single-handedly destroyed the Giants, leading to the New York *Daily News* headline "Browns Rip Giants, 38–14; Jim Runs, Catches, Hurls.")

Now, with decades of historical perspective, it is clear that Cleveland's victory over New York did more than give the Browns first place in the division. It symbolized the end of the days when the Giants, now an older team in a rebuilding mode, were screaming out Paul Brown's plays before they were run, and getting inside the heads of Cleveland players. The Browns were intimidated by the Giants no more.

As the season progressed, the Browns continued to engage in their Age of Post-Paul Democracy, with Jim and quarterback Frank Ryan serving as the epicenters. In the huddle, they occasionally drew up plays in the dirt. As noted in Pluto's book, Collier often appeared in the team's meeting room and drew up some twenty running plays on the blackboard, just a fraction of the total number, but those were the plays that Collier thought might work best against that particular opponent. Collier would then go to Jim and ask his preference. Which ones do you like? he'd query. Such maneuvers by a head coach were not just unheard of for a Paul Brown–coached team, they were almost never done by any team, anywhere, in that age.

What Ryan did was serve as team referee, walking the balance beam—being quarterback and leader, but also deferring to Brown and keeping him happy. "I remember one day when Frank and Jim Brown disagreed in the huddle," former Brown Monte Clark told Pluto. "He told Jim to watch out for something, and Jim said, 'I'm standing back here with you. I can see things just fine.' Frank didn't press the issue, but he did get the message across to Jim without making Jim feel as if he were challenged. And Frank also didn't see a need to challenge Jim, when Jim seemed to dismiss what he had to say. It was a fine line, but Frank walked it well."

"Jim was the big star," Modell tells me, "and the Cleveland players realized that, but they also knew that Jim needed them as much as they needed Jim. There was always this delicate balancing of egos."

After the tenth game of the season, the Browns were 8–1–1. They were bordering on great, but they were not perfect by any stretch. In the eleventh game against Green Bay, Cleveland lost because the Packers held Brown to 8 yards rushing. Throughout his entire NFL career, Brown rarely had back-to-back poor days. He was too prideful, too resolute. The week following the Packers loss he ran for 133 yards against Philadelphia, more than the entire Eagles team.

After losing to St. Louis in the thirteenth game, the Browns won the division the following week by blasting their nemesis, New York, 52–20, allowing the Browns to reach the NFL championship. Otto Graham, the former Browns quarterback who was critical of Brown's blocking and had stated that the team would never reach a championship with Brown as the center of its offense, was forced to eat his words.

Sportswriters and fans deemed the championship game an upset if Baltimore won by fewer than two touchdowns. "No one, and I mean no one, outside of Cleveland gave the Browns a chance," says Accorsi. The reason? The Colts had Unitas. Plus, Unitas had top receivers like Raymond Berry and tight end John Mackey, who was perhaps the premier player at his position. Unitas had beaten out Brown for Player of the Year in an Associated Press poll voted on by writers by a whopping tally of 32–8.

"Baltimore was the pick by the writers," says Wooten. "Baltimore was the pick by most of America."

"The prevailing thought was that Unitas would score so many points that Cleveland would not be able to keep up," Accorsi says. "They would nullify Jim Brown."

The Browns possessed a quiet confidence, particularly Brown. The Browns were one of the few teams that stayed in a hotel the night before home games—another Paul Brown innovation. Paul always felt that isolating the team twenty-four hours before games would prevent distractions.

Jim and Wooten were on their way to the hotel in Wooten's car, along with both men's wives. As the car buzzed along, Brown casually leaned over, and quietly told Wooten: "We're going to kick the shit out of these motherfuckers."

Wooten and Brown were roommates, and inside the hotel room Brown did as he had done many times before: he became withdrawn and quiet. The day of a game, he would sleep in much longer. He and Wooten would barely talk. The reason was because Brown was analyzing the future contest. "He was always thinking," Wooten says.

As usual, there was no speech to the team from Brown. He despised such things. There was another symbol of normalcy: Brown played through pain and produced his usual pile of yards despite the dirty tactics he had seen so many times in his career.

One of the least known aspects of that game, all these years later, is the abuse Brown fought through for that entire contest. As had happened to him once in a game against the New York Giants, when Brown would go to the ground, Colts players would step on his hands and kick him in the legs or ribs. Hands and fingers probed through his face mask, which had two bars that protected the lower portion of his face, leaving the eyes exposed, and the Colts attempted to gouge them out. All of the abuse and pain only served to make Brown angry.

Sports Illustrated described how Brown got revenge. He did as he always had in the past. "Then Ryan took advantage of a peculiar defect in the Baltimore defense," wrote the magazine's Tex Maule. "The Browns ran one play to the right from a conventional formation. Then they came out in a double wing, with Ernie Green set as a flanker to the left. The only man behind Ryan in the backfield was Jim Brown. The Colt linebacker on the left cheated in a little toward the middle; the defensive halfback opposite Green was playing six or seven yards behind the line. The play was a quick pitchout to Brown, swinging to his left, and he swept around the pinched-in linebacker with three blockers in front of him. The halfback was too far back to come up and stop him before he gained momentum. He ran for 46 yards, down to the Baltimore 18-yard line.'"

In *Sports Illustrated* a large black-and-white photo shows Brown, his white uniform muddied, football in his left hand, his slim waist and large shoulders a study in contrast.

The staggering upset was eloquently summed up this way by the magazine: "Frank Ryan is a tall, slender man with the ascetic face of a Catholic priest, prematurely graying hair and, at last, the cool, quick mind of a great quarterback. Last Sunday afternoon in Cleveland he engineered one of the biggest of all football upsets, and in that improbable destruction of the Baltimore Colts, by the implausible score of 27–0, his choice of plays was both flawless and daring. He used the incomparable running talents of Jimmy Brown with maximum effectiveness. With his quick right arm he sailed three long and lovely touchdown passes to Flanker Gary Collins, the third of Cleveland's triumvirate of particular stars." The *Plain Dealer*'s headline declared in bold print: "Collins, Ryan Shock Colts."

Ryan was the sexy star of the game and Collins was the MVP of the game, but it was Cleveland's ability to shut down the Colts offense and the team's use of Brown as a clock-controlling battering ram that won the game for Cleveland. Brown finished with twenty-seven carries for 114 yards, which was more rushing than the entire Baltimore offense.

In the Browns locker room afterward, there were hugs and chaos. Reporters surrounded Brown and saw something they had rarely seen before: the usually guarded and solemn Brown was smiling and laughing. He revealed to the media that he'd had a small cold in the days leading up to the game. If the Colts were not going to slow him, neither were germs.

"It's the biggest thrill of my career," Brown told reporters. "I have had better days as an individual, but this is the most satisfying of all." Browns coach Blanton Collier approached Brown, leaned in close, and whispered something in his ear. Pluto says that Collier told Brown: "Jim, thank you for your leadership."

This is why many of Brown's close friends remain so loyal to him, why despite his at-times crusty, even mean-spirited demeanor, he is often described as charitable and loving. A longtime Cleveland writer says in *When All the World Was Browns Town*: "You know what Jim Brown did right before he went to bed the night of the game? He called Western Union and sent a telegram—not to Blanton, but to his wife, Forman Collier. He thanks Mrs. Collier for allowing her husband to spend so much time with the team. To me, nothing could have been more thoughtful than that."

Brown was unlike any other football player and any other athlete with the exception of Ali. Brown did not simply go to football practice or games and then go home, remaining silent or inactive when it came to social issues. He purposely used the clout accumulated from his years of football stardom to try to enact social awareness and change. In other words, that football capital was bargained like money or gold bullion, and helped him get into the doors of the rich and powerful—from bankers to American presidents— that would otherwise have been firmly closed to a black man who grew up poor. After the championship game, he was on top of the athletic world, his face recognized by millions. Brown met with congressmen, business leaders, mayors, and Hollywood producers, while also personally responding to many of the 150 letters a week he received from fans.

There was no question in the mind of anyone who knew Brown: he was not going to be just one of the great athletes of his generation, but one of the distinguished men as well.

What those people underestimated, or did not know, was the effect that Brown's troubles with women and the law would have on his budding legacy. Those problems would slowly whittle away at his greatness. While the FBI's actions were unpardonable and unforgivable and may have hurt Brown in ways that are difficult to see or calculate, the main cause of Brown's troubles was Brown.

SUE AND JIM Brown were married in Cleveland not long after he joined the Browns. She was a petite beauty with dark hair and light brown skin. Sue's smile was what often caught the attention of people she met; it was wide and glowing.

Sue believed strongly in faithfulness and the sanctity of marriage. Jim, to say the least, did not. Sue knew about Jim's carousing, but she tolerated it for the sake of the children. Hers was a far simpler life than Jim's. She gardened and sewed and took the kids to day care while Brown went to practice. He'd get home around three thirty and she would be waiting.

What is certain is that she kept up appearances of a happy Brown family. A December 24, 1964, picture of the Browns appeared in the *Plain Dealer* and showed Jim with his two young sons, Kevin, then five years old, and Jim Jr., just over three years old, and five-year-old twin daughter Kim. The boys held between them a Christmas present draped in striped packaging. The Browns were seated in front of a glistening Christmas tree. The portrait was impressive and pretty, if not altogether accurate.

Brown was not concerned about discretion. Many of the Browns players and coaches—going back to Paul Brown—were aware of what Brown was doing. Some didn't care, because they were involved in the same kind of behavior, while others privately thought that Brown was playing with fire. To be certain, Brown underestimated his booming popularity. There was a curious blend of arrogance and naïveté at work. In those days, reporters did not discuss the private lives of the athletes they covered. Yet Brown had to know that he was no ordinary athlete, and any mistake or indiscretion would be highly publicized. That was the case when in March of 1965 a twenty-one-year-old former Ohio State student claimed that Brown had raped her in Whitehall, Ohio. Any potential case was dropped because the woman refused to press criminal charges.

Then came a June night in 1966 when an eighteen-year-old woman named Brenda Ayres knocked on the door of room 520 at the Howard Johnson Motor Lodge on East 107th Street and Euclid Avenue near Western Reserve University in Cleveland. It was about three in the morning. Behind that door was Brown. What happened next—or did not happen—became big news in Cleveland.

Ayres was a woman whom Brown had seen several times at various functions around the city. Though she bore a resemblance to Sue, Ayres was much different, and was portrayed in the Cleveland media by Brown and his lawyers as a gold-digging liar. Soon after that night, she accused Brown of striking her in the face, and Brown was charged with assault and battery.

The news rocked the city and led to a months-long period of intense headlines, charges, and countercharges. Brown told the *Plain Dealer* after the accusations became public: "I am not that small that I have to beat a girl." Modell told the press: "I will reserve my opinion until I have a chance to talk with Jim. It is easy to level charges, but as far as I'm concerned, Jim is innocent until I have further facts."

At the time of the charge, Brown was twenty-nine years old, and though he denied having any kind of physical relationship with Ayres, she fit the profile of the kind of woman Brown often pursued: she was petite, pretty, and much younger, the kind of woman Brown would ogle while driving his Cadillac convertible up and down Superior Avenue. Sometimes he was driving that car to meet Wooten and a few other teammates at the Carnegie Hotel

Lounge or Dearing's Restaurant, two local hot spots; other times the Cadillac, with a young woman inside, pulled into a motel. There was almost no one who did not believe that Brown had sex with Ayres, but most people also felt that Brown did not strike her. The understanding of domestic violence at that time was primitive, if not nonexistent. Brown was handsome and wealthy, and if he wanted a woman, the thought went, he did not need to resort to violence to get her. Of course, the issue of men's violence against women is far more complicated than that.

The charges and impending trial opened a public door into Brown's private life. In the barbershops and bars across Cleveland, the whispers about Brown's womanizing grew louder. When the assault and battery trial began in July 1966, Brown's personal life became one of the hot topics discussed by Clevelanders. Media coverage was extensive, particularly when Brown took the stand and was cross-examined by prosecutors, who earlier had told the jury that Brown had to abide by the rules of society just as he did the rules of football. "You decide who is telling the truth," Assistant Prosecutor Albert Corsi told the jury. "There are no witnesses. Just remember, Jim Brown is in a courtroom. He's not on the football field." Brown's lawyer, Norman S. Minor, said that Ayres was a confused child who was a product of a dysfunctional family.

The pivotal moment in the trial came when Brown testified in his own defense. According to media reports and court testimony, Brown denied he ever struck Ayres or was intimate with her. As the examination continued, the courtroom was quiet, and everyone was riveted on Brown. When Corsi asked how many times Brown had rented the hotel room before, he replied, "Several times in the last few months." The answer hung over the court like dense smog. Was Brown using the motel to have parties and meetings with women other than his wife? It was indeed the 1960s, when America's attitudes about sex were beginning to change, but people still had an idyllic view of their athletes, especially in Cleveland.

"Did Mrs. Ayres [Brenda's mother] tell you to leave her daughter alone?" Corsi asked.

"No, she did not," Brown replied. Ayres's mother claimed that on several occasions she told Brown to end his relationship with her daughter because she was too young and Brown was married.

"Now, the night of Saturday, June 19, did you see Brenda Ayres that night?" Corsi asked Brown.

"Yes, I did, at Mrs. White's [a personal assistant]," Brown said. "I played golf till dark and I usually pay Mrs. White [for handling fan mail] on Fridays. So I just went over there without cleaning up to give her [a paycheck]. All the kids were there and they asked me to take them to Manners drive-in. Usually I wouldn't do it, but the little kids begged me so that I decided to do it."

After establishing that Brown then drove to White's house, the prosecutor asked about his passengers when he left White's house, and Brown replied, according to one newspaper account of Brown's testimony: "Brenda Ayres. . . . She stayed in my car and asked for a ride to St. Clair and Eddy Road. I drove her there, then went to my motel room, took a shower and went to bed."

"Were you ever awakened?" Brown was next asked.

"Yes, about three a.m.," Brown testified. "I heard a knock. At first I thought it was someone else's room. They have thin walls there. Then I realized it was my door, but I didn't open it. I asked through the door who it was and it was Brenda."

Brown testified that she wanted the two to talk, though he did not tell the court what they spoke about. Brown said he later became irritated and asked her to leave. She refused, Brown said. "I was a little upset and said again I was going to call her mother,"

Brown said. "I took a $5 bill out and threw it on the dresser and told her, 'When you're ready to leave just call a taxi.' I left."

Corsi asked Brown again about earlier testimony that he had once put Ayres out of his car. When asked what Ayres said to Brown before he asked her to leave the vehicle, Brown said, "Well, I don't remember specifically. It was generally that she wanted money and if I gave her money she would give me love."

"And what did you say to her?" Brown was asked.

"I told her that I would have none of that and put her out of the car," Brown explained.

There was testimony that Brown had given money to young women he had known only a short time. This point was not covered extensively, but it was clear that the prosecutor was attempting to establish Brown as a womanizer. "Do you normally give money to girls you've known only [a short] length of time?" asked Corsi.

"To some, on occasions," Brown replied.

"Did you ever give Paula White money?" Corsi asked.

"I gave her mother money to get her a prom dress," Brown testified. White, sixteen years old at the time, was a friend of Ayres's and his assistant's daughter.

The trial lasted ten days and went to a jury of seven women and five men. On July 23 they acquitted Brown. He was also later cleared by a juvenile court of being the father of the fifteen-month-old daughter of Brenda Ayres, Shelly Monique. Brown had denied that the child was his at the time, but years later would admit he was indeed the father.

Publicly, Brown kept a strong, controlled front, hugging Sue and laughing with her in the courtroom hallway in the moments following the acquittal. When practice began in Hiram in late July, a proud Brown spoke to reporters. He was asked if sitting in a courtroom was tougher than playing in a football game and Brown replied, "Not really. In fact, I was thinking about that in court. The pressure is so great at times in football. I remember the first St. Louis game last year when Frank Ryan and Gary Collins teamed up on that great pass play in the last quarter down to about the 2-yard line. I knew I was going to have to take it over for the touchdown. And so many things could have happened. What if I had fumbled? In the courtroom I knew I was innocent. I felt that if I had patience, everything would come out all right."

Privately, Brown fumed about the trial to friends, saying he was targeted unfairly because he was famous. Brown is not incorrect in those assertions. Yet what was a sordid case for that time also showed Brown's untoward side. He was a high-profile athlete, but he was also a man who apparently regularly pursued young women who were not his wife. He kept motel rooms on the side and used them for parties and romantic encounters while his wife and children were home. While these disclosures would seem mild today, then they were seen as blockbuster tidbits, normally never discussed in public. Remember, the press even turned a blind eye toward the Kennedy shenanigans in that era.

In a short but incendiary commentary, the *Cleveland Press* wrote: "Legally, the assault and battery charge against the Browns' Jim Brown is closed. Under the U.S. system of justice he is exonerated. Although the band has stopped playing, the melody lingers on, and it isn't a very pretty tune. For the good of his own personal life, for his family's sake, and for the welfare of the football team, which he has represented so spectacularly in the past, Jim Brown should take a good long look at his way of life. And this includes the company he keeps."

Brown would write decades later: "As promiscuous as I have been, I've always looked for relationships of value. Just to fuck every night with no meaning, with a blank face, gets hollow quickly, and I find I want to do some fucking with meaning. I don't mean I want to marry the girl I fuck, but I want something happening that's spontaneous and alive and makes us both feel somehow special. . . . I look at the practice of marriage two ways: it's designed by society to keep emphasis on the family, which is good. Marriage is also designed to give the woman the lawful right to take most when she gets rid of you. If a woman lives with me for a significant period, gives me everything on Earth I want from a woman, totally backs me up, even sometimes when I'm wrong, then maybe I'll get married. If she does that, she deserves all my stuff when I die, and I'll marry her to make sure she gets it, and to show my appreciation, if that's what she needs to perceive it. To me, though, the piece of paper means nothing. You're married when you're married in the mind and heart and soul, not by government decree."

Sue had long known of Brown's carousing and his almost resentful view toward her and their marriage. Friends of Sue's informed her of the rumors of Brown's cheating and how people spotted him with this different young woman or that one. Several years after the trial, Sue, apparently weary of Brown's increasing distance from her and their three children, his flings, and an even bigger Brown controversy involving another woman, filed for divorce in a Cleveland court, citing gross neglect of duty.

TIME MAGAZINE IN 1965 was not reserved in one of its many descriptions of Brown: "Jimmy seems to be shooting for still another title: Most Controversial Athlete of the Year. Flashy, arrogant, casually indiscreet, he drives a red Cadillac Eldorado, brags that he owns so many suits that 'I might lose one in the cleaners and never miss it.' He does not care much for people in general ('I've met three or four beautiful people in my life. The rest all have an angle')—and he does not care what they think of him. 'I do what I want to do,' he says."

Before the breakup of the Brown family, Jim lived in a modest home in the Shaker Heights neighborhood of Cleveland, next to a doctor and near other black professionals. He could have afforded a larger house, but he enjoyed the idea of living in an unpretentious area of the city where other black professionals resided. That part of Brown, the humble aspect of his personality, would never change. What would also never change was that for every part humility in his soul, there were equal parts confidence and self-importance. Brown's status inflated, and so did his superciliousness. It is in this period, the mid-1960s, when that extravagant sense of self-confidence almost destroyed him, nearly ruining so many of the things he had worked so tirelessly to accomplish.

INCREASINGLY, EACH TIME a microphone—or a pen—was put in front of Jim's face, he spoke of societal ills and racial injustice. He criticized the government for its treatment of blacks. The country was changing and so was Jim's verbiage, becoming more radical by the standards of those times, and more fearless.

Brown's constant talk of racism and the powerlessness of his people irked some in the media who followed the team closely. A Cleveland sports broadcaster named John Fitzgerald said during one newscast that Brown should cease talking about racial matters and concentrate only on football.

Fitzgerald later pulled Brown aside in the Cleveland locker room. "I've always admired you as a football player, Jim," he told Brown. "I've never looked at you as a Negro."

Brown refused to let such a silly statement pass so easily. "That's ridiculous!" Brown responded. "You have to look at me as a Negro. Look at me, man! I'm black!"

Unlike other athletes, Brown did not water down his views as he became more popular, and other than Ali, no athlete's repute grew faster than Brown's. In January of 1965, just as the Browns were receiving their game checks for beating the Colts in the championship contest, monies valued at a record $8,000, Brown signed a new contract with Cleveland for $200,000. Brown's deal was unique in the league; he structured his payments so he would still receive money from the Browns after he retired. "Most athletes did not think that way at that time," former teammate Bobby Mitchell explained. Before the multiyear deal, Brown had signed a one-year pact with the Browns for $50,000, which was the highest salary ever paid a football player.

Brown was making another impression in Hollywood. In August 1964, a small item ran in the Cleveland newspaper about a unique movie billed as a "super Western" made by film giant 20th Century Fox. The movie was called *Rio Conchos* and starred Brown. The grand opening of the movie was in Cleveland on what was billed as "Salute to Jim Brown" night. Outside of the Hippodrome Theatre in October 1964, Brown did a red-carpet interview, thanking his guests, many of whom were Browns players, and then walked inside. In an almost comedic moment, two FBI agents, the former government source claims, slunk into the premiere as well, and jotted down notes through parts of it. What those in attendance, including the G-men, saw was the beginning of a Hollywood leading man and the creation of a brave new action hero.

At a time when Hollywood turned out dreamy and almost exclusively white Adonis figures like Ford automobiles on an assembly line, Brown was refreshingly different.

In *Rio Conchos* Brown blasted his way onto the screen, bare-chested and biceps bulging, getting into gunfights and saving damsels in distress. He played a sergeant from the United States Cavalry attempting to track down stolen weapons in a post–Civil War America. He was not a thespian, not a superb speaker of dialogue;

he was all testosterone and guts. In other words, he was like every other action star of the time, except he possessed a different skin color.

"The big question around here is, how does Brown do as an actor?" wrote Emerson Batdorff in reviewing the film for the *Plain Dealer*. "The answer is, pretty good, although possibly not as well as he does as a football player. He is entirely adequate in his part. . . . One of the film's problems is how to treat a Negro in a principled part, in accord with the practice of that day, and yet not make it offensive to an audience today. This problem has largely been resolved in favor of human dignity."

Brown's entrance into moviemaking started somewhat accidentally. During his stay in Los Angeles for the Pro Bowl in January 1964, Brown met a film studio representative, who asked if he was interested in reading for the part of Sergeant Franklin. "I'm no actor," was the blunt response from Brown. The studio persisted. After the Bing Crosby celebrity golf outing that same weekend in Pebble Beach, he agreed to read the script. Brown recognized instantly the anomaly of a black man playing that kind of heroic action champion. He agreed and, with the help of Modell, negotiated a contract to do the movie.

As much as Brown had starred on the football fields, appearing in a movie had escalated his fame even more. The previously unseen combination of gigantic football star and hunk actor took Brown from prominent to lethally illustrious. There was more money, more power, more prestige, more women, and more trouble.

HE WAS BACK.

The man on the cover of the August 12, 1968, *Sports Illustrated* looked oddly out of place. He wore an orange-and-black baseball cap with "CB" etched on the front. Behind him were orange football helmets with the word "Bengals" emblazoned on them. Out of place indeed. It was Paul Brown, and the "CB" on his hat did not mean Cleveland Browns. It stood for the new team he was running, the Cincinnati Bengals.

Since his unceremonious departure from Cleveland, Paul had mostly worked on his golf game and traveled with his wife, Katy, to Europe and Asia. As much as he enjoyed the new freedom and lowered blood pressure, there is little question that Paul missed professional football, and the sport missed him.

The magazine told a story about Paul that showed just how miserable and lost he was without football. Paul attended a Packers-Rams contest, and as the pregame approached, those old juices began flowing, and he became even edgier when he saw Vince Lombardi patrolling the sideline, getting ready for the game. Paul left his seat in the stands and called to Lombardi and a writer who was speaking with the Packers' coach. The two men approached Paul, the group began conversing, and suddenly Lombardi walked off to start the contest. The writer stayed and continued speaking with Paul and noticed the pain in Paul's face. "Is it that bad?" being away from football, Paul was asked.

With tears forming in his eyes, Paul responded, "I can't tell you how bad it is. I can't tell you."

It was the kind of emotion Paul had rarely shown with his Browns players.

Other offers to coach came in the years following Paul's leaving, but none of the NFL teams interested was willing to hand over the total control he now craved. If there was ever a lesson learned from the disaster that was his firing with the Browns, it was that control was a necessity if he was to get back into coaching. The Bengals did not balk at giving the legend what amounted to a blank check.

The cover story on Paul did something else: it regurgitated and cemented the prevailing thought that Jim Brown was the leader of a rebellion that led to Paul's demise. "The break in Cleveland came after a strong clash of personalities between Brown and Arthur Modell, the new owner," wrote Tex Maule. "A small coterie of Cleveland Browns players, headed by All-Pro fullback Jim Brown, indicated to Modell that they would not play another season under Paul Brown. Their reasons were rather vague: some accused Brown of having let modern pro football pass him by, others said he was cold and distant. In any case, Brown was out as coach."

The rebuilding of Paul's professional life had begun in an unusual locale, Cincinnati, of all places, but not without Paul's meticulous touch, as he carefully screened assistant coaches, sites for training, and even administrative assistants.

BROWN'S NEGRO INDUSTRIAL Economic Union, despite what some government officials thought at the time, had indeed changed the financial fortunes of hundreds and possibly thousands of black people by providing loans to small businesses that otherwise would never have received them. Brown's organization had ballooned to hundreds of employees and played a significant role in starting twenty-five to thirty small to midsize businesses. One branch in Kansas City was mentioned by President Richard Nixon as a brilliant example of how a charitable organization should work. Brown supported Nixon's 1972 campaign—to the chagrin of black leaders, since Nixon was seen as hostile to minorities. Brown's backing of Nixon was part of a complex political quid pro quo in which one black-owned business wanted to do business in Africa and Nixon said he would help, but only if these black businessmen, including Brown, supported Nixon.

Brown may have backed Nixon for political purposes, but he did not tone down his feelings on civil rights. In yet another moment, and there were many, when Brown showed dramatic courage and leadership, he gathered many of the country's top black athletes in Cleveland for what was called a "Muhammad Ali draft summit." Brown wanted to bolster Ali, since Ali had shown such public and financial support for Brown's group. Ali's decision to forgo the draft was inflammatory, and turned Ali, almost overnight, into one of the most disliked athletes in the nation. White sports fans who had formerly hung on every Ali couplet now repudiated him and his decision to bow out of the service. On November 10, 1966, at a press conference inside the Negro Industrial Economic Union head-quarters, Ali explained his decision in detail while surrounded by Brown and eight other high-profile black athletes, including Lew Alcindor, Bill Russell, Wooten, and Mitchell.

"Jim felt strongly that we should support Ali, since he was so good to us," remembers Wooten. "I can't stress enough just how controversial what Jim did was at the time. There were a lot of people that hated Ali, and because Jim supported Ali, they now hated Jim. Jim really stuck his neck out."

Before the announcement, the group met privately for more than two hours. Ali told them he felt his decision was the moral one, and he would not change his mind. "The bottom line was we were going to support him," says Mitchell. "We all listened to what he had to say and knew he was sincere. We were really touched by what Ali was doing."

The racial tensions in St. Louis were as intense as almost anywhere in the country and manifested themselves in Brown's organization's dealings with entities in the city. The Black Economic Union de-manded that the three largest radio stations in the city better serve the black community with news coverage of black nationalists.

The FBI's documents show that the bureau became heavily

involved in June 1968. The St. Louis chapter had become more radicalized than others, but still retained its core mission of bringing economic change to black communities. FBI documents show that the bureau viewed the St. Louis Black Economic Union as a clear danger. One four-page document showed just how concerned the FBI was.

The memo, declassified in 1986, almost twenty years after it was written, and now publicly disclosed for the first time, read:

On June 17, 1968, a source, who has furnished reliable information in the past, advised that Charles Koen of the Black Economic Union, East St. Louis, Illinois, together with three unknown Negro adults and three Negro teen-age boys had presented the following demands to Radio Stations KXLW, KADI and KATZ, St. Louis, Missouri:

The radio stations in St. Louis are inadequately covering Black News. The Black Nationalist Organizations in this city have banded together to rectify this injustice wantonly inflicted upon the Black Community.

Radio Stations KXLW, KADI, and KATZ are oriented toward [the] Negro Market, and we the Black Nationalists demand that the above stations serve the Black Community with the true voice of Blackness and not the voice of indoctrination toward the White Culture.

We the Black Nationalists demand that the following demands are complied with by the above listed radio stations:

1. We demand: One hour of broadcasting centered around Black Nationalism.

2. We demand: That the Black Program be broadcasted at ideal times.

3. We demand: That the Black Nationalists be interviewed at least two hours per week.

4. We demand: That the program director be given
   the flexibility to institute the Black programs. No
   White has the insight to censor his program.

5. We demand: Promotion of drives for Black Nationalist Organizations.

6. We demand: More positive news coverage for the
   Black Community.

The letter was signed "Black Nationalist Movement endorsed by the Black Economic Union of the Mid-West Leaders."

According to the documents, the FBI had five moles in the Black Economic Union and other groups, attending meetings and feeding information to the FBI supervisors. In less than a year, however, the situation went from fiery to cold. The organization simply disintegrated. Once the Black Economic Union in St. Louis was disbanded, the FBI turned its attention to other entities. "Since it has been established the Black Economic Union is no longer in existence as per St. Louis Airtel," one memorandum says, "this file is being closed in this office." Phrases like "Agitator Index" and "Security Index" are sprinkled throughout the file.

The documents show no evidence of any arrests, and there was little media publicity. It is unclear why this St. Louis chapter of Brown's group shut down. Did Brown do it? Did the FBI have some sort of detrimental effect? The only thing that is clear is that though it took years, the FBI stopped seeing Brown's Black Economic Union—and to some degree Brown himself—as a threat.

The FBI source says his spying on Brown ceased in the late 1970s, though he believes agents on the West Coast may have continued using informants and infiltrating various Brown projects after that. "I am not certain of that, but it was the scuttlebutt among some of the agents that did this sort of thing," the FBI source says, "that the agency never really let go of Brown."

The intensive spying may have stopped once stronger laws preventing illegal wiretapping were put into effect by the government. "But laws didn't mean shit to the FBI then," the agent says; "we probably would have been ordered to spy on him anyway and eavesdrop on him whether there were laws in place or not. We were that arrogant."

In Spike Lee's documentary about Brown's life, Brown talks about his FBI file, saying the bureau tried to tie Brown to the Nation of Islam and focused on his various run-ins with the law. While there is no hard proof beyond the agent's claims that the FBI did more, it is naive to believe that everything the agent states is false. He is extremely believable, particularly since these kinds of privacy abuses were common in the later J. Edgar Hoover era of the FBI.

Where was the moral compass of the men who spied on Americans? It is a question being asked only now by the former spies themselves. Melissa Boyle Mahle, a retired CIA officer, was a key speaker at a conference in early 2006 about the ethics of spying, according to the New York Times. "As an intelligence officer, you are confronted with ethical dilemmas every day," she told the newspaper, adding that morality is an important quality but one possibly lacked by spies.

Others say morality and ethics in intelligence do not mix. "Depending on where you're coming from, the whole business of espionage is unethical," Duane R. Clarridge, a former CIA operations officer, told the newspaper. Clarridge stated that "intelligence ethics" is an "oxymoron. It's not an issue. It never was and never will be, not if you want a real spy service."

While most of these former spies were speaking of today's climate, in which intelligence officers attempt to snag members of al

Qaeda, this argument should clearly have been held decades ago as the government spied on its own. J. Edgar Hoover had achieved success in the earlier years of his almost half century at the head of the FBI—with his agents gunning down Dillinger and capturing Nazi saboteurs sneaking onto East Coast beaches—but slipped into persecution of what he called "subversives," like the Black Panthers, John Lennon, and Martin Luther King Jr., in the 1960s and 1970s.

When I contacted an FBI spokesperson at the bureau's main headquarters, she declined to comment.

If the government can, according to legal experts, violate the rights of citizens in the twenty-first century by using the National Security Agency to mount wiretaps against its own citizens making calls outside of the country—in the name of catching terrorists—then what was the government doing in the 1960s and early 1970s, when the laws to protect citizens from these kinds of abuses were not explicit and the morals of some of our highest leaders were lacking?

A former intelligence official familiar with these laws and with the acts of surveillance committed by various government entities explained that the Foreign Intelligence Surveillance Act was passed in 1978 to regulate the kind of wiretapping that President George W. Bush authorized after the September 11 attacks. Executive privilege, argues the Bush White House, authorizes electronic surveillance without going to the FISA court, the expert explains.

"Keep in mind, however," the official says, "that another whole set of laws applies to human intelligence [humint]. Humint would include physical surveillance to gather intelligence on American citizens [e.g., by following someone]. Much of the law related to the latter has developed over the years through judicial interpretation of criminal laws, although there are specific statutes that provide constraints on physical surveillance as it relates to the intelligence community. . . . I think you mentioned the FBI doing both electronic and physical surveillance with regard to black athletes. I don't think any of these laws were in effect during the time frame you mentioned."

In other words, there were very few rules at the time preventing the FBI from spying on Brown and other black athletes. FISA was originated as a way to prevent such abuses the agent claims occurred, but it came much too late to help people like Brown.

"I'll go to my grave regretting what I did," the former agent says. "At the time you get swept up in believing what you are doing is right for the country. Years later you know it was a wrong thing to do."

BROWN SAT AT a 1965 meeting of the Cleveland Touchdown Club, his frame snuggled into a seat that seemed too small for him, still looking dapper in his charcoal suit that was perfectly tailored, the vest he was wearing buttoned up tight. The rolls on the table were split open by his large hands, and there was no fussing over the veal cutlet. He was introduced succinctly by the host. "Gentleman," the man stated, "I give you Superman."

Everyone in the room knew that Brown could not bend steel and that bullets would not bounce off his chest, but they still applauded him as if he were an immortal. The anecdote about the Cleveland club was told in a lengthy cover story by *Time* magazine that ran on November 26. The cover art was a detailed and splendid drawing showing Brown wearing his number 32 jersey while holding a football. "Cleveland's Jimmy Brown," read the words under the picture. That a football player was on the cover while a war waged in Vietnam was an indication of how Brown's actions on the football field were clearly rippling from football into popular culture.

"After nine seasons in the league, Brown is regarded as a genuine phenomenon in a sport that shares the language ('blitz,' 'bullet,' 'bomb') of war," read the story. "Pro football's stars are the samurai of sport—immensely skilled, brutally tough, corrosively honest mercenaries who respect each other almost as much as they respect themselves. In the critical company of his peers, the Baltimore Colts' Johnny Unitas is considered 'a great quarterback, but if you beat his blockers, you beat him.' Rookie fullback Tucker Frederickson of the New York Giants is 'strong right now, but in a year he'll hit a little less hard.' And flanker Bobby Mitchell of the Washington Redskins is already 'slowing down fast'—at the age of 30. There is only one player in the game today whose ability on field commands almost universal admiration, and that is Jimmy Brown."

The magazine called Brown a "fire breathing, chocolate covered monster."

The reason for the Brown cover was the year he'd just had. In the 1965 season, Brown led the NFL in rushing for the fourth straight time, blistering the league for 1,544 yards. "He just kept cranking out great season after great season," says his onetime teammate Mitchell. "There was no sign he was going to slow down." Brown's *Rio Conchos* had received good reviews, and it was clear that his movie career was moving to an entirely different level.

Modell did not care. He wanted Brown the football player, not the actor, to appear in training camp. When Brown began production on *The Dirty Dozen,* filmed in London starting early in 1966, much of the film's initial days of shooting were delayed because of rainy weather. When training camp began in the summer of 1966, Brown did not show up, and the relationship between Brown and Modell was officially no longer chummy.

But no one expected what would happen next, not even people close to Brown. Newspapers in Cleveland speculated that the sudden rift between Brown and Modell would smooth over, just as it had before. After all, Modell had once referred to Brown as his "senior partner."

"Even a man of Jim Brown's many business interests undoubtedly can find use for another $65,000," wrote the *Plain Dealer*'s Charles Heaton in July 1966. "And that sum may be an underestimate of his remuneration from the Browns. On the other hand, the Browns can find room for the game's finest running back despite the presence of some very talented performers on the 1966 roster. So it's my guess that some compromise will be worked out and that No. 32 will be in the lineup Sept. 11 when the club opens its Eastern Division title defense in Washington. Meanwhile, however, those negotiations should prove mightily interesting."

They did. Modell, hating the fact that Brown was publicly challenging his authority, issued equally public ultimatums, stating that if Brown did not show up to training camp, he would be fined $100 a day for each day of camp he missed. (Some media reports said Modell threatened to fine him $1,000 a week, while others stated it was as much as $1,500 a week.) Modell may have thought he knew Brown, he may have believed he understood who Brown was, but by threatening Brown, he showed a profound ignorance of Brown's internal makeup. The minute Modell took an aggressive stance toward Brown and attempted to embarrass him publicly, the relationship was doomed. There is even some question whether Modell had the right to fine Brown, since Brown was technically not under contract.

It was a bold move by Modell that totally backfired. Now challenged, Modell had left Brown no choice. Brown was going to retire.

Once Modell realized his mistake, he secretly attempted to woo Brown back, but it was too late. Modell dispatched a friend and fellow owner to hunt down Brown on *The Dirty Dozen* set, talk with Brown, and discuss his return to football. The conversation was brief and Brown's mind was unchanged.

Brown phoned his wife, Sue, from London and informed her of

his decision, though she already suspected what he was going to do. They spoke of his thoughts two weeks before Brown made his decision public. "Whatever you decide, I'm behind you," she told him. Though Brown was increasingly an absent husband and father, Sue remained loyal. She enjoyed watching Brown play, but she also saw the other side—Brown would toss and turn many nights, trying to find a position in which the bruises didn't keep him awake.

After telling Sue, Brown wrote two letters: one to Blanton Collier and another to respected Cleveland columnist Hal Lebovitz, who broke the news publicly. The headline in the *Plain Dealer* was bold and succinct: "Jim Brown Quits Football."

"I am leaving the Browns with an attitude of friendliness and cooperation," Brown told Lebovitz. "Once I return to Cleveland I'll do everything I can to help the Browns—other than playing. The Browns have a great organization and a great team. One man won't make the difference. I leave with great respect for Blanton and Art. I'll help them any way I can."

Perhaps Brown's public statement was the right thing to say, but it wasn't what he believed—except for the part about Collier, whom Brown liked personally. Brown did not possess similar feelings for Modell. "Our relationship changed after that," Modell says. "I think we both made mistakes. I may have acted somewhat hastily."

From the movie set, Brown held a formal press conference on July 14, 1966, while seated in front of a World War II tank replica. In the war between Jim and Modell, Brown had fired the final shot, and won. Brown has portrayed his decision to retire as a complicated one, but it was simpler than he would like to admit. His decision was indeed partially financial. He was on the verge of becoming a significant motion picture star and was earning far more money as an actor than football could ever have paid him. Some Hollywood reporters called him "the Negro Clark Gable" because of the strong sex appeal Brown oozed in his movies. "When the Cleveland Browns' Jim Brown quit pro football to become a movie actor," penned writer Joseph Gelmis from Hollywood, "a press agent predicted: 'He could become a black Rock Hudson.' "

Hollywood called, but Brown's retirement was mostly about ego. Brown responded belligerently to any perceived challenge. To him, there was no difference between a linebacker attempting to tackle him and an owner trying to coerce him back into football. Brown's estrangement from Modell would continue for years. One year after his retirement, he blasted Modell—from another movie set—for what he felt was Modell's unfair treatment of a group of Cleveland players. Five Browns players were holding out for better contracts and being fined by Modell $100 a day. When Modell declared publicly that the Cleveland organization had historically treated black players with respect, an angry Brown fired back: "Before I get to the only important issue involved in negotiations between owner Arthur Modell and players John Wooten, John Brown, Mike Howell, Sidney Williams, and All-Pro Leroy Kelly, let me make it clear that Mr. Modell is completely off base in telling the press what the Cleveland Browns have done for Negro players. Let it be known that Negro players are no different from white players in seeking economic betterment. So if Mr. Modell feels that this is a racial matter, let him be informed that the players involved are not concerned with charitable contributions made to them on the basis of race." Modell responded that Brown's claims were "completely inaccurate."

While it is true that Brown's interjection into Cleveland's contractual dispute was in part fueled by a genuine sense of irritation at the treatment of the holdouts, Brown's response was mostly just a way to jab his former owner. Their decades-long feud had begun.

When Brown departed professional football, he ripped an immense hole in the sport that would not be filled, even to this day. He finished with league records in almost every rushing category, including yards gained in a season, with 1,863 in fourteen games, two fewer regular-season contests than today. He set the career rushing mark at 12,312, in just nine years. Brown also finished first in total career yards; had the most rushing attempts for a season and a career; was tops in yards per carry at 5.29; and had the most career rushing touchdowns with 106, the most years leading the league in rushing at eight, the most consecutive years leading the league in rushing with five, and the most career touchdowns. He was second in a number of other pertinent categories.

It was on November 19, 1961, when he was twenty-five years old, that Brown pummeled the Philadelphia Eagles for 237 yards. It was the kind of game that running backs no longer have. He had thirty-four carries and his longest run was only 18 yards, mainly because each time he touched the ball, five or six Eagles defenders instantly swamped him.

Once, he broke through the line so quickly, and the blocking was so efficient, that only one Eagles player had a chance to tackle him. Newspaper accounts described Brown and Philadelphia player Bobby Freeman colliding. Freeman ended up being tossed on his back.

After the contest, a newspaper photographer spotted Brown walking off the field, as many of the 68,399 fans stayed to continue cheering Brown. The photographer then asked Brown to do something. "Hold this," the man told Brown. He handed the runner a football.

"Give us a smile," the photographer requested. Brown complied and posed, giving one of the few public smiles he ever did as a Cleveland player.

Brown was probably capable of playing at least three more years and possibly five, all at a high level. If he had played three, he would still be first or second in total rushing yardage in history. If he had played four or five, he would still hold the record for most career rushing yards. No other runner would have come close. And imagine if Brown had the same advantage as Emmitt Smith, the current all-time leading rusher, who was able to play half of his games under Texas Stadium's partial roof. Barry Sanders played many of his games inside a comfortable dome on a quick artificial turf.

The lone but substantial caveat in assessing Brown's career is that he dominated in an era when defenses were far smaller and slower. There is indeed some truth to this argument. Some defensive ends were two hundred pounds, the size of a safety in today's football. Brown was larger in many instances than almost any defensive player. Thus the NFL was completely unprepared for someone who combined his speed and power. Still, Brown would have routed on the field in any era because his level of athleticism and mental toughness is unmatched.

"As one of the thirty-nine Hall of Fame selectors, I am inundated with numbers every year," says longtime great *Sports Illustrated* writer Peter King in an interview. "Art Monk deserves to be in the Hall because he caught 940 balls, I am told. Warren Moon threw for a jillion yards; how can he not be a Hall of Famer? And what I've said to several people who've made these arguments with me is, basically, we shouldn't be looking at players in a numerical vacuum. Numbers matter, of course. But we should be looking at players with our own eyes and asking: Was this player truly one of the greats of his era?

"And I use Jim Brown as an example. He'd pass the eye test and the numbers test, surely, but I tell people I wouldn't care if he rushed for 5,000 fewer yards. He was the best running back of his day, and there is no doubt in my mind he remains the greatest running back of all time. I interviewed Emmitt Smith near the end of his career, and he told me he wanted to rush for 20,000 yards so he could leave his footprints on the game forever. Fine, I thought. Admirable goal. But that still wouldn't have made him Jim Brown's equal. To be able to steamroll linebackers and juke past cornerbacks is rare enough. Doing it while having every eye on the defense focused on stopping him was rarer. Doing it week after week, carry after carry, for a decade . . . it's never been done before. And it never will again, in my opinion. I always thought it was amazing that a man at the absolute top of his game would retire to pursue something else he liked doing. Imagine LeBron James quitting at 27 to act, or Albert Pujols retiring at 28 to act and then not going back! We as a society hate to see the plug pulled on greatness. But if anything, retiring with three good years left in him only added to the Jim Brown legend. To me, there are a few singular players in pro football history. Don Hutson, the incredible and eternally underrated receiver for Green Bay in the '30s and '40s. Otto Graham, who led the Browns to ten straight championship-game appearances in the '40s and '50s. Jim Brown. Jerry Rice. Lawrence Taylor. There's five. Notice something: There's only one running back on that list. And there's a good chance there will only be one ever on that list."

1970

LIQUID

For the first time since Clark Gable's days, Hollywood thinks it has a genuine he-man star—a man who brings out the love-to-be-knocked-around quality in women. This time though, he's a Negro.

—**Dick Kleiner,** Newspaper Enterprise Association writer, in a 1968 article about Brown's film career

Big Jim never drank or smoked. His only weakness was the chicks.

—**Roy Simmons Sr.,** Brown's former lacrosse coach, to *Sports Illustrated*

Brown was in Los Angeles in January 1967, filming an episode of the TV show *I Spy*, when he heard from the Cleveland Browns that they were going to retire his number 32 jersey and honor him at a Jim Brown Farewell Day. Brown was not sure how his retirement would be handled by Modell, since both men were still angry with each other. Fan reaction was mixed. Some praised Brown for leaving at the top of his game, while others fumed at what they thought was Brown's leaving the team in a difficult situation. How were the Browns going to cope, fans wondered, without Brown in the backfield?

The country itself was in an uproar. Recent years had seen Freedom Riders beaten and lunch-counter sitters hosed; Klan members were awaiting trial for shooting three civil rights workers in Neshoba County, Mississippi; and organizations like the Black Panthers and the Student Nonviolent Coordinating Committee had been formed. When the appreciation day took place on January 29, 1967, at an arena in Cleveland, a smiling Modell presented Brown with one of his jerseys. "We won't be using it," he told Brown and the crowd of about 4,500 people. The attendance reflected fans' unhappiness with Brown's decision to retire, as well as anger over his controversial book and perceived role in the dismissal of Paul Brown. The organizers of the event had hoped for a packed house, or 12,000 people, but just one-third of that number came. The large number of empty seats was shocking considering the magnitude of the event and who was retiring.

Still, the night was special. Modell had prepared an eight-minute film—in color, the *Plain Dealer* raved—showing some of Brown's career highlights. The moment from the film that elicited the loudest cheers showed a game against Dallas in 1965. Inside the 5-yard line, Brown was able to avoid or run over six Dallas defenders.

Athletes from across the country flew into Cleveland to attend the event. Boston Celtics star Bill Russell arrived after his team beat the New York Knicks, landing in town around nine that night. Bobby Mitchell told the audience that Brown had taught him how to "return to the huddle with dignity. I hope he is my friend forever."

"My trip here is to make sure Jim Brown won't come back," said Sam Huff. Muhammad Ali told the crowd that Brown was "the greatest athlete in the history of sports next to me." Then, aware that the small crowd made for a partially awkward moment, Ali gushed, "This arena should be too small for Jim's farewell. He is still pretty. I am glad to see him retire undefeated."

When Brown spoke—for over twenty minutes, without notes—his words were so intense and authentic and inspiring that the *Plain Dealer* published the entire speech the following day. Brown told the arena crowd in part:

> I know that this is a farewell to yours truly, and that's very wonderful of you. But I think of it more as something else. I

think of it as a point wherein the Negro Industrial Economic Union can be brought forth, and then move on to greater things.

Now there is a struggle going on in this country. There is a struggle. We all know about this struggle. We know what we want, and we know that one day we're going to get it. The confusion has come about because of the methods that have been applied in trying to gain this freedom. The Constitution of the United States says that all of us should have freedom of speech, religion, and so forth. It does not say that one portion of our society should have more freedom than another. In fact, the theory and the philosophy that built this country is a very, very wonderful one. But as you all know, this theory and philosophy is not always carried out. We know the methods that have been employed to bring about freedom—a lot of them have failed. A lot of them have caused trouble in the streets. . . .

Now, what I'm saying to you in closing is that we all have an opportunity to better ourselves. We all have the opportunity, believe it or not, to go on to much, much greater heights. We cannot be lazy, we cannot sit back and let someone else do it for you. We can't say, "Well, that's Jim Brown's organization, let him do it, we'll see if he is going to succeed, or if he is going to fail." You are going to have to get out and participate. Really, I'm very tired of hearing all of our problems blamed on the other man. We know about discrimination, we know about all of the hardships that our people have gone through. We know about the castration of the black male. We know about the strength of the Negro woman because the mother became an image in the house. We know that our black women have been taken advantage of throughout history. We know that we do not get the big part of the stick. But we also know that we don't take advantage of the opportunities that we do have.

It would have been very nice if we had had a full house tonight. It would have been a very nice thing. But somehow, when things like this happen, they sort of test your courage. It sort of lets you take a look at yourself and see where you're really at. It lets you look at yourself and say, "Well, am I going to hold up? Am I going to get discouraged? Or what am I going to do?" Well most of you know my history. You know that I've probably been involved in almost everything there is to be involved in. You probably know that I've been fighting ever since I was a little boy. And when I leave here tonight, I'm not going to think that we didn't have 12,000 people—I'm going to think that we had all you people. I'm going to think that when I leave here that all of you are going to dedicate yourselves to self-help and betterment. And I'm going to go down to Jamaica to finish a movie and make a little more money, and I'm going to come back here and dedicate myself all over again. And we're going to win. Thank you very much.

Most athletes speaking at their retirement would simply have told the crowd a few funny stories, thanked them, and then departed for the bar to get drunk. Not Brown. He used his retirement as an opportunity to make a social statement, speaking fervently of race and economics. Such moments were what made Brown spectacular, even when he did not have a football in his hands. In the coming years he alternated between those special instances and ugly moments, shifting, bending, committing hideous deeds and humane ones, a fluid and indefinable presence.

. . .

HIS MOVIE CAREER in full swing, his conscience unblemished by guilt, Brown was making movie history, and having relationships with other women despite still being married to Sue. He left Cleveland to buy a party house with a pool high in the Hollywood Hills, and to say that Brown was comfortable with his sexuality, well, that is like saying he was a pretty good runner. Soon the Brown party house included women and orgies and drugs—though Brown never used; the cocaine was there for the women, almost as a lure, and to help them perform.

Brown was not alone in being promiscuous. This was Hollywood in the 1970s. Men had women, women had men, and all the combinations thereabouts. Once he became a star in the movies, he was no different from any other heterosexual action hero. Women flocked to the stars, and the stars took advantage.

And there was no question: Brown was a star. The movie press and periodicals were filled with stories about Brown's acting abilities and potential. With historical perspective and after decades of racial growth, it is easy to see what journalists wrote about Brown in that era as condescending and offensive, and in some instances scandalously racist. His race was a constant topic in the media because he was so unusual—a black action star who was allowed to have depth and intelligence. He also spoke his mind when interviewed and did not shy away from discussions about race.

"Jim Brown isn't the first Negro star," wrote journalist Dick Kleiner in 1968. "Sidney Poitier is still one of the top box office draws in the movie business. But Poitier's bag is urbanity; Brown's is action and, increasingly, sex." Kleiner later wrote: "The only two questions about Brown's ultimate position at the top of the heap are his color and his acting ability. So far, the color of his skin does not appear to be affecting his box office draw. Producers these days are willingly paying him $300,000 a picture—and they wouldn't do that unless they were reasonably sure they'd get it back."

By 1968 Brown had starred in or was filming five movies. He played an assassin in *The Dirty Dozen,* in which twelve violent soldiers—sentenced either to die or to life in prison—are given a pardon in exchange for being trained by Lee Marvin's character for a suicide mission. Brown starred with the man who was supposedly his white counterpart, Rock Hudson, in *Ice Station Zebra,* a cold war movie about competing American and Russian submarine crews racing to the North Pole to retrieve secret documents. He played a craggy seafarer in *Kenner.* The film *Dark of the Sun* (also called *The Mercenaries*) was the first movie to deal with the slaughter that occurred in the Congo in the early 1960s. *The Split* was about a rogue thief who designs an ill-fated plot to rob the box office of the Los Angeles Coliseum. He starred with Ernest Borgnine, Jack Klugman, and a then lesser-known actor named Gene Hackman.

Brown brought to acting his sense of professionalism and a stern work ethic honed in football. Producers and actors praised him. Mary Murray, producer of *Kenner,* called him "very good—a natural talent."

"Let's put it this way," actor Lee Marvin, who starred with Brown in *The Dirty Dozen,* told the press. "Brown's a better actor than Sir Laurence Olivier would be as a member of the Cleveland Browns."

"He's seemingly more believable to the average Negro than guys like Poitier," Marvin added. Director Robert Aldrich said at the time: "There isn't another Negro actor around quite like Brown. Poitier, Belafonte, or Ossie Davis aren't Brown's style."

In the 1968 *Playboy* interview with Alex Haley, Brown talked of his significance to Hollywood. "I don't know; maybe I *am* shaping a new movie personality. I'm just being myself; that's all I know how to do. I'm sure not taking anything away from [other black actors]

and others like James Earl Jones. But there's a crying need for more
Negro actors, because for so long, ever since the silent screen, in
fact, the whole world has been exposed to Negroes in stereotype
roles. Have you ever been to any Negro theater with a movie going,
with a Negro in it? Well, you can just *feel* the tension of that audience, pulling for this guy to do something good, something that
will give them a little pride. That's why I feel so good that Negroes
are finally starting to play roles that other Negroes, watching, will
feel proud of, and respond to, and identify with, and feel *real* about,
instead of being crushed by some Uncle Tom on the screen making
a fool of himself. You're not going to find any of us playing Uncle
Toms anymore. In my first picture, *Rio Conchos,* I played a cowboy
who fought not only Indians but white guys, too. And I played a
realistic Negro in *The Dirty Dozen*. And in this picture I'm shooting
now, *Ice Station Zebra,* I play a Marine captain on an atomic submarine. It's not a part written for a Negro, or for any race in particular;
it's a part with no racial overtones whatever."

"I'm an ardent civil rights advocate," John Sturges, director of *Ice
Station Zebra*, told the *Press-Newsday* newspaper, "but that's not why
Jim Brown was cast in a role that didn't specify a Negro or white actor. He was picked because he's an actor with steam. He's got presence. He's playing the part because he's a big, rough, tough cookie
and he's right for the part. He's got star potential, let's face it."

Brown, always with his sense of humor intact, though he often
refused to show it publicly, made a joke about why his characters die
in the movies: "Most of my friends ask, 'Why you dying in all the
flicks? I say, 'Look, man, I die well. They give me beautiful deaths.
And the part in this film, at least, wasn't written specifically for a
Negro. So it's not like they were deliberately killing off the Negro."

"I know that this is only Jimmy's third picture," actor Rod Taylor, who starred with Brown in *Dark of the Sun*, told reporters in
1967, "so all I can say is that he must have inherited an awful lot of

experience. Added to which he is a big, good-looking guy, extremely sensitive and intelligent. Playing in scenes with him is a pleasure."

What Brown had accomplished in leaping from great football player to accomplished actor was simply astounding. Imagine if New England quarterback Tom Brady suddenly quit football and then starred in five movies. At the time, it seemed Brown's feat was respected, but some in Hollywood still did not know what to make of the athlete turned actor. "Women are afraid of him," Robert Chartoff, coproducer of *The Split,* told Kleiner, "but they're attracted to him at the same time. He satisfies women's masochistic need."

Pop psychology and sexism aside, moviegoers were at times as split as Hollywood. While his movies made money, studios still received bags of hate mail about Brown. His love scene with Raquel Welch in *100 Rifles* caused a stir and was the main prompt for angry complainers.

An interracial love scene even now would generate a slight commotion along racial lines, but it cannot be overstated just how big a controversy was generated over what Brown and Welch did almost forty years ago. The publicity for the movie played off the differing ethnicities, with movie studio PR people writing in press release blurbs that the film paired "two beautiful animals." One newspaper ad declared: "Negro and White Love Scenes That Will Shock-It-to-You!"

"Critics agree that, whether or not the casting is explosive, the movie is a bomb," wrote the gossip rag *Uncensored* in 1969. "However, it is also a solid financial success, for millions of people—including bigots and racists seeking to stimulate their hate glands—are willing to pay to watch those 'beautiful animals' mate."

Late in 1968, Jim Brown sat on the reddish veranda at the Aquadulce Hotel, just outside Almería, Spain, only a short ride to the *100 Rifles* movie set and a long way from coastal Georgia. Lovely young Spanish women bounced and giggled around him, but for the time being, none interested him but one—Eva Maria Bohn-Chin, a stunning young model and his mistress of the moment. Bohn-Chin had accompanied him to Spain.

At the hotel, sometimes he simply lay by the pool after a lengthy day of filming, wearing tight white swimming trunks, just enjoying the sun and quiet. Other times, when on the terrace, he sported a dashiki, a pair of black pants, and bare feet; he could relax, knowing that his spacious two-room penthouse that ran $750 a week was being paid for by 20th Century Fox. With the Mediterranean in the background, Brown would sip orange juice or nibble on half a watermelon cooled to his desired forty-five degrees and brought to him by a young Spanish boy. As if the beautiful scenery were not enough, Aretha Franklin and sometimes Lou Rawls crooned from a battery-operated Singer record player.

He had made it. He was a millionaire. He was a movie star. He was also controversial, and the making of *100 Rifles* with Welch was both a rewarding and a tense time for Brown. His increasing salary showed that studios did indeed think he was a bankable star. Brown earned $37,000 for *Rio Conchos,* his first film, and $40,000 for *The Dirty Dozen;* for *100 Rifles,* his eighth movie, Brown was paid a handsome $200,000 in salary and 5 percent of the film's box-office gross. On the set, Brown was active, doing many of his own stunts, and he was also demanding, even bullying. After one scene called for Brown to dangle over the side of a cliff, causing dust and debris to build up over his Afroed hair and elegant face, eventually settling into his eyes, Brown was testy. An assistant did not make his way to Brown quickly enough with some water and towels. "I'm sorry, Mr. Brown," the production assistant sheepishly said. Brown was not tolerant. "Just do your damn job," he told the assistant. "It's not the first time it has happened, and if it happens again, you won't be around."

Probing reporters increasingly began to focus on Brown's love life and what appeared to be a disintegrating marriage to Sue. A splendid and jaw-dropping *Ebony* magazine profile on Brown quoted him about just that subject: "You see, there are cases of a man advancing and a woman not advancing; she just sort of stands still, afraid to move out of her safe, comfortable spot. But a woman has to keep up with her man, educationally and every other way. As a man switches careers and moves up, his woman has to do the same. She has to move right along with him; she has to move up, too. Right?" The candid Brown sometimes did not realize how cruel his words sounded, and this was one of those moments. Brown did not appreciate how Sue had stood by his side when Brenda Ayres accused him of battery.

Brown continued: "Now at this point in my career, I need a woman who is educated and charming and able to hold her own anywhere. So much of my career now involves meeting people, traveling all over the world and things like that. So when I have to go some place on a film, I need a woman on my arm who's able to meet all kinds of people, who makes a striking appearance and who can help me in all kinds of situations. She has to be the kind of woman who isn't happy with the way she was ten years ago. She has to be the kind of woman who's constantly seeking to improve herself and improving herself in a way that's an asset to her man. It's like a man leaving his old neighborhood and going off to college to better himself and then returning to his old neighborhood and meeting his old pals who're still in the same rut that the man got out of a long time ago. The man still likes his old pals, but he can't afford to let them pull him back down to their level once he has risen above that kind of life. . . .

"Sue's a great, great woman. A fantastic woman. But she's not interested in the kind of life I want to live right now. See, she's the kind of girl who likes the kind of man who comes home every evening at a certain hour and shuts the gate on the white picket fence and relaxes in his favorite chair with his favorite pipe and watches the kids feeding the goldfish and playing with the dog. Well, I'm not that kind of man. I've never been, and Sue has known this and we've talked about it lots of times. I tried to be like that at one time, but I didn't fit the mold and I decided I wasn't going to make life miserable for both Sue and myself just in order to conform to some kind of convention and have people saying 'Oh, aren't Jim and Sue the ideal couple' and all that kind of crap. There are a lot of phony people living together like that and they're just as miserable as they can be."

For much of the making of *100 Rifles* Brown and Welch were not speaking to each other off the set. Brown had decided that Welch was shallow and silly. Welch felt Brown lacked sensitivity. Their differences became profound when the subject of nudity came up early in the shooting.

The love scenes in *100 Rifles* were anything but electric. Making out with Welch was, as Brown told *Ebony*, like "lying up in bed with a piece of wood. That's just how she affects me. Cold. Nothing." People on the set speculated about other reasons why the two had a contemptuous relationship. Welch did not swoon at Brown's feet as some of Brown's previous leading ladies had, causing Brown to act defensively. He also thought Welch was snobby and elitist. "I think she has the idea that I ought to be grateful that she agreed to make this picture with me," Brown chirped to *Ebony*. "You know, just because we go through all that sex business in the film. If that's what she thinks, she can go to hell. This is a picture that has a heavy man-woman theme. I'm the man; Raquel's the woman. We'll both make a lot of money out of it, so why the hell should I be grateful to her for anything? To me, the whole thing is just a business deal. That's all. Some white reporters have been down here asking me all kinds of silly things about how I feel to be making love to a white woman. I have one standard answer: 'It's not like this is the first time I've done it, baby. You know what I mean?' That's what I tell them and it shakes the hell out of them."

The biggest reason Brown and Welch clashed, however, was probably nudity. Welch disliked the idea of being naked on-screen, it caused friction between her and the studio, and that bitterness eventually seeped into Brown and Welch's relationship. The original script called for Welch to appear in two nude scenes. One was supposed to be in a shower and the second in a bed with Brown. Welch insisted on remaining clothed, and her representatives and the studio sent terse telegrams back and forth attempting to negotiate Hollywood's most attractive leading lady out of her top. Welch would not relent, and the nude scene was instead filled by a body double.

"I wouldn't take my clothes off in front of 300 extras," she told the media in 1969. "It was a very personal thing to take off your clothes. Besides, this wasn't exactly the part of a lifetime. To go the limit for a second-rate film would be playing a sucker's game."

When the movie moved to the bedroom, Welch insisted that while shooting the love scene, a towel be placed between her chest and Brown's. This irritated Brown, who took the act personally, and it was not long before a great chill affected their relationship. Once, while eating lunch on the set, Welch asked Brown to pass the salt. "Get it yourself," Brown replied. "It's not black." The trashy *Uncensored*—in which one issue had a front-page story titled "Those Ugly Rumors About Jim Brown"—stated that several media outlets had reported that Brown had spat on Welch after a nasty argument, something Brown vehemently denied. "That's terrible," Brown said; "you don't even spit on a dog."

"Jim just sort of withdrew into himself," Welch said at the time, "and he never came out. I hate animosity myself, but if somebody wants to keep up the silent thing, that's all right with me."

Brown moved on from his *100 Rifles* experience and discovered there was an interesting irony at work in his early films. "More and more, in his films, he is being given love scenes," wrote Kleiner. "So far, he had none with an actress playing a white girl. In *The Split* he has some torrid scenes with Diahann Carroll, a Negro playing a Negro. In *Kenner* he is romantically linked with Madlyn Rhue, a white actress playing an East Indian. In *100 Rifles* there are some rough love scenes—so rough that both *Life* and *Look* decided not to print pictures of them—with Raquel Welch, a white actress playing an American Indian."

That changed when Brown performed an intense love scene with actress Stella Stevens in the 1972 film *Slaughter*. When Stevens was contacted about doing a nude love scene with Brown, she was not hesitant, despite the taboo of interracial love on the big screen. "Before we shot that scene they cleared the room except for a few key people," Stevens recalls. "It was very intense.

"It was definitely an issue at the time that I was white and he was black," she says now. "I thought it was a great public statement at the time that we made it. We were saying that the color of skin is irrelevant. It was a public statement of common sense. Some people in Hollywood hated me for what I did and some people loved it. I did have some irate people say some nasty things to me after the movie. They criticized me for enjoying the scene too much. There were ugly men in Hollywood calling me a 'nigger lover.' There were men screaming at the movie screens, yelling at my character.

"There were good and bad things about making that movie," remembers Stevens, who would go on to star in *The Poseidon Adventure*. "One of the good things was working with Jim and his professionalism. He was wonderful to work with. I enjoyed my time with him. One of the bad things was that *Slaughter* was low budget."

The reviews of Brown's performances ranged from calling him an average actor to praising his abilities. "Jim Brown bulls his way through *The Split* in acceptable fashion," wrote *Plain Dealer* movie reviewer Emerson Batdorff, "neither adding a lot, except for his big physical presence, nor distracting at all. Brown, who used to push other fellows around on the field for the Cleveland Browns, now pushes people around in the movies. He took up movie acting in an intensely wooden fashion a few years ago and it is a pleasure to be able to report that in this one he has relaxed quite a bit and even carries a certain amount of conviction."

Brown's life had changed drastically, in some ways for the better. There were no longer muscled-up men trying to decapitate him on frozen football fields. He had entered a new world and was faring well in it. But he would once again run into two old adversaries that mixed to produce a poisonous concoction: his übercontrolling nature, particularly when it came to women, and his ugly, violent temper.

IN THE EARLY 1960s, Brown was cited for driving without a license. As that decade came to a close, there was another insignificant traffic case involving Brown. Though there is no way to prove this, Brown's traffic stops were probably a result of his being black and driving a nice car, his 1966 Cadillac convertible, or simply being a star and piloting a nice automobile. Maybe it was some combination of the two. When Brown returned briefly to Cleveland, he was stopped by police and charged with speeding, driving left of center, and driving without a license. He was clocked at 39 miles per hour in a 25-mile-per-hour area. He was eventually fined for the speeding and improper passing, while the license accusation was dismissed when he produced the license in municipal court.

Back in Los Angeles, at his party palace, Brown was not free from legal woes or run-ins with the cops and his many women.

Brown dated models and feminists, drug-using babes and strait-laced church women. He dated all races, all religions. Jim liked his women beautiful and young and thin and smart, but those were his only prerequisites. In 1968 he was dating both Gloria Steinem, the magazine journalist and budding feminist, and Eva Bohn-Chin, the stunning model who would later pose in *Playboy* for its special "Girls of Munich" edition, and someone who would surely never have guessed that she would one day lie sprawled under the balcony in Brown's condominium, with a dislocated shoulder and head trauma, and that Brown would be charged with assault and intent to commit murder.

Bohn-Chin and Brown met in London while Brown was filming *The Dirty Dozen*. She was his type: a beautiful woman with a slight build and small breasts, and ten years younger than the thirty-two-year-old Brown. In the 1972 *Playboy* edition she stands in front of a mirror, wearing only a long-sleeved yellow shirt and red socks, leaving her ample rear end uncovered. "In a reflective mood," the magazine says, "TV bit player Eva Maria Bohn-Chin—at her flat in the Schwabing district—confesses a desire 'to be the ideal of other black German girls.' " Their physical attraction was instant and intense, with their differences serving as a sort of igniting fluid. She was the daughter of a Jamaican diplomat who had married a baroness. She was born in Germany and educated in Switzerland, and for most of her life she jet-setted around the world, modeling in Rome, London, and Paris, while Brown was breaking records in Cleveland.

Their relationship was sometimes volatile, even violent; yet, as Brown has stated in his second autobiography and media reports illustrate, they still fell in love. They went together to London's pubs, clubs, and restaurants, and had sex not just with each other, but with other women they invited into their sexual trysts. There were nasty arguments followed by peace and sex. Brown says he has slapped her several times (Brown had slapped other women as well), and she hit him. Their relationship vacillated in this way for many months.

With his wife and three children still in Cleveland, Brown moved Bohn-Chin into his West Hollywood condominium. The passionate fights, the violence, the sexual highs, continued. In June 1968, what seemed inevitable occurred, as a fierce argument led to the police being called by a neighbor. According to police and media reports, two officers appeared at Brown's door, stating that a neighbor had heard screaming and what sounded like loud thuds, which the neighbor thought were bodies hitting the walls. "We'd like to come in," one of the officers stated.

Brown was arrogant and defiant. "No," he replied, "you're not." Brown was sweating and breathing heavily, police said. "There's nothing wrong in my apartment. You people can't seem to find enough wrong in my apartment." He then slammed the door in the officers' faces, police reports state. When they knocked again, an angry Brown returned and opened the door a crack. "What?" Brown reportedly said to the police. He argued vehemently, saying, according to them: "You big white cops and your goddamned system. Everything is against the Negroes. If you're coming in you're going to have to shoot me first. Well, come on ahead, but you're going over me."

Did Brown really state those words? They certainly reflect how many blacks felt about some people in law enforcement. Brown was close friends with an officer in the Los Angeles Police Department, but it was clear Brown still distrusted some cops.

When one of the officers attempted to shove his way inside, Brown hit him with a right forearm, the police claimed. The police maintain that Brown's shove sent the five-foot-nine, 165-pound deputy back seven feet. It is possible that is exaggerated; it is also possible that Brown was strong enough to knock a smaller man much farther than seven feet.

When other police showed up, Brown reportedly said, "You got the rest of your white help here now, don't you?" Brown finally relented and let the officers in. He was handcuffed and moved to the police car. When officers searched the house, the police report states, a five-inch patch of hair was discovered on a large rug. There was blood on the rug, on the walls, on a towel, and on a bedspread, the report states. Police say they found Bohn-Chin sprawled and barely conscious underneath the balcony, wearing a partially bloodied long white dress. Police estimated she had fallen twenty feet. She had landed near a tall plant and a fence, on hardened concrete. When the police reached her side she started moaning, "No, no, no, no." They moved her to County-USC Medical Center with a left shoulder separation and a number of bruises across her face and head.

The question became, how did she get there?

"I did not throw her off anything," Brown told me when I interviewed him while he was in prison. "I did not throw her off that balcony. I was not accused of that. That was totally fabricated. It was a lie. I have never thrown anybody off of anything. She was trying to protect me.

"Much of what the media has written about me and the things with women have been either exaggerated or totally false," he said. "I do think there have been times when I should have been in more control of myself. But a lot of the things that have been said about me in the press have been said only because I'm Jim Brown."

"I loved life," Bohn-Chin says in Spike Lee's *Jim Brown: All-American*, with a heavy German accent. "Why should I jump? To become a cripple or whatever? Why should I do this?"

She says of the aftermath of her experience: "I'm a damaged person."

"I treat people with respect, and that includes women," Brown told the author. "I'm not the person people often portray me as. I'm not the violent monster that people claim I am."

Bohn-Chin was urged by prosecutors to press charges against Brown, but she refused, claiming then she had not been tossed off the balcony, but instead fell accidentally while crawling down the balcony to escape the police, which would be amusing if the incident were not so disturbing. Investigators were highly suspicious of her story, but there was nothing they could do. She insisted there was no violence involved and what happened to her was an accident. Brown has always maintained that she jumped.

"There was not sufficient evidence to convict," one of the city's district attorneys, Phillips Mueller, told the *Los Angeles Times* on June 11, 1968. "This is aside from the fact that the woman would not sign the complaint." The case remained open, but the charge of assault with intent to commit murder was dropped. Still, what happened to Brown was constant news in Los Angeles and Cleveland. Brown kept mum after making bail, but for years afterward newspapers across the country were filled with stories about Brown's scrapes with the law, his various court hearings, and other lawsuits and accusations of violence. He pleaded no contest to the charge of resisting arrest stemming from the confrontation with the LAPD in his West Hollywood apartment, and in January 1969 a judge fined Brown $375 for striking the deputy. In 1972, after the Internal Revenue Service filed a $92,366 tax lien against Brown, claiming he owed money from his moviemaking in Europe, among other things, the divorce action filed by Sue finally wound its way through the court system. According to court records, Judge John L. Maxwell ordered Brown to pay Sue $2,500 a month in alimony and $100 a week support for each of the three children and to pay for their medical bills until they turned twenty-one years old. He was also ordered to finance their college education. Brown had to relinquish ownership of their Cleveland home and pay for the $45,000 condominium Sue and the kids had lived in since their separation.

When a soft-spoken Sue addressed the court in one of the hearings, she stated that Brown had supported the family adequately for some time, but that had changed in February 1971, when Brown, she alleged, sent very little financial support. Beginning that August, she told the court, he sent nothing at all.

The press followed all of Brown's various escapades, smelling a juicy story. There were as many photographs of Brown's various dates as there were stories about his brushes with the law. He was photographed by United Press International at the Western White House, an estate overlooking the ocean in San Clemente, California, that Nixon had bought in 1969, shaking hands with President Nixon and Mrs. Nixon as Brown entered one of their parties. The story made certain to point out Brown's date, who was obviously much younger than Brown. Later the following headline appeared in the Cleveland *Plain Dealer*: "Jim Brown Slated to Wed Girl, 18." Her name was Diane LaVerne Stanley and she was the daughter of a Philadelphia lawyer. Stanley herself was a prelaw student at Clark College in Atlanta. Brown was thirty-seven years old. They never married.

Nothing tantalizes the media like arrests, sex, and violence, and Brown would give reporters their fair share of each. When he was inducted into the football Hall of Fame in Canton, Ohio, in 1971—a foregone conclusion indeed, but still a special moment—the event was almost relegated to insignificance. (But his former costar and friend Stella Stevens came to Canton and, during a Hall of Fame dinner, greeted Brown by sitting in his lap.)

"I'm loyal to Jim, and he and a bunch of us from the Browns

days remain close friends to this day, so I say this in that context," says Wooten. "I don't get into his personal life. But I do think a lot of the troubles Jim went through were invented by people. They took advantage of the fact he was famous. None of us is perfect and we all make mistakes, but I really do believe a lot of that stuff was bullshit. I'm not going further than that."

While Brown did have a violent temper that could become dangerous, and he did use violence against women, inexcusably, some of the accusations against him were questionable. One such moment happened in August 1970. When Brown was driving back from a round of golf in Beverly Hills with basketball star Bill Russell, Brown's car hit fifty-two-year-old Charles Brush's vehicle from behind. A confrontation ensued. Brush contended, media reports show, that Brown refused to provide his driver's license to Brush, got back into his car, and began to speed off. Initially, Brush maintained that as Brown drove away, Brown's car collided with him, planting Brush on the windshield, and as Brown increased speed, Brush claimed he clung to the wipers. When Brown stopped the car, Brush claimed, Brown threw him from the windshield onto the ground.

Brown was arrested and charged with felony assault and misdemeanor battery. Photographers snapped shots of a handcuffed Brown being escorted into prison, shackled to a group of rapists and robbers and thugs. "I walk tall," Brown told reporters as he was taken into the jail. "I do my thing. I feel I stay within the law. Being who I am, it is all out of proportion."

On February 5, 1970, a jury of seven women and five men, who had listened to Brown testify on his own behalf on the witness stand, took just thirty minutes to acquit Brown of all charges. It probably did not help Brush's case that he sued Brown for $1.25 million soon after the charges were filed.

Brown may have been the victim of an at-times voyeuristic

public, overly aggressive law enforcement, and racially insensitive media. A friend of Brown's says that Brown once referred to the press as the "nigger-baiting media." But Brown also consistently repeated mistakes and sometimes allowed his rage to control him. People who were close to Brown knew which buttons not to push. In arguments with friends, teammates, and lovers, Brown would announce when he was on the verge of losing his temper, and some of those people knew when to back off, and some did not. That is when Brown was indeed at times inexcusably abusive and violent, particularly with women. Once that line had been crossed, his anger could rarely be assuaged until it was too late.

In public, with perfect strangers who did not know any of this, that line was crossed constantly. Some people wanted to test the tough Brown, test to see if that reputation was indeed warranted. A few found out the hard way that it was. "There were times when I would see him put on that mean face with other people," remembered his onetime costar Stevens, "and when he did that, look out, he was fearsome."

In yet another scrape, Brown served a one-day sentence in the Los Angeles County Jail following an altercation with golf pro Frank Snow. The golfer maintained that Brown slapped him in the face, punched him in the ribs, and wrapped both of his hands around his neck. Brown maintained that Snow initiated the fight by picking up a golf club and threatening Brown with it. The argument was triggered by a dispute over where to place a ball. Whoever started it, what was clear was that Snow had suffered a concussion and other injuries. Following a two-day trial, a judge found Brown guilty of misdemeanor battery.

Each arrest, each negative article, seemed to make Brown more angry and bitter. His rhetoric publicly became more challenging and pungent, even when it was well meaning. Brown initiated a decades-long cold war with his alma mater, Syracuse, by accusing football coach Ben Schwartzwalder—Brown's old nemesis—of not just racism but of paying white players cash in violation of NCAA rules.

The turmoil started when eight black Syracuse football players were suspended by Schwartzwalder after missing portions of spring practice in 1970. They claimed the coach had punished them because they were black, and they requested help from Brown to resolve the matter. Brown responded by blasting Schwartzwalder and accusing the school of violating NCAA rules. University officials were furious with Brown.

Though he spent the decade continuing to be a groundbreaker in the areas of entertainment and civil rights, the various charges and countercharges and legal actions sapped integrity from some of the great deeds he was accomplishing. One news article in a Cleveland paper even wrote about how Brown's mother, Theresa, faced eviction from her home for being five months behind in her rent. Though an eviction notice was filed in municipal court, Theresa was quoted by the media as saying she knew nothing about the problem.

In August 1969, Brown returned to Cleveland to support a rhythm and blues band called Friends of Distinction, which he was bankrolling. Brown entered Public Hall wearing a gaudy white silk suit, flaring bell bottoms, and a long scarf. He was stunningly handsome, and also irritated. When a reporter asked about the Bohn-Chin incident, Brown responded angrily. "Bill Russell said it all," Brown stated. "I have nothing to add." Russell believed that Brown had been mistreated by police.

Brown also took a swipe at the city of Cleveland, which had grown increasingly frustrated with him, as he had with the city. Brown spoke to several people on his way into the show, and one of them was a teenager interested in getting into the music business. "First you have to get out of Cleveland and out to the West Coast," Brown told the young man. "There's a lot more freedom for Negroes there." Some Clevelanders were angered by those words.

More people in Cleveland became infuriated when later he told the *Plain Dealer:* "The only thing I miss about Cleveland is the fans as they related to me on and off the field. I never got booed. They treated me very nicely on an individual level. Other than that, Cleveland reminds me of a bombed-out racist city that needs revamping. It's the only city I've been in where I feel totally separated on a racial level—the whites on the West Side, the Blacks on the East Side." That of course was not the case. Brown had seen plenty of racially divided metropolises in his time, including cities like Dallas, where he was well aware of the humiliating segregation suffered by college and professional athletes. Part of Brown's motivation was to strike back at the city that sometimes treated many of the black Cleveland players—away from the playing field—quite poorly.

Brown did not stop there. When told by the reporter that blacks had integrated several suburbs, Brown replied, "That's only money. Blacks pay an extra $10,000 to buy a house." In another interview, Brown said something that encapsulated his views about his various legal issues. "I'm no angel," Brown told reporter Will Grimsley. "If I was a goody-goody, I'd be a psychological wreck by this time. I'd be in a straitjacket. Do you think I could keep throwing girls out windows, knocking policemen forty feet in the air and running down guys on the turnpike without them nailing me for it one day? I'd have to bribe every jury and judge in town. But I've never been convicted. I've just been harassed. I've been hit so much I don't sting anymore. They can call me a nigger. It doesn't bother me.

When a controversy comes up, I take it and look my accuser in the eye. I don't look at my shoes when I talk to anybody. I know what I am. I only have to live with myself."

MANY OF BROWN'S movie roles still centered on his physicality, and Brown did not shy away from using his attractiveness as a draw. In one of the more interesting moves he made during his decade of mutability, Brown posed nude in the September issue of *Playgirl* in 1974. When photographers arrived at Brown's home in Los Angeles, they were greeted by a relaxed Brown, and it was not long before the clothes came off, and he was posing nude in various positions and locales. In one, Brown leans against a piano, standing tall, his abdominal muscles rippling, his legs cut, his bulging manhood swinging freely, and his eyes starring upward. It is odd to see the player football historians call one of the toughest men in the history of sports the focus of a four-page centerfold.

The photographs were accompanied by hokey text, since, of course, people only read such magazines for the articles. The woman reporter wrote: "I ask about women and relationships. What are his expectations? He has, after all, been accused in the past by numerous journalists of beating up lady friends—being domineering, unreasonable, and just in general, all-around male chauvinist."

Brown's response was not surprising. Brown did not care if his words offended or appeared to be dogmatic. "Well, I guess I'm sort of old fashioned," he told the magazine. "I expect my lady to be loyal to me, to be feminine, to be interested in having my babies, to be interested in being with me—not to be off doing her individual thing. Because if she's off doing her thing, I can mess with a thousand chicks. Why should I give up a thousand chicks for her to be off developing her own career? Why should I have one woman if she's going to be away from me all the time?"

While posing for *Playgirl* was billed as Brown demonstrating his sensuality as well as his comfort with his sexuality, it was neither of those things. The shoot was simply one indication that Brown was searching for a niche and, in some ways searching for himself.

While Brown was still no Academy Award winner, he was also no longer all gams and no acting game, even if the reviews were not exactly gushing. *Plain Dealer* movie reviewer Emerson Batdorff wrote about Brown's film *Dark of the Sun,* "It is a melodrama of an expedition in the perilous Congo in which Jimmy Brown, late of the playing field of Cleveland, makes more of a mark than in his previous films. He's less wooden." In *Slaughter* Brown is far from stilted. He's smooth, talented, and commanding, playing a former Green Beret soldier whose parents are killed in a mysterious bomb blast. Brown shot the film in Mexico City and was paid about $750,000. He also does a fine job in the sequel, *Slaughter's Big Rip-off.* In a third movie shot in the 1970s, Brown is a nightclub owner who takes on the mob in *Black Gunn.*

However, the acting jobs for Brown were quickly drying up, despite his improved acting skills. In an interview with journalist David Elliott in 1972, Brown explained why he thought his career was stalled. "The whole movie business went into a slump," Brown said. "But that wasn't the reason I didn't work. I was blackballed from the business. In fact, I actually saw the letter that was circulated among the producers in Hollywood, telling them why I ought to be kept out of pictures."

Whites were fascinated with Jim Brown's race for much of his movie career. Too fascinated, actually. Though his achievements on the field and in Hollywood were historic, some could never get beyond his ethnicity, with some Hollywood producers nixing Brown for challenging acting roles. A book written by a Brown admirer named

James Toback, who was white, exemplified the ridiculous obsession with Brown's skin color by Hollywood and the white media. It was called *Jim: The Author's Self-Centered Memoir on the Great Jim Brown.* The *New York Times* book review stated in part:

He is a Jew with a Harvard education who is insecure about his manhood and who, he says, believes that the black man, or at least Jim Brown, is the most sexual thing going in America. Associating with Brown constitutes a sort of proving ground for Toback's sexuality. He has played at being a Norman Mailer "white Negro" and failing at this—"O funny, too-hip, freaky Jew"—now feels it absolutely necessary to encounter the genuine article. Richard Wright has written that the Negro is America's metaphor, specifically, I submit, America's sexual metaphor. Similar to Jack Johnson, whom midget-sized Jack London felt he had to meet, Jim Brown's image as an athlete and more recently his image as a movie star, fits this metaphor. Black males become sex fetishes, objects of sexual divination. They are credited with possession of a sexuality that whites feel they lack and can somehow acquire through lynching and castration or through intimate association with black males. Toback freely admits this. Writing about Brown, getting to know him, he would not only hopefully learn of and perhaps acquire some of those sexual powers, but could also hope to approach and to understand certain mysteries in America, as well as to measure one of her largest and darkest heroes. For the true stranger, the true sexual outlaw and source of power in America was not the Jew but, once removed, the boo. All of which calls to mind the familiar stereotype of the black man as "brute nigger" or "King Kong," the beast, the monster, before whose awesome animal powers we tremble and quake.

The seeming novelty of a black man—intelligent, rogue, and sexual—eventually wore off in Hollywood. Brown's scrapes with the law, and this phenomenon of the movie industry becoming bored with Brown, led to his movie career quickly dying by the end of the 1970s, and Brown's bitterness increasing exponentially and just as rapidly.

"I'm blackballed from movies now, at least those that produced my major motion pictures," he told the *Plain Dealer* in June 1979. "They don't like me because I can't be controlled. I've always been outspoken. If too many whites in America love you, you aren't doing anything. Watch O. J. Simpson in the next two years. Now that he is getting a divorce and dating white women, they'll find a way to discredit him."

1980 AND 1990

LOST

Richard [Pryor] was one of the few people in life that ever hurt me. He hurt my heart. Because I was genuine with him and I respected him and I never thought that he would ever double-cross me.

—**Jim Brown**
in Spike Lee's *Jim Brown: All-American*

I look at South Central L.A. and see those bars on the windows, and I have to look at my people. Because if my people were doing the right thing, those bars wouldn't be on those windows and kids wouldn't be killing each other. People say to me, "Why would you talk about black guys?" Well, truth is truth.

—**Jim Brown**
to the Newhouse News Service in 1993

Jim Brown was flailing. Without football, without major movies, there was little to propel him. His flaws stood out in relief, as his muscles once did. He still had his troubles with women, he still had his hubris and his temper, he still had his dander up against the police and the media.

At this point in his life, Brown found himself in the same place as many other NFL players who walk away from professional football: he was searching for his fix of adrenaline, the next thing that could captivate him the way football did. Some ex–NFL players searched for jobs; Brown searched for a purpose.

He seemed at times to wander aimlessly, moving in and out of ventures both civic-minded and important, while dabbling in other things that were frivolous. The great football legend, the civil rights leader, was on television hawking celebrity bowling tournaments for $20,000 a pop.

The Black Economic Union had faded, though Brown's civic-minded nature and genuine care about the poor and underrepresented had not. Increasingly, with little attention at first, Brown continued to visit some of the most dangerous and decrepit neighborhoods in Los Angeles, places far from his towering home in the Hollywood Hills. Of course, Brown could not proceed far without some gripping controversy interrupting the historic good he would create.

ON JUNE 11, 1980, a solemn Brown entered the burn center at Sherman Oaks Hospital in California. In one of the rooms, lying on a sterilized bed, was Richard Pryor. From the waist up, his body was disfigured with third-degree burns—he was seared. Little shocked Brown at this point in his life—he'd been seared himself by his high-intensity life, from racism at Syracuse, to an NFL title victory in Cleveland, to his role as a black Hollywood sex symbol, to beating, first, a sexual-assault rap, and then, attempted-murder charges.

This sight . . . this was different from any of those things. Pryor looked almost inhuman, and when the comedian spoke, it was barely above a whisper. One day after Brown and Pryor met, a doctor would tell Pryor he had a fifty-fifty chance of survival. Pryor looked pained and stiff and fragile, as if, should Brown touch him, he might splinter into pieces.

The two friends spoke, and media reports at the time portrayed the conversation as remarkably emotional. It was more than that. It was intimate. Brown and Pryor vowed protection and friendship. Pryor promised Brown that he was ready to fight for his life, and Brown in turn told Pryor he would be there for him. The two had been friends for fifteen years, through Pryor's and Brown's many linkings with women, their breakups, their similarly volcanic angers. As he gazed at his friend, tears came to Brown's eyes.

Brown was not helping Pryor recover from a horrific freebasing accident out of some self-serving need to be in the public eye. This

facet of Brown showed him when he had full control of his aloof
and arrogant personas. Brown had evolved into the kind of distant
father to some of his children that his father had been to him. Yet
inside the stern Brown was the man who cared deeply about friends
and the downtrodden. Though Pryor was a significant star, he was
now reduced to a human being in unbelievable pain. That pain triggered Brown's protective instincts. Brown could be violent and
shallow, while being equally intuitive, kind, and loving.

According to Brown's book *Out of Bounds* and media reports,
over the next few months Brown helped Pryor recuperate from his
ruinous wounds, but in the end Pryor, a brilliant but self-hating
person, turned on Brown, shunning Brown once he regained his
health.

Pryor used Brown as material in his stand-up routine *Live on the
Sunset Strip,* which was made into a movie in 1982. In one scene
Pryor speaks of his drug addiction and how it nearly destroyed him,
to the point where he became a recluse and began having an imaginary conversation with his crack pipe. Like all of Pryor's splendid
comedy, the humor is ripe and true. "I ain't been out my room in
eight weeks," Pryor says in the film, speaking of how the drugs controlled him. "Funk is my shadow. Funk be just hanging all over me
talking about, 'Hey, don't wash.' Then finally my old lady called Jim
Brown up. 'Jim going to come over and talk to you.' "

" 'Fuck Jim Brown!' " Pryor says he responded. " 'I'll show Jim
Brown. I'm the man. I don't give a fuck. Ain't nobody afraid of
Jim Brown here.' Jim was coming in the driveway. I got all
nervous. . . . Pipe said, 'C'mon, Rich, we'll show Jim. Shit, Jim don't
scare nobody. That's right, Rich.' I started smoking. 'Hey, Jim.
How ya' doin', bro'?' Jim had psychology. Jim would go, 'Wanna go
roller-skating?' [Then] Jim say, 'Whatcha' gonna' do?' "

Through his humor, Pryor was telling a basically true story, in
which Brown sincerely and passionately attempted to save his

friend, though, in the end, unsuccessfully. Pryor would continue to sink into his drug-induced chasm.

When Pryor ostracized Brown after the accident, it wasn't the last time he would disappoint Brown. After some months of not speaking, the two men would go into business together, and on June 9, 1983, at a crowded press conference in Los Angeles, Brown and Pryor announced the birth of Indigo Productions, which Brown hoped would become a home for black writers, actors, and producers, where they could attempt to make movies, even if they were smaller-budget films. With Brown as president of the company, and a five-year contract worth $40 million with Columbia Pictures, as well as the backing of Coca-Cola, the company seemed to have a serious chance to help black filmmakers.

The resulting confusion and disbanding of the company were inevitable. The breakup went beyond the standard Hollywood euphemism of "creative differences." Despite his declarations to friends and family, Pryor was a troubled soul, possibly still an addict, and addicts do not always make the best business leaders.

The split between the two men and the embarrassing firing of Brown from Indigo was ugly and public. The press was orgasmic at the sight of two powerful men brawling, and eventually race became part of the coverage. In addition to Pryor firing Brown, three other black staffers from the production company were also dismissed.

The Associated Press reported that the NAACP was extremely irritated at the outcome, and though Pryor publicly apologized for the firings and declared the enterprise a mistake, the NAACP was not convinced that the firings were Pryor's doing. Willis Edwards, executive director of the Hollywood–Beverly Hills NAACP, told the AP in December of 1983: "It's a slap in the face because we were working very hard with Jim Brown. Richard Pryor couldn't just fire Jim Brown by himself when a major company [Columbia] is putting up the $40 million. I think they're using Pryor as a scapegoat, making everybody think he did this when it fact it was Coke and Columbia making the move." The AP contacted Stan Robertson, identified by the news organization as the highest-ranking black spokesman for Columbia, who promptly denied Edwards's claims. "To say Coca-Cola or Columbia Pictures put pressure on Pryor is totally untrue. Pryor is his own man. His deal with Columbia gives him the right to hire and fire."

For his part Brown publicly stayed quiet, refusing to engage in a nasty discourse with Pryor. It took remarkable restraint for Brown to stay silent and let it go, two things he never does easily, but in this instance he did both.

THE TWO MEN who had despised each other for so long and said such malevolent things about each other for so long finally made their peace in a hallway outside of a suite at the Pontiac Silverdome in Detroit, right before Super Bowl XVI.

Brown has described in his second book the almost accidental meeting between him and Paul Brown. But the words Jim uses are dispassionate, almost pasteurized, and do not do justice to how important the brief meeting was between two of the most important men in football history. Paul's son, Mike, the Cincinnati Bengals' general manager, saw Jim, and invited him to their suite. Brown writes that he knocked on the door, and out stepped Paul.

They spoke for a few minutes and told a few stories. Then it was over. As short as it was, it was vital. Paul and Jim had officially and quietly ended their bitter quarrel.

ON OCTOBER 2, 1984, President Ronald Reagan, from aboard Air Force One, placed a phone call to a man in the bowels of Soldier Field, home of the Chicago Bears. "Congratulations," Reagan began.

The man on the other line listened attentively, and when Reagan finished speaking, Walter Payton thanked him, and then told the president: "Give my regards to Nancy." Then he added: "This call really means a lot to me."

Payton's 154 yards on that day pushed him past Brown's career mark of 12,312 yards. Brown's career rushing record had stood since 1965 and had been considered almost unbreakable. But two runners closed in on it. One was Payton, and the other was Pittsburgh Steelers great Franco Harris. Brown admired Payton, and as Payton approached his mark, Brown was extremely complimentary. He told Charles Heaton from the Cleveland *Plain Dealer*: "Walter tries. He gives it his all. You have to respect that. He doesn't take the easy way out. I wouldn't mind if Walter breaks my record." Payton once told the author before sadly succumbing to cancer: "Jim Brown was always very gracious to me and I always appreciated that." (Conversely, Brown intensely disliked Chicago Bears coach Mike Ditka, now an ESPN analyst, whom Brown referred to as "fascist, loud, could talk a streak of paramilitary bullshit, but [was not] exactly Phi Beta Kappa.")

Brown did not treat Harris with the same deference, however, openly mocking his running ability and saying that Harris did not belong in the same conversation with Brown and Payton. Brown looked aimless and sounded bitter, occasionally publicly ripping the NFL as soft and glamorous instead of what the league had been when he played, which was gritty. He thought television was destroying the game. "I think Jim was stating what a lot of the older players felt," says his friend and former teammate John Wooten. "Players that played in the 1950s and 1960s think the game was tougher then. Jim was the only one with the guts to state it."

Brown was not wrong. In his day, players did not shimmy after scoring a touchdown. They did not leave games to take short breaks after long runs; instead, they played through all kinds of breaks—broken ribs, broken toes, broken noses, broken everything. Television did not command the game. Players were not as obsessed with money.

It was just football. It was just men in love with the sport.

Nevertheless, his public words still sounded angry. In fact, it is likely that Brown was aggravated that mediocre runners with a fraction of his skills were making millions of dollars, while the players of his generation had to fight for a few thousand.

His attacks on Harris were brutal. Brown despised it when Harris ran out of bounds to avoid a hit. Brown never did that. He did the opposite. Once he saw the sideline, Brown would stutter, slowing to avoid it, and jam his forearm or shoulder into a tackler. Each time Brown would watch a Steelers game and see the 230-pound Harris scamper toward the sidelines to avoid a tackler, Brown became bothered, almost taking it personally. He began to publicly challenge Harris, and when the exceptional football writer Paul Zimmerman from *Sports Illustrated* penned a story on how the game had deteriorated, it played right into Brown's mind-set. He talked of making a comeback, and the magazine put him on the cover, wearing a Los Angeles Raiders uniform. There was no way Brown was making a return, but he enjoyed the public speculation and attention, especially the headline, which proclaimed "Just What the Boring NFL Needed."

"Once giants like Brown roamed the NFL. Every team had an identity," Zimmerman wrote. "The Packers against the Lions—the mere thought of that battle made you tingle. Alex Karras and Joe Schmidt laying it on Paul Hornung and Jim Taylor. Ray Nitschke and Dave Robinson and all the rest of those superstars. These days Robinson would be a designated blitzer. Schmidt and Nitschke would be situation linebackers; they'd come out on passing downs. Karras would be a noseguard, Hornung would be the single back in the one-back offense and Taylor would come in for short-yardage plays."

"Why would a 230-pound man run out of bounds?" Brown told the media. "Why is everyone dancing, mugging for the camera? Where's the danger in the game? Where are the characters and the warriors? You talk about records. Why even compare me to Franco? He played thirteen years, I played nine. He played something like fifty more games. Man gets four strikes to my three, where's the significance? My performance spoke for itself. I don't want to hear any shit about Franco."

In Cleveland and around the nation, few people took Brown seriously. "We can save money because we still have his chin strap and his helmet," Cleveland Browns owner Art Modell told the *Washington Post*.

The story continued: "Certainly out of admiration and respect I would be willing to listen to whatever he has on his mind," Raiders owner Al Davis said after hearing that Brown had in mind to ask Modell to relinquish his playing rights, now that he was eighteen years retired, to the Raiders. "But quite frankly, right now, our total concentration has to be on this season. . . . Yesterday, I thought it was just a passing note. This morning, I've had all sorts of calls." The article added: "Yes, the Cleveland *Plain Dealer* spurred lots of telephone activity by getting on the horn with Brown, now a long-time Hollywoodian, and interviewing him about the threat to his NFL career rushing record by Franco Harris and Walter Payton. "I have the greatest respect for Franco Harris, but he is just hanging around to try to break my record," Brown said. "Even if Franco beats my record by 500 yards, I will come back."

Eventually, the entire episode became a circus, unworthy of the dignity with which Brown normally carried himself. Brown would lose to Harris in an atrocious 40-yard dash that was supposed to be some kind of challenge between two great former runners, but instead tarnished the images of both. Harris would depart football before he broke Brown's all-time rushing mark. (The record is now held by Emmitt Smith.)

BEFORE HE BECAME a nationally recognized lawyer, before his name was linked with one Orenthal James Simpson and the murder trial of the twentieth century, Johnnie L. Cochran was known in Los Angeles as a man who fought for the poor and took on the police in numerous inner-city police-brutality cases.

"People think of me only in terms of the O.J. trial, but I was a lawyer long before that," he told the author in a brief interview several years ago. (Cochran died of an inoperable brain tumor in March 2005.)

An experienced attorney, a popular man, and a man of principle, Cochran was contacted by Brown, who was, yet again, accused of violence against a woman.

"The case was weak from the beginning," Cochran told the author. "I believed Jim, but I don't think many people in Los Angeles did. When you spoke to people about it, in the grocery store or in the barbershops, they would tell me, 'Jim done did it this time. He's not getting out of this one.' "

The media did not initially disclose the woman's name, instead describing her as a thirty-three-year-old schoolteacher. But she was Margo Tiff, a friend of Brown's for several years. Tiff claimed that in the winter of 1985 after an argument involving her and another female friend of Brown's, Tiff was angrily told by Brown to leave his Hollywood Hills home. Soon after that, she filed a complaint with police, accusing Brown of sexual assault. Though there were serious questions about the veracity of her claims, the legal system moved forward, and the media spit out damaging headlines about the incident, seizing on the history of allegations of violence against Brown. It was, once again, an ugly moment in Brown's life, though this time, it is likely, he was unjustly accused.

When Cochran became involved, he said in an interview that he never doubted Brown, though in Brown's second autobiography, Brown portrays Cochran, a former Los Angeles prosecutor, as too political for Brown's liking, treading too carefully, in order to avoid angering friends in the prosecutor's office. Their differences became obvious when Brown wanted to call a press conference to declare his innocence and Cochran wanted Brown to stay silent. "In handling my case, Johnnie was proceeding with a certain ambivalence," Brown wrote. "Johnnie was a capable, scrupulous lawyer, but he was also a political creature, in a political profession. It seemed as if he wanted to keep me under wraps because he didn't want to embarrass the prosecution, which consisted of former colleagues."

Brown won out, and at one press conference in the halls of the courthouse, surrounded by reporters and gawking onlookers, he told the media: "This is ridiculous. Everybody is lying. I want the total truth to come out. My name has been totally destroyed."

During the press conference, Cochran did something he had done many times before and would do again: he eloquently defended his client when almost everyone felt he had to be guilty. "Basically we feel real strongly that these charges should have never been filed," he told a gang of reporters. "Jim Brown will be acquitted. You can count on that. The district attorney's office has a witness who was there, who clearly exonerates Jim Brown, and we're going to try to get that evidence before a proper tribune as soon as possible."

A preliminary hearing ensued; by its third day, some four months after newspaper headlines and television programs had portrayed

Brown as a rapist, court testimony from police and witnesses, medical evidence, and other facts indicated that Tiff's allegations were not true; in fact, she was caught in several serious contradictions. The most important witness was Tiff herself, who police claimed changed her testimony about key facts regarding the events of that day. Police detective Tom Maioli testified that what Tiff had stated in court was different from what she had told Maioli when he interviewed her.

Cochran interviewed Dr. Jonathan Ching, the emergency-room physician who examined Tiff on the night of the alleged attack. Ching testified that there was no evidence of vaginal trauma, but there were bruises on Tiff's left wrist and on one of her eyes, and she may have suffered a perforated eardrum. He also stated that Tiff had suffered a bloody nose.

Ching's testifying that there was no physical evidence of a sexual assault severely hurt Tiff's credibility. One of the few pieces of physical evidence was a semen-stained towel, and it could not be determined when the semen was deposited on it, so it was basically useless.

Dino Fulgoni, the deputy district attorney, stated in court, according to an Associated Press report, that the evidence "tends to contradict the allegations. I would not want anyone to be forced to stand trial with the contradictory nature of the proof that's come forward here." He asked municipal court judge Candace Cooper to dismiss all charges, and she granted his request. After the decision was announced, Brown met with the press. "First of all," he said, "I'm glad to be an American because we have a chance in our system, if we're innocent, for the facts to come out."

The media, as usual, excoriated Brown, despite the charges being tossed out of court. A significant number of the country's sportswriters now saw Jim as a troubled soul and a violent man. Elements of both were indeed true, but the articles written about Brown grew extremely nasty in tone and marked a distinct change in how the media viewed him.

Cleveland *Plain Dealer* columnist Bob Dolgan, on February 24, 1985, wrote a scathing, sarcastic piece about Brown under the headline "C'mon, Guys, Leave Poor Jim Alone." The column is run in its entirety to demonstrate just how much some in the media began to mock and dislike Brown:

What do people have against Jim Brown?

Why are they always picking on this clean-cut pillar of American sport, this stalwart hero of the football generations?

It must be jealousy. Brown has been so successful on both the gridiron and in the movies.

You remember some of those immortal films he made, like *Kenner* and *100 Rifles* and *Slaughter* and *Slaughter's Revenge*.

His enemies started on him back in 1963, when he was charged with assault and battery, for allegedly slapping around an 18-year-old Cleveland girl, Brenda Ayres, in a hotel room.

In one of the more memorable quotes that emerged during the case, Brenda said Brown threatened to put her in a room full of naked men.

How terrible. What a rotten thing to say about a full-fledged idol of athleticism.

It was no wonder that Brown was found not guilty.

But Brenda still wouldn't leave the great man alone. She had the nerve to charge him in a paternity suit.

Aghast, a shocked jury acquitted him. It was so logical. How could a man who averaged a magnificent 5.2 yards per carry in football be guilty of such uncouth behavior?

The persecution continued. In 1968, a 22-year-old girl was found semi-conscious under the balcony of Brown's Hollywood apartment.

The police had the bad manners to suggest that big Jim had thrown her off the balcony. He was accused of assault with intent to murder. Holy Jack Armstrong, what a rotten thought.

Fortunately, the charges were dropped when the woman said she had fallen off the balcony by accident. Of course. People fall off balconies every day, don't they?

But the police still claimed a victory. Brown was fined $300 for resisting a police officer in the same case. Some guys never quit when they set out to get you.

Jim was allowed to live in peace for a few years, but then in 1978, the harassment began again. Brown was sentenced to a day in jail and fined $500 for beating up a golf pro in an argument over the placement of a golf ball.

This was unjust. A guy who picks up a golf ball and puts it in an advantageous position deserves to get beat up. Especially when he does it against one of the most magnificent athletes of all time.

Now they are at it again. The other day, Brown was arrested for allegedly raping a 33-year-old woman in Los Angeles. What will they think of next?

Good old Jim says he is innocent. He has always prided himself on telling the truth. The bet here is that the woman who accused him will say it was all a mistake, just the way that other woman did when she fell off the balcony.

Brown is understandably angry over the whole matter. "I'm the last revolutionary of the 1960s," he said. "When my back is broken, the vendetta is over."

What a revolutionary he was in that crucial decade in American history, the 1960s. How can we forget Brown's forays into the civil rights and anti–Vietnam war protests?

When Abbie Hoffman was out there in the streets, Jim

was supporting him by getting rich and making such movies as *Dark of the Sun* and *The Split*.

When the Chicago Seven was put on the rack and the college kids were getting hit on the head by the cops in the Days of Rage at the 1968 political convention, Brown was creating more movie history with spectacles such as *Ice Station Zebra* and *One Down, Two to Go* and *El Condor*.

When Martin Luther King was marching against brutality, Jim was walking around in his Edwardian suits, appearing on Hugh Hefner's TV *Playboy* show and filming landmark pictures such as *Black Gunn* and *Slams*.

Yes sir, old Jim sure was a revolutionary. Remember how he always said he was more interested in green power than black power?

He was always so good, projecting a noble image. He never smoked or drank. He ran up and down hills to preserve his sculptured body, played tennis and basketball. He pontificated against drug users. A godling of that kind cannot be destroyed by mere balconies and loose women.

Now, when he is in his old age, having been defeated by Franco Harris in a 40-yard footrace, the envious continue to pinch and nip him, like Lilliputians tormenting a Gulliver.

They won't even give him a Hollywood Life Achievement Award for his classic movies such as *Take the Hard Ride* and *Escape from Devil's Island* and *Three the Hard Way*.

Why can't they leave him alone?

Dolgan's column illustrates perfectly how badly Brown's arrests and acts of violence had eroded his greatness. His messages had become distorted. When Brown spoke of green versus black power, he was speaking of how in America's capitalist society, blacks needed financial clout more than they did the right to sit in the same diners as whites. If blacks had more economic power, Brown thought, they could buy their own businesses, and racism would not be as stinging a factor.

While Brown did not participate in war protests or win movie awards, he was still iconic in sports, civil rights, and cinematic history. That someone of such heroic proportions as Brown could be treated so flippantly—albeit justifiably so, considering some of his actions—was shocking. The writing shows just how lost Brown had become in the minds of some and how injured his reputation now seemed.

Perhaps realizing that he needed more allies, Brown slowly and deliberately began to rebuild bridges he had burned so easily. He began this process before the rape charges, but intensified the effort afterward. One of the people he reached out to was Modell. After seventeen years, Brown simply picked up the telephone in September 1984 and called Modell at the Browns' team hotel in Los Angeles when Cleveland was in town to play the Rams at Anaheim Stadium.

They went to the game together. They talked about the old days, the old Cleveland Browns, the championship, the greatness of football as it used to be. Football writer Tony Grossi wrote about the meeting and quoted Modell in the *Plain Dealer*. "You know," Modell explained, "he did not leave the Browns under the friendliest of circumstances. He retired in the spring of 1967 after promising he would come back for at least one year. Left us high and dry.

"He announced his resignation in London, England, which I thought was not fair to the people of Cleveland," Modell continued. "So we sort of parted not on the friendliest of terms. So when he called me in Los Angeles at the hotel and asked to go to the game with me I was very, very pleased. It was like renewing old days. I saw Jim Brown in a different light. He wanted to patch up any differences that might exist. And I respected him for that. I said as far as I'm concerned there have never been differences. There's no point in rehashing seventeen years ago. He wanted to come out and make friends again."

BROWN'S RECONNECTION WITH his old team continued in earnest when his second autobiography, *Out of Bounds,* was published in 1989. Brown appeared at Ohio bookstores and made the media rounds in Cleveland in late September and early October of that year. Fans flocked to see him. The ones who had been angry with Brown for his harsh words for Cleveland years before forgave him. The younger fans either didn't know or didn't care.

The team's organization also welcomed him back with open arms, and Brown returned with his usual vigor and, in some ways, his usual outspokenness and bluntness. Upon his return, Modell took Brown on a tour of the facility, and the two men were joined by Ernie Accorsi, then the Browns' general manager. When they reached the training room, the team's sturdy running back Kevin Mack was seated on a table. Mack was a hard-hitting runner who would become one of the best in team history. That didn't matter to Brown. When the two were introduced, Brown looked at Mack, shook his hand, and said: "Quit running out of bounds." Then Brown continued on as if nothing had happened; Mack had just been dealt a stinging hit-and-run insult.

Mack was incredulous, and Accorsi stepped in. "Before you get angry," Accorsi told him, "that's the greatest running back in the history of the NFL."

AFTER HIS CLEVELAND visit, Brown returned to Los Angeles, where he continued his work with the disenfranchised. On the day in 1992 when four police officers were acquitted of using excessive force in the severe beating of Rodney King, parts of Los Angeles went up in flames. There were riots and mass protests. The city would eventually suffer billions of dollars in property damage, fifty-five of its citizens were killed, and more than eight thousand were arrested. As the riots went on, Brown hit the Los Angeles streets, where he traveled with a former gang member who had joined with Brown to try and ease the gang tensions across Los Angeles. The two men ended up in a part of South Central Los Angeles where there were houses destroyed and cars set aflame. Brown was in danger—thousands of people were on that day—but he left un-harmed. The riots that caused so much destruction led to a sort of calm. Brown had been able to strengthen the trust he had formed with gang members.

Nothing had affected Brown as much as seeing young black and Latino men killing one another in the gang-ridden parts of the city and, to some degree, the entire country. It reinforced Brown's thinking that his Amer-I-Can program was desperately needed. He had been billing it as a self-help plan for gang members and the im-prisoned. In many ways, there was little difference between Amer-I-Can and the Black Economic Union. As with the group he began in the 1960s, Brown invested a great deal of his own money into Amer-I-Can, this time some $600,000. The core theories of the two organizations were also similar. Brown did not want gang mem-bers to receive handouts or pity; instead they would work with a network of educators and teachers who would raise the self-esteem of people who had few, if any, role models in their lives.

For years Brown had invited gang members into his Hollywood home. Hundreds, in fact. None of them ever challenged Brown. No one threatened him. Though it was impossible to save everyone, no one ignored his words. He was Jim Brown. He was respected even in that world.

Brown's home was considered neutral ground, so youths who would usually kill one another on sight respected the temporary truce each time they visited his home. It was an unthinkable scene at times: members of some of the most violent gangs in Los Angeles—the Crips, the Bloods, the Blackstone Rangers—walking throughout Brown's home and talking. Gangsters talking instead of killing.

They trusted Brown because they knew he wasn't working for the police and was no punk snitch. If you wanted to change your life, Brown wanted to help you, but only if you were going to help yourself.

Soon, he had convinced the state of California to institute his program into the state's penal system. By 1992, the California Department of Corrections had agreed to a $294,000 contract with Brown, and almost three thousand inmates were participating. Prisoners learned lessons in anger management and bill paying. They learned basic skills that most people take for granted.

By the mid-1990s, Brown's Amer-I-Can had spread to cities and prisons across the country. Brown's actions caught the attention of Capitol Hill, and on February 9, 1994, Brown sat before Senator Herb Kohl and his Subcommittee on Juvenile Justice. The senator wanted to know about Amer-I-Can, and Brown came with a prepared speech, which he read to the committee. Members listened patiently to what was a blunt but enthralling oration.

Chairman Kohl and committee members, my name is Jim Brown. Although I am well known as a former professional football player and movie actor, I am most proud of the capacity in which I speak before you today—as founder and president of the Amer-I-Can program. I am honored to present testimony before the U.S. Senate Judiciary Committee

Juvenile Justice Subcommittee on the topic of what the federal government should be doing to reach out to gang members and other youth at risk to provide them alternatives, opportunities, and support. . . .

. . . Amer-I-Can offers a solution. Not only is the program effective in dealing with behavior that leads to criminal activity, it is effective in offering a positive alternative to individuals that have already become involved in criminal activity. Amer-I-Can is an eighty-hour life-management skills training curriculum which enhances the ability of the individual to become a more productive member of society. It has been developed after consultations with technical experts, behavioral scientists, human resource professionals, psychologists, educators, ministers, former addicts, convicts, and gang members. Amer-I-Can's philosophy is an outgrowth of current and past rehabilitation/community services programs that I have administered, including the Vital Issues Project, Coors Golden Door, and Jobs Plus. It is also a part of my long-term interest in the economic development and collective empowerment of individuals and communities at large, which manifested itself as early as 1968. The Black Economic Union, a nonprofit corporation which I founded, promoted economic empowerment of minorities. . . .

. . . By enlarging the scope of individual lives; by introducing self-determination techniques; by motivating people to have goals; by showing them how to improve and to achieve success and financial stability, Amer-I-Can has literally and figuratively saved lives which would have been lost. As an example, two graduates of the program, ex–gang members lacking high school educations, were the architect and the author of a truce between the Bloods and the Crip sets in four housing projects in the Watts area of Los Angeles. This truce will soon celebrate its second anniversary, and has been directly responsible for a reduction of intergang violence in this area. There are few international truces of such duration. The truce agreement, which was based on the 1948 Arab-Israeli peace accords, is the subject of a scholarly law review article currently being written by Professor Adrien Wing of the University of Iowa College of Law. Professor Wing has accompanied me here today and is prepared to address any questions you may have about her research. The truce agreement is also being revised for possible use by other gangs across the nation. The two remarkable young men responsible for this agreement are not only alumni of our program, but are currently employed as full-time facilitators teaching other participants.

Brown's speech continued as he outlined the program's exact protocols. Many of the committee members were impressed, but others had doubts, particularly after an issue of *GQ* magazine portrayed Brown's Amer-I-Can as a bloated organization that could show few actual results of changed lives. The magazine said Brown's group charged a 40 percent "administrative fee." Brown was irritated about the inference.

Was it true? I was shown one contract from that time period by a business representative who worked with Brown and Amer-I-Can in the 1980s. There was nothing in the contract that indicated any type of fee, let alone a 40 percent one. The representative, who asked not to be identified, said his dealings with Brown were "just fine."

"I would say the best proof that Amer-I-Can is pretty solid," said the businessman, who maintains contacts with both Brown's group and city government officials who do business with Brown's organization, "is that it is still around, has expanded, and there are few complaints about it from what I am told."

The most important aspect of the magazine story was that it showed, yet again, that Brown had trouble controlling his temper. *GQ* writer John Lombardi described how it took him three weeks to gain permission to speak to Brown, and when he did, Lombardi was forced to jump through a series of preinterview hoops by who was then basically Brown's spokesperson, Allysunn Walker. She had warned Lombardi to refer to Brown as "Mr. Brown." He was to "ask permission" before meeting Brown for scheduled appointments and to initiate any "lines of inquiry" that Brown might find irritating with an advance apology. Then she warned: "He might get sick of you at any moment."

Brown was more difficult to arrange a meeting with than a U.S. president. He could also be infinitely more nasty. When Lombardi began treading into sensitive areas about Brown's past, Brown exploded. "No interview!" Brown said. "I don't need no magazine story, big guy. Y'all came to me! I'm not like these sorry-ass motherfuckers sitting around remembering their fame, these old black athletes. Y'all wanna write about me pushing women around twenty-five years ago—which never happened, proven in court—you do it without my help! I'm living my life. I'm doing my work. Sheeit!"

When the writer attempted to reason with Brown, he interrupted. "Your mind is on too low a level," Brown told him. "You write for a commercial-ass magazine! How are you going to climb up?" When Lombardi further attempted to reason with Brown, wearily trying to cite the magazine's street creditability by referring to a *GQ* story about Rodney King, Brown didn't initially bite. "Don't talk to me about Rodney King," Brown said. "He don't represent nothing. He don't even know who he *is*—they caught him in an alley with a damn transvestite . . . And Morgan Freeman's a honky motherfucker. He's an establishment actor."

A friend of Brown's says that Brown was angered by the portrait of him as a foulmouthed, arrogant hothead and his program as illegitimate. He was also perturbed, the friend claimed, that the magazine quoted an unidentified Cleveland *Plain Dealer* reporter who covered Brown as saying that during Brown's playing days, owner Modell "would go crazy" over reports from team personnel and others that Brown's Cadillac was frequently seen parked near East High School. The implications of that statement are indeed repugnant although the magazine offered no proof they were accurate.

When Cleveland *Plain Dealer* reporter Paul Shepard traveled to Los Angeles in 1994 to profile Brown and asked him about the controversy involving Amer-I-Can, Brown erupted, displaying his arrogant side. "This is my home and I don't have to hear this!" Shepard quoted Brown as saying. "Man, I don't need no approval from nobody for nothing. I'm J.B., man. I don't need no approvals from anybody! EN-NEE-BOD-DEEE!"

Brown later said, referring to the alleged administrative fee: "That's crazy. I don't charge nobody nothing for nothing. I provide a service, run this business and pay my men." Curses rolled out of Brown's mouth before he suddenly morphed into the emotional Brown rather than the belligerent one. "Every other program is out there getting millions and they don't have to justify shit," Brown said. "I work 55,000 times harder than any of those and I got to answer questions about some 40 percent fee. All the contracts we work on are public record. So check the record."

Then it was back to the angry Brown. "I've never taken a nickel from anyone I didn't work for," he said. "I don't sit around and hustle any rich people I know. You have never seen me get on the air and tell people to send no money to no number on TV. You don't see me selling no hats with Amer-I-Can on them or no shit like that. . . . Why the hell should this be a charity while everything else out there is about economics and making a living? The Cleveland Browns ain't giving away no tickets. Doctors ain't operating for free. Hospitals don't operate for free. People must think Jim Brown gets his money from God. But I got to pay the pool man if he's going to work for me. I got to pay my pool man."

FRIGHTENED AND BREATHLESS, she fled her own home, sought refuge in a neighbor's house, and phoned for help.

911 emergency operator 987.

Who's this?

Hello?

Who is this? Hello?

This is 911 emergency, how may I help you?

Yes. This is Monique Brown calling.

Huh? This is who?

Monique Brown.

Monique, what's going on?

My husband . . .

What'd he do? Did he hit you?

He smashed things, and he's [unintelligible].

What's your address?

1851.

Huh?

18 . . .

Yes.

18-5-1 . . .

Yes.

Sunset . . . Plaza Drive.

Okay, what's, okay what—where is he?

He's inside the house. He just beat my car with a shovel.

He what?

He beat my car with a shovel.

Okay. And just one minute. Is he . . .

And I'm at a neighbor's house.

Is he black, white, Asian, or Hispanic?

He's black.

What color shirt and pants is he wearing?

He's wearing a black T-shirt and blue-black shorts.

What color shorts?

I think dark shorts.

Is he tall, short?

His name is—well, he's tall. He's like six foot, six foot three maybe.

Yes.

He's an ex–football player.

Okay. Okay, Monique?

Yes.

Okay. So he's armed with a shovel?

Yes, and he had a gun in the house, but he didn't use it. And I just want to go and get my things and leave. I'm at a neighbor's house. I ran here with my dogs, though.

Okay. Just a moment.

What's the address? Could you please close the door? Close the door. Please, please close the door. I'm calling the police so they can come and get me.

Okay, ma'am?

Yes.

So he beat your car with a shovel? Was this today?

Yes. I was out.

Okay, Monique? Monique? Monique, do you need a paramedic?

No. He hasn't hit me.

He didn't hit you today?

Not today.

Okay. But there is a history of domestic violence, right?

Yes.

And he threatened to kill you today?

Yes.

So where are you going to be at?

I'm—what's the address, sir? 1823? 18 . . .

1825. Okay. Are you—is he going to let you stay there until the police get there?

Will you let me stay until the police come here? He said yes.

Okay. So I'm going to send them there, and then you're going to go and direct them to where he is, okay?

Okay.

He's still there, right?

Yes.

Okay.

I don't want to go there, though.

No, but—no, the police are going to come and you just tell them where to go.

Okay. And they'll let me—they'll make him leave so I can get my things?

Right, right.

Thanks a whole lot.

Okay.

And, you know, if that's fine—it's no danger there, I'm okay.

Well, he has weapons inside the location, ma'am, and he threatened you. Okay?

Okay.

Okay. Good-bye.

Bye.

MONIQUE AND JIM had been married for two years before that night in 1999. They had a fervent, at times scorching relationship, not so different from the relationships Brown had with some of his previous wives and lovers.

The incident with Monique was instructive and showed both the stubbornness and excuse making Jim was capable of. Jim Brown does not apologize. Jim Brown does not confess his ills. Most of the time, he refuses to acknowledge his ills, thinking it shows weakness, when the act of denying the obvious makes him look far more feeble than if he publicly showed his human side and the frailties that every person possesses. "I wanted to be a bad motherfucker," Brown once said about his football career. In many ways, that has been his attitude as he has stormed through life.

For once, just once, you would like Jim Brown to say: "I'm terribly sorry for what I have done." But those are words he will likely never utter.

According to various published reports, court testimony, police records, and public statements by Jim and Monique, their fight began with accusations by Monique that Jim had been having an affair. Actually, the larger issue was the death of a close friend of Jim's, George Hughley, a former LAPD investigator whose specialty was exterminating fraud within city government. The two men initially became close by exchanging stories about the extensive racism each faced in their lives. Hughley was also an athlete, and Jim respected that.

Before his death, Big George, as Jim called him, was Jim's best friend and greatest ally, one of the few men who could curse at Jim and tell him he was full of shit without catching that Brown glare—or worse.

Following Hughley's death, Jim sank into a terrible depression, isolating himself from Monique and almost everyone else. According to Brown, Monique took the isolation as proof of an affair and confronted him. Brown denied he was being adulterous and attempted to withdraw, knowing he was reaching his breaking point.

This is what Jim does to avoid unleashing his temper, which he has difficulty controlling.

He retreated to the couple's bed and sprawled out across it. He was thinking about Big George. He was thinking about his ten thirty flight that night to Ohio to speak with state officials about Amer-I-Can. He was thinking about so many things, and the pressure built. That is what happens inside of Jim. The pressure builds and there is no release valve.

Monique continued her aggressive probing, and Jim continued his aggressive silence followed by his stern denials. "This is ridiculous," he told her.

In Jim's mind, from his perspective, Monique wasn't satisfied. After a horrific argument, Monique departed the home, took the couple's dogs, and went for a walk. Soon after that, Brown left the house as well, but he had a different way of cooling off. He went into the garage, and as Monique continued away from the house, still exchanging words with her husband, Jim picked up a shovel and smashed in the windows of Monique's car, in what was several seconds of unfiltered rage.

By the time Brown was done whacking Monique's automobile, the windows looked as if they had been covered by a light snow. The shovel had hit the glass so hard that the rear and side windows had been reduced to a fractured, crystalline mess, with the shovel creating what looked like gashes across them.

It was not the first time Jim and Monique had gotten into an argument that led to Monique angrily departing their Hollywood residence. Just a short time before Brown's angry act, the two had a disagreement that led to Monique going to Hughley's home and staying there until both of the Browns had cooled off.

This was different. Monique's call to emergency services had raised the intensity and profile of this particular fight. It is true that the Los Angeles police, perhaps reliving O.J. all over again, completely overreacted in their response. Brown had said in the past that whenever he or some other high-profile black man was caught in a situation like this one, police would swamp him with overwhelming and unnecessary force. "Ten helicopters and fifty cars," is how he said it would happen. He was not far off. According to published reports, approximately fifteen squad cars stormed Brown's property, with dozens of officers running toward his home, some with shotguns drawn.

Monique's mentioning that Brown had a firearm in the house triggered the massive police action for one sixty-three-year-old man. She had also claimed prior abuse, which contributed to the police and 911 operator's aggressive mind-set.

Brown was arrested and faced misdemeanor charges of vandalism and making a terrorist threat. Because the accusations and charges were so profound, Jim and Monique launched a massive public relations counterattack, with Monique speaking to the press and claiming that she had fabricated the abuse allegation because she was pressured by the 911 operator, and was desperate for attention from Jim.

Jim spoke at a press conference and said that the reason for the charges filed against him and the massive police response was because he was an outspoken black activist who had tussled with the police before. Indeed, the police involvement reminded Jim of his encounter with officers three decades before when Eva Maria Bohn-Chin was found unconscious under Jim's condo balcony and he was accused of giving a forearm to one of the officers attempting to enter the premises. "I don't want to play the race card," Brown said at the press conference. "I don't want to play the independent black man. I don't want to play that particular game. But it is a fact in this country that all over this country policemen have been killing people for having screwdrivers in their hands. There has been brutality in New York. There are cases all over this country wherein African Americans and Latinos are being harassed. I'm not blatantly saying that every policeman is against me or against the black community. I am saying that the black community [has] no trust in law enforcement."

Monique also spoke: "I did call 911, but it was simply just, you know—I kind of overreacted. And in those situations, you know, you get emotional and you do things and you're not thinking straight. I mean, I was in no harm. There was no threat toward me, and that's pretty much it."

On Wednesday, August 4, 1999, the couple appeared on *Larry King Live* with their attorney and a host of other guests, ranging from world-famous defense attorneys to advocates for domestic-violence victims. The hour on King's show was one of the more surreal moments in a great life that has had many of them.

"So you've been bum rapped in the past, Jim. I mean, why you?" King asked.

"I won't call it that, Larry," Jim responded.

"What would you call it?" King said.

What I will say is that I have been an independent man in our society," Jim said. "I have been an activist. I have been a community person. I have been outspoken. I have been around Malcolm. I have been around the Nation of Islam. I have been in what you might call volatile situations."

"Correct," King responded.

"I have fought all of my life for freedom, equality, and justice when there was racism up to here in this country," says Brown. "I am sixty-three years old. I have not ever succumbed to the authorities. I have always been known as an outspoken, independent individual."

They talked about PMS. They said the PMS made her do it. It made her make up false accusations of violence against her husband.

"What was this about premenstrual?" King asked Monique.

"I have been—over the past four years, I've dealt with it more, because it's been—I've been suffering from PMS," she responded. "I've consulted with my doctor about it."

"It gets worse?" King asked.

"It gets worse," she said. "Me and Jim have talked about it. It's documented. He's said . . . recommended certain things. You know, we've talked about exercise. We've talked about diet."

"Isn't there medication too?" King asked.

"We have talked about possibly medication," she said. "I don't like taking medication, yes."

"All right," King said.

Then the callers phoned in, and they saw what likely everyone watching did, which was a woman deeply in love, in all probability covering for her man, and searching for every excuse to do so.

"For Monique," the caller into King's show began. "Monique, it sounds to me that you're making everyone else responsible for your husband's actions, including PMS, and a very large man smashing windows is real scary. You seem like you're kind of in fear. Anyway, this is nothing to do with PMS. I want to know what he's taking responsibility for. I haven't heard him take responsibility for basically anything."

"Jim?" King said. "Well, you have taken—you shouldn't have broken the window."

"Absolutely," Jim responded. "I mean, this is not our life, Larry. This is an incident wherein my wife had an attitude about what I was doing. I broke a window. She went up the hill and called 911. I take responsibility every day of my life. You know that I am the kind of person that would never lie to you about breaking the windows. If I had hit my wife or threatened her, I would say that and take responsibility. There's nothing else I can do. I didn't hit her."

"Have . . . you've never hit a woman?" King said.

"Of course—not of course I have hit a woman—yes, I've hit a woman in my life, Larry," Jim said. "I have admitted that before. I admitted that in my book. But I have never touched my wife, and since 1988, I have not said a loud word to anyone based upon the work and the people that I am dealing with, because I deal with violent people every day and I must set an example and I must have them believe I'm not a hypocrite or a phony."

Another caller phoned in and talked excitedly. "Please have Mr. Brown address the incident thirty years ago where he threw a woman from the second-floor balcony into my—I repeat my—patio in West Hollywood, California," said the caller, referring to the Bohn-Chin accusation.

"Do you live next door, sir?" King asked.

"I lived below him," the caller responded.

"Okay. What happened with that? I think you wrote about that, didn't you?" King said.

"Absolutely," Jim responded. "This is what I'm talking about, the attitude . . ."

"Well, he lived next door and he saw it happen," said King. "It's a fair call." Actually, no one had seen the incident, and the caller had stated that he lived below Jim, not next to him.

"He didn't see it happen, Larry," Jim responded. "It never happened. I've never thrown anyone off of a balcony. I never was accused or charged with throwing anyone off a balcony."

"How did that story come about?" King asked.

"The story came about because we were having an argument," Jim responded. "She went over the balcony to protect me, and the police said that I threw her over and they tried to browbeat her into saying I did it. It's that simple."

"Things come . . . do you wonder . . . have you got a gray cloud following you around?" King asked.

It was the best question of the show.

"Well—" Jim began, but he was cut off by King, who asked another query before Brown could answer the most important one.

The question went to the core of something many Brown detractors say. Either he has serious issues with anger or he is the unluckiest man in the world.

FOR MANY YEARS, the front door to the Brown home remained open, even at night. This was Brown's way of letting the people he was helping know that his house was always a sanctuary. Come in any time. "If you are in a gang or you are poor and you live in L.A.," says friend John Wooten, "basically you have a place to go. Jim's house is a safe haven and everyone knows it."

There are moments on any given day when some of the city's most notorious killers and gangsters will be reclining on Brown's sofa or hanging out on his back patio, which overlooks the Pacific Ocean. The peace accord between some of the gangs that Brown was able to broker is one of the more remarkable accomplishments of his remarkable life. He was able to convert dozens, maybe hundreds, of murderers and thugs into citizens who would then go on to save the lives of other gang members. Some celebrities use their clout to save the Kodiak bears or raise awareness about global warming; Brown has used his power to save human lives.

On any given day, the leaders of these gangs would make their way into Brown's home. Their names sound like something out of a comic book or Greek mythology, but make no mistake: they were gangsters. There was Apollo, a leader of a gang called the Jungle. The man nicknamed Batman had been the O-G or captain of the Eastside Crips. Rockhead had spent a decade in the notorious hellhole known as Folsom Prison and had been shot, by his count, almost a dozen times.

Brown had saved all of their lives. He may be better than anyone at fighting inequity and, what's more, getting wealthy people to pay attention to killers and thugs and make people believe that they can be saved.

Brown has connected with poor neighborhoods across Los Angeles by displaying a soft, sensitive, and nonjudging side that often catches the gang members by surprise. They see how he refuses to judge them, and they quickly trust him.

Why a man of such remarkable intelligence and vision could be so shortsighted in other aspects of his life has always been a great conundrum that no one has been able to properly decipher or adequately explain. By September 1999, anyone following the trial of Jim for his attack on Monique's car must have been wondering the same thing. Defense witnesses called Jim a hero and a savior of lives, while the prosecution portrayed him as a violent monster.

Jim's defense was spirited and at times extremely emotional. His attorneys called Big George's widow; Shirley Hughley, who sobbed so much at times that she was unable to speak, testified that in the forty years she had known Brown, she had never seen him commit a violent act. "I have never seen him angry at a human being," Hughley testified.

She described a Jim Brown who was not the detached brute who some have portrayed him as. Hughley testified that after Big George's death, Brown retreated, and she did not see him for two to three months. Then, suddenly, Jim resurfaced, and when they did begin talking again, she said, they spent time "holding each other and talking about George and crying."

During a brief recess in the trial, Jim held his head in his hands, covered his face, and sobbed uncontrollably.

Then, at the end of the day, Jim's alter ego returned. "Regardless of what happens, you will never see this black man on his knees," he said. "I'm not a slave. I am a free, strong black man and that may be an issue with a lot of people."

The prosecution argued that Monique had recanted her allegations of abuse because she was a classic domestic-violence victim, crying for help and then, because she wanted her marriage to stay intact, claiming she had lied about Jim abusing her. Other than people close to Jim, however, few people believed Monique's recantation. Even after a psychologist working for the defense testified that Monique had been molested as a child and had a personality disorder that may have caused her to lie to police, many observers of the trial felt that Brown was losing and would face some sort of punishment. One of the key issues was Monique's testimony that she had given Jim permission to break the car windows. It was a claim that seemed implausible, and even if it was true, it did not mean that Jim still had to do it.

Perhaps sensing Jim was in trouble, the defense moved to have the judge, Dale S. Fischer, removed from the case because Jim alleged she was a member of what he said was an extremist group, named American Inns of Court, that hated minorities. The group describes its mission as one of promoting legal ethics. When speaking to reporters, Brown referred to it as a "radical and extremist group of white upper-class women who target men of color, including Jim Brown." The defense's motion was denied by a superior court judge, and there is no evidence that the group is racist.

In January 2000, after a jury had convicted Jim of vandalizing Monique's car—but acquitted him of the more serious charge of making a terrorist threat—and after Jim had refused to accept several deals and probation offers from the prosecution, a fed-up Fischer sentenced him to six months in prison.

Brown reported to the Ventura County Jail and started serving his prison sentence on March 13, 2002. He was sixty-six years old.

In prison, Brown was respected but not feared, and there were people considering testing just how tough the legendary Jim Brown truly was. That is what is done in prison. New cons are tested and probed for weaknesses, even someone like Brown, who was still physically imposing, with a large frame and bulging biceps, despite his advanced age.

Any potential predators were quickly dissuaded by a career criminal named Michael Monzano, who helped to protect Brown. "Let him do his thing," he told other prisoners, "then let him go home."

That's exactly what happened. Brown served his sentence without one significant incident or write-up. When he left prison, Brown, surrounded by dozens of supporters, held a press conference. He was as defiant as he had been before entering jail.

"It was a fantastic experience for me," Brown said. "I knew two years ago that I'd have to go to jail to prove my point."

There are very few people who would describe prison as a "fantastic experience." The comments were a way of telling the judge, and anyone else who was listening, that his stint in prison had not changed his views about the judge or what he thought of the judicial system.

"No one is going to break me," Brown told the author.

Throughout the black community in Los Angeles, he was indeed seen as a hero who had stood up to an unfair judge who attempted to steal his dignity. The fact that Brown had committed a crime was lost on some. Brown had thumbed his nose at a judicial system—particularly in Los Angeles—that had discriminated against the black and the poor for decades.

"Jim told the judge to go fuck herself," says one of Brown's friends. "He did something that other black people would like to do to a judge or a court that they feel has treated them wrongly, but don't have the balls to do. But then again, that has always been Jim. Nothing has changed, which is why so many people close to him, particularly black people, admire him so much, despite the troubles he has been in and the mistakes he has made."

NOW

HERO

Jim Brown goes into the roughest places in the country, the ugly places, and he pulls people out. He saves lives. He has saved hundreds of lives.

—**James Box,** Cleveland activist

We go into the belly of the beast. We get to know the predators and we challenge them to change.

—**Jim Brown** to the Cleveland *Plain Dealer*, speaking of his Amer-I-Can organization

Bill Belichick, the best NFL coach of all time, was having dinner in the Boston area with the best running back of all time, soon after Belichick had taken the job as leader of the New England Patriots. They were finishing their meal and a long discussion about Amer-I-Can when a woman approached the table where Belichick, Brown, and a few political leaders were sitting.

The woman sheepishly asked Belichick for his autograph. "Sure," Belichick said. While he signed, she looked at Brown but did not recognize him. "Who are you?" she asked.

Belichick finished signing, and the woman left, but the coach fumed inside. Belichick and Brown have become close friends, and Belichick, a student of history, believes Brown is one of the most important figures the sports world has ever seen. "I couldn't believe it," Belichick remembered. " 'Who is he? Who is he? Who the fuck are you?' I mean, this is Jim Brown we're talking about."

Years earlier, when Belichick was head coach of the Cleveland

Browns, he asked Brown to speak to the team's rookies. "I saw Jim and I was totally in awe of him," Belichick said. "What a presence. He is a great speaker. I figured he needed no introduction, because it's fucking Jim Brown. But I could tell some of the rookies were not so familiar with who he was and what his accomplishments were."

So the following year, when Brown spoke to a different crop of rookies, Belichick recounted all of Brown's past civil rights achievements. Then, when Belichick showed a highlight tape of Brown's runs, the eyes of the rookies sparkled with awe.

"My concern with Jim is that as time goes by, people will forget just how important he was to sports and society," Belichick said. "I just hope people don't forget that or remember him only for some of the controversies he was involved in. He is without question one of the top two or three human beings I have ever met. He makes me proud to know him and proud to be his friend. What is important about him is how he relates to people in the community. He can talk to anybody whether it is the owner of an NFL team or a kid in the projects. I just hope his life, and how impressive it was, is never forgotten."

Jim Brown turned seventy years old on February 17, 2006, and on that day Brown's wife, Monique, did something that seemed impossible: she caught Jim Brown from behind.

She startled Brown by throwing him a surprise birthday party in California, and Brown had no clue until it occurred. There were dozens of guests, including some of Brown's closest friends. One of them was actor Donald Sutherland.

Brown and Sutherland met early in both men's movie careers and formed a friendship while on the sets of *The Dirty Dozen* and *The Split*. They have remained friends, and Sutherland has stayed loyal to Brown throughout all of Brown's troubles because of Brown's secret act of kindness. Some time ago Brown loaned Sutherland $3,000 so Sutherland could continue his acting career. Sutherland stayed in the business, going on to perform in over one hundred films. He never forgot what Brown did for him.

Cleveland activist James Box walked around the party as well, taking it all in. Eventually Brown learned Box was there. They greeted each other, and Brown asked, "How did you get here?"

"I flew," Box told Brown.

"No, I mean how'd you pay for it?" Brown said.

"I bought a ticket," Box responded.

Brown was slightly irritated. Knowing Box's financial situation, Brown decided to reimburse him immediately.

They continued to talk, and Box could not help but think about where he was now and where he had been just a short time earlier. Box had come a long way—from hell to the Hollywood Hills is how he put it—and he owed much of the change in his life to Brown.

There are literally hundreds of stories of the lives Brown has changed. Brown's recent visit to San Quentin State Prison, one of perhaps fifty prisons he has visited, exemplified what he does. He speaks to prisoners about hope and the future, two words they rarely hear. In San Quentin on that day, he stood before a room of black and brown faces. "Just a country boy," he says when beginning his talk to them, referring to himself. "National Football League, all that. But y'all know me, don't you?" Heads go up and down in agreement. "Y'all know I'm dead serious and I work with those that a lot of people don't like to work with. . . . And for the rest of my life that will be my work."

He has turned gang leaders into social activists, thugs into religious men, the uneducated into college attendees. Hundreds of stories, hundreds of lives saved by Brown.

The story of James Box might be one of the most impressive of them all.

———

Box's mother was a heroin addict. It did not take long for him to fall into gangs and drugs and then into crime. As a kid, he was taught that whites were evil and not to be trusted. "I didn't believe in America," he says. "I hated white people. It was my childhood. My family taught me hate. I think Jim noticed that right away, because he was always telling me, even before we got to really know each other as well as we do now, 'You really have to love all people.' "

Brown and Box met at city hall over a decade ago. Box was there with his young daughter, and Brown saw the two together and approached them. "This is Jim Brown," Box told his daughter. She said: "You mean James Brown?"

That is how simply their friendship began. Brown was taken with Box's burgeoning activism, and Box was enthralled by Brown's commitment to help the underprivileged. "The only thing I knew about Jim was what my father told me," Box says. "He said he was a great running back. As I got to know him I could sense he was not one of these guys in it for a headline or publicity. He was in it to save people's lives."

They became even closer when Box's mother succumbed to difficulties arising from her drug addiction. When Brown was informed that Box did not have the money for his mother's funeral, he contacted Box. "Let me do this for you," Brown told Box. He paid the expenses for Box's mother's funeral.

Brown invited Box to Los Angeles soon after that, and they spoke in Brown's home for five hours, talking about ways to solve the ugly gang violence that was rising across the country. Brown took Box out to meet current and former gangbangers throughout the city. Box saw people like himself: people that society had abandoned and viewed as animals. Now, some of them had jobs and were going to school. They had changed everything. "The key was Jim," Box says.

Brown soon asked Box to join Amer-I-Can. Box was perfect for Cleveland. He had been a troubled youth himself, and that gave him credibility in Cleveland's rough neighborhoods. Besides, Amer-I-Can was back strong in the city after Cleveland partnered with Brown's organization and provided Brown with $300,000 in funding. Box set up in Cleveland, and Brown flew representatives from Los Angeles to instruct Box on how Amer-I-Can worked. "Now we talk all the time, I see him all the time," Box says. "He's still on the streets, in the prisons, talking to gang members. I do the same thing. I can't think where I would be if it wasn't for Jim."

When Box visits Los Angeles, he plays chess with Brown for hours, sometimes until three or four in the morning, the game peppered with talk about Amer-I-Can and gang problems. They speak so much on the telephone that Brown was once able to trick Box. A short time ago, Brown phoned Box and informed him that he wanted to fly Box to Miami for a business trip. When they met in Florida, Brown had a surprise. "I'm going to teach you how to play golf," he told Box.

"I had no idea how to play," Box says, "until Jim taught me."

Box and others say they see the personal and compassionate side of Brown that few people outside of Brown's circle of friends and family do, like Brown watching *Barney & Friends* with his two young kids. Belichick has spoken at an Amer-I-Can graduation. "He was emotional, I was emotional, everyone was emotional," Belichick said. "It was very moving. I would say right up there emotionally with winning a Super Bowl."

"People have no idea how good a family man he is," says Box. "When I am in his house, I can't believe sometimes what I'm seeing. He is such a good father, and his household is so different from the one I grew up in. If I dropped a dish, or dropped something, I got yelled at, and I probably got beat. I saw his daughter drop this glass sculpture, and Jim said, 'Now, honey, you have to be careful with these things.' Jim was so calm and caring. I didn't grow up in that kind of environment. I didn't know that sort of household existed."

HELPING PEOPLE IS not what is different about Brown now. He has always done that. His demeanor is what has changed. Brown no longer lobs insults the way he once did his forearm. His temper, it seems, is less supernova, more controlled. He no longer refers to the city of Cleveland as a bombed-out shell or actor Morgan Freeman as a "honky motherfucker." He repairs personal relationships damaged from past neglect instead of inflaming the damage. Age has mellowed Jim Brown. Slightly. For most of the past nearly fifty years, Brown's constant refrain was that Brown did what he wanted, and if you did not like it, well, too bad. Now, Brown is much more communicative and pleasant.

That does not mean he is free from controversy or still not intensely opinionated, and the arrogance that at times infuriated people around him has not dissipated entirely. Brown could not resist taking a generous swipe at the NCAA when stories arose about the University of Southern California and the possibility of several of its football players receiving improper benefits. He told Sporting New Radio: "I think the NCAA is probably the most hypocritical organization ever that's been on the face of this earth. These guys live high off the hog. They have a convention; they live on the top floor; they have the best food, the best suites; they make these laws; and they're all hypocritical because a lot of these kids can't afford a doggone thing. Everybody knows that most of the kids that go to college have to get some kind of financial assistance. So instead of doing it legally, it's always done illegally. And then what they do is they crack down on certain individuals. All of us went through college poor and had some alumni that gave us $10 a week or $20 a week so we could survive; they're in a survival situation. So I don't want to hear anything about this organization and what they rulings are because I don't respect any of their rulings."

A New York *Daily News* gossip columnist reported in 2006 that Brown's former assistant, Duane Moody, who says he worked for Brown at Amer-I-Can, sued Brown for wrongful termination. The newspaper states that court papers say: "Jim Brown listed the following as a reason for terminating plaintiff: (A) Attending Johnny Cochran's funeral with O. J. Simpson; (B) Failing to secure a wiretap of the telephone of Jim Brown's wife, Monique Brown, in violation of Jim Brown's request." Brown's lawyer vehemently denied the accusations.

In terms of today's athletes, Brown still sees many of them as lacking social consciousness and being woefully ignorant of their power. Brown believes that if only a fraction of today's players pooled their wealth and resources, they could change the fortunes of perhaps thousands of poor people.

"Jim has done basically his entire life what many other athletes, not all of them, but most of them, won't," Box says. "The black athletes today don't know their history. Jim does. The athletes today only want instant gratification. The cars, the jewelry, that stuff. They don't think long-term."

Brown also clearly believes that NFL players in the twenty-first century are not nearly as tough and resilient as the players from his era. In 2005 Brown taped an ESPN show with former NFL runners Gale Sayers, Eric Dickerson, and Herschel Walker in which moderator Jim Gray asked each of them a series of questions about the past and present NFL. Brown was asked, as the others were, if there was a runner today on his level. He politely responded that there were about a dozen good backs in today's game but none as good as he and Sayers had been. Then he launched into a persuasive, if convoluted, answer to the question of what it takes to be a great runner.

"God gives a runner his gift," Brown responded. "You don't teach it. You don't acquire it. You don't imitate it. And you don't worry about the other guy." Then, looking at the other former backs, Brown said: "Because each one of us is totally different and it's a gift. You can't really explain it. We admire each other. We have no problem with who we are because we are all different. When I brought up Gale earlier I have so much admiration for him because I never thought of myself like him because he was totally different. He did things I could never do and that's how it is with runners."

"These guys that play now they'll go out there and have 1,100 yards, 1,200 yards," said Dickerson. "They'll have two or three good games and all of a sudden [the media] puts him on this pedestal. 'Aw, he's the greatest. We've never seen anything like him. Look at his footwork. I haven't see this in twenty years.' I'm like, 'This is a joke.' I start laughing at it. Even at the decline of my career, I could outrun some of these guys. If Jim and Gale [had played today], with the media attention the way it is now, they would have been phenomenal."

Dickerson's more expansive comments must have gotten Brown's competitive juices flowing. After being asked by Gray if players celebrate too much in today's game—excessive celebrations irk Brown—Brown's criticism intensified. "The media drives all of that," Brown said. "The media covers it. They cover it upside down. The guys say if I don't do it, I'm not going to be at the top of the show. Money—you get a $20 million bonus that's guaranteed and you haven't played one play. It's upside down. The players association is playing along with the owners, etc., etc., etc. So it is entertainment now. It's not true sport. They're not really gladiators out there, because a true gladiator could not jump up after every play and do a dance. That means that you are saving energy for the dance and your energy should be dispelled on each play, and when you finish that game you should be totally exhausted.

"The quality of the game has gone down," Brown asserted, getting more animated. "People have accepted losing. They have accepted making mistakes. What do guys do when they drop a ball? What do you do in a dressing room after you lose a game? The most exciting thing about a game is when you play it hard and you win it. Then after you win it, go celebrate if you want to celebrate. The champions do not celebrate. [New England coach Bill Belichick] is looking toward the next Super Bowl and his players on TV are different than all the other players. So the players should take note of the New England Patriots and try to emulate that because they are the successful franchise."

Gray switched to the topic of O. J. Simpson and asked if the double-murder charge had injured his legacy. "The take I have [is] when you do it on the field, that's what it is," Brown said. "They kept me out of the college Hall of Fame because they didn't like my character. They kept me out of the lacrosse Hall of Fame because they didn't like my politics. When I finally got into the collegiate Hall of Fame they brought Paul Robeson in [the same Hall of Fame class]. . . . They kept him out all those years because they didn't like his politics. Yet I was a great admirer of Paul Robeson. Because the legacy of the country was slavery, so those fighting against . . . injustice [were] controversial and always kept out of things. Eventually they came around and put both of us in the Hall of Fame. . . . So we can't put the politics into the performance because the performance is the performance. . . . The man was a great football player."

The greatest indication that Brown has softened—slightly—is that he had a free shot at Simpson and did not take it, which he had done many times before.

• • •

DESPITE A PROPENSITY for aiding perfect strangers, Brown mostly used to ignore his own flesh and blood.

After the Brenda Ayres trial, in which he was accused of assault, Brown said he was unaware the relationship between him and Ayres had produced a child, Shelly. Still, just several years later, Ayres phoned Brown and asked him to meet Shelly. Brown has said that when he saw the little girl he knew immediately that the child was his. Brown still remained mostly out of Shelly's life and did not publicly acknowledge her existence until decades later, in 1989.

Many of Brown's early relationships with his kids were not much different. Brown named his son Jim Brown Jr., and along with that name came unrealistic expectations, and Brown the father was not present to help guide his son through what would inevitably be a troubled childhood, because Brown the Movie Star and Brown the Football Legend were bigger personas than Brown the Dad. In Spike Lee's movie, the various Brown children speak of lost opportunities with their father. Kevin Brown, the other son, and perhaps the Brown child who is most like Jim, rebelled against his mother, became addicted to alcohol and cocaine, and was eventually imprisoned. At one point Kevin, who can recall being hugged only once by his dad in his entire life, broke into his own mother's house and stole from her, selling off her personal items. "Initially, for the kids, I don't think it really affected us," says Kim Brown to Lee. "But later on, when, you know, we really wanted a dad, needed a dad, somebody to talk to, you know, it kinda started messing with our heads. I wanted to be daddy's little girl. I wanted to be held, touched, you know, taken places. I wanted him to come to some of my ballet recitals, things like that. And you know, he wasn't there."

Now he is there, in what is a period of major reconciliation in Jim Brown's life. Now he does hug his children. Now he expresses that emotion, that support, at the right time, which he did not do in the past. By all accounts, Jim and Monique are doing well. Brown has a daughter, Morgan, and a son, Aris, from his marriage to Monique, and there is little question he is now an excellent, dedicated father. "You should see him with his kids," says Box. "He's a great dad. He's gentle and loving with those kids."

The stimulation Brown once received from sex and power and control of women—and some men—has been replaced by the high he receives from taking a ferocious gangbanger and turning him into, as Brown has said, "a guy who can be proud of who he is."

When Brown spoke to me from prison, he made it clear he was just such a man and that jail had not changed a basic aspect of his personality.

"I'm a fighter," he said then, "and I always have been. That will never change."

AUTHOR'S NOTE

I SENT JIM BROWN several letters via FedEx, requesting a second interview, and heard nothing. I called him on the phone. "Let me call you back," he said. I never heard from him. Then I sent him more letters, including this one: "I hope you are well. I wanted to tell you that I am going to be in Los Angeles for a few days beginning on October 8 [2005]. I was wondering if I could meet with you for a short while to introduce myself, and you can meet this crazy person who is sending you Federal Express letters. I can meet with you anywhere, anytime. Thanks and take care." Again, nothing.

This is of course not atypical Brown behavior. Brown speaks when he wants to speak.

I must admit, I was sometimes scared out of my mind when writing this book. I envisioned a seventy-year-old Brown kicking my ass *Mars Attacks* style and the whole brawl ending up on *SportsCenter*.

Jim Brown is an intimidator with heroic qualities, possessing both a temper and a tender soul as big as his legend. He is a great man with great flaws. Most of all, Brown wants to control every aspect of his life, as most of us do; but Brown is hypersensitive, almost fanatical, about how he is portrayed.

It is interesting to note that a short time after I sent Brown an initial letter, editors in the publishing world began to receive book proposals from Brown for a book to be written by Brown himself. Brown was attempting to do what he has always done: beat an opponent before the opponent beats him. I was not an adversary, of course, but in Brown's mind, anyone outside of his inner circle is exactly that. He also feels, according to his close friends, that many people have made money off of his football career, a fact that has made him extremely bitter. Indeed, on eBay there are literally thousands of Brown memorabilia items for sale. He is like many famous athletes and people: hundreds profit off his current or past efforts. Brown is not one of them, and that has irritated him.

Overall, I have no idea how Brown will react to this book.

Despite the book being extremely fair and mostly complimentary of him, he is likely to react angrily.

As he has said many times, Brown feels he has met only a handful of beautiful people in his life. Everyone else has an angle. Mine was to present Brown as he is—real and raw—though most of all, despite his horrible flaws when it comes to women, I believe Brown is the biggest combination of influential athlete and generous social activist in sports history. I am certain many will feel differently and have their own candidates for such a nomination, but I would put Brown's athletic accomplishments and contributions to society against any current or former athlete's.

Penetrating Brown's inner sanctum was the toughest assignment I have ever encountered in my nearly twenty years of writing about sports. It was more difficult than convincing a gay NFL player to talk about his life, as I have done in a previous book, and more tricky than getting sexual-harassment victims at a major television network to open up to me, which happened in another book I wrote. I believe Brown put up roadblocks to try and stop me. In the end, I was able to write an accurate portrait of Brown because some of his closest friends cooperated with me. For that I am extremely grateful, and I was able to keep my promise to them that I was not writing a tasteless book that only trashed Brown.

The FBI source who spoke to me did so at great risk. Although he was sometimes frustratingly vague, I am appreciative, since he took serious chances in submitting to an interview. His believability will be an issue to some. Not to me. When I asked for proof of his activities, the agent showed me several photographs of Brown entering a nondescript dwelling accompanied by two women. The agent says the home was the house Brown referred to in his biography as "Headquarters." The photos were yellowed and wrinkled and had an FBI stamp on them. The former agent would not allow the photos to be kept or examined for authenticity. I was able to verify, however, that the source was indeed an FBI agent during the 1960s.

A note about sources. There is a great deal of public information in the media about Brown. I read approximately a thousand newspaper and magazine articles about Brown and watched each of his movies. Several dozen interviews were conducted. One of the more difficult aspects of writing this book was determining proper attribution. When in doubt, I quoted the source directly. In some parts of the book, scenes were re-created using interviews and public-record sources, a common writing technique.

The descriptions of how Brown ran the football came in part from a 1960 *Sports Illustrated* cover story on Brown as well as from watching archival footage of Brown several dozen times. A 1956 issue of *Life* magazine provided some colorful details about Brown's Syracuse days. The *Ebony* profile on Brown and a *Sport* article regarding Brown's best five games were helpful. The book

PB: The Paul Brown Story provided Paul's version of coaching Jim. Bill Pennington's excellent book on the history of the Heisman Trophy, *The Heisman,* helped provide some historical information about the award. Paul Brown's training-camp speech was originally chronicled by Cleveland *Plain Dealer* writer Gordon Cobbledick. A 1989 article that chronicled Paul's rise to stardom by Lonnie Wheeler in *Ohio* magazine was helpful, and some of Paul's views and quotes about race came from this article. Several quotes from Otto Graham were also taken from this article.

Statistics about the Great Black Migration came from Nicholas Leman's excellent book *The Promised Land.* Information about the FBI spying on John Lennon was originally published in the book *Memories of John Lennon* by Yoko Ono.

Art Modell's behavior was interesting, to say the least. He was at first enthusiastic about submitting to an interview, then suddenly hesitant. However, he still allowed me to interview him three times over several years.

The U.S. National Archives and Records Administration was timely in providing the Black Economic Union documents I requested under the Freedom of Information Act. The FBI, however, put up roadblock after roadblock when it came to requested documents, at times improperly, I believe.

A small amount of background information from Brown's two autobiographies was used. They are *Off My Chest,* published in 1964, and *Out of Bounds,* written in the 1980s. The letter from Kenneth Molloy to the Manhasset community was taken from *Off My Chest.* Information about "the Headquarters" came from independent interviews with former Cleveland Brown players and *Out of Bounds.* Information about the scene describing Brown having his eyes poked when playing against the New York Giants came from *Out of Bounds* and interviews with several of Brown's former teammates. All information from Brown's books has been properly sourced. Information from the documentary show *Beyond the Glory* on Fox was used to re-create the prison scene in San Quentin.

I was helped in writing this book by a group of highly talented friends. My editor at HarperCollins, Mauro DiPreta, is the best in the business, and I am eternally thankful to him for giving me the chance to work with him again. Associate editor, Joelle Yudin, was her usual hard working and tremendous self. My agent, John Monteleone from Mountain Lion, Inc., is a superb advocate and adviser.

I would like to extend my appreciation to the research staff at the Cleveland *Plain Dealer,* one of the great American newspapers, particularly Patti Graziano. I would also like to thank the archives personnel at the Cleveland State University Library.

Editors at the *Florida Times-Union* newspaper in Jacksonville, Florida—particularly editor Pat Yack and sports editor Chet Fussman—were quite gracious in allowing me some occasional time away to work on this book while also being extremely supportive. I also want to thank *Times-Union* editors Carole Fader and Mike Richey for being constant sources of inspiration.

Stacey James, executive director of media relations for the New England Patriots, is one of the best PR guys in football or any other sport. Bill Belichick has always been quite gracious with me, and for that I will always be thankful.

Most of all, my appreciation goes out to Susan Thornton Hobby, who proofed my manuscript before submission with her usual skill and tirelessness, while putting up with my tardiness and smart-ass e-mails. Quite simply, there is no better word editor, fact checker, or childhood friend who used to kick my butt in touch football.

INDEX